second edition

# Latin America
since 1780

**second edition**

# Latin America

## since 1780

Will Fowler

**HODDER**
EDUCATION
**PART OF HACHETTE LIVRE UK**

First published in Great Britain in 2002 by Arnold.
This second edition published in 2008 by Hodder Education,
part of Hachette Livre UK, 338 Euston Road, London NW1 3BH.

**www.hoddereducation.com**

© 2008 Will Fowler

The advice and information in this book are believed to be true and
accurate at the date of going to press, but neither the authors nor the publisher
can accept any legal responsibility or liability for any errors or omissions.

*British Library Cataloguing in Publication Data*

A catalogue record for this book is available from the British Library

*Library of Congress Cataloging-in-Publication Data*

A catalog record for this book is available from the Library of Congress

ISBN-13: 978 0 340 95873 5

Impression Number      5

Year                            2011

Typeset in 9.25 on 13 Lucida by Phoenix Photosetting, Chatham, Kent
Printed and bound by CPI Group (UK) Ltd, Croydon, CR0 4YY

What do you think about this book? Or any other Hodder Education title?
Please visit our website at www.hoddereducation.com

**For Caroline**

# Contents

# List of figures

# Preface

The idea for this second edition came from Tamsin Smith. In the autumn of 2006 she persuaded me to write an updated version of my textbook, *Latin America 1800–2000*. The political landscape of a considerable number of Latin American countries had indeed changed significantly since I submitted the original manuscript in September 2001. Hugo Chávez survived an attempted coup in 2002 and was re-elected president of Venezuela in 2006 for a third consecutive time, with 63 per cent of the vote. His Bolivarian Revolution has become increasingly resonant in Latin America as a novel, albeit contested, challenge to US hegemony in the region, and as a potential alternative to neoliberal practices. Michelle Bachelet became Chile's first female president and Evo Morales became Bolivia's first indigenous president. Their electoral victories coincided with a noticeable shift towards the 'left' in their neighbouring countries. Brazil, Uruguay, Argentina and Ecuador acquired socialist-sympathising governments. Alan García and the APRA returned to power in Peru, as did Daniel Ortega and the Sandinistas in Nicaragua. The extremely close electoral victory of Mexico's conservative Felipe Calderón was tainted with allegations of fraud. The only country in which a right-wing president won the elections with a resounding victory was Colombia. Latin America's allegedly populist response to globalisation and neoliberalism deserves to be studied. It made sense to bring the final chapter up to date so that this course book remains fresh and relevant.

The objective of *Latin America since 1780* is the same as it was in the first edition: to offer a clear narrative history of Latin America, broadly chronological in its approach, that will give students of Hispanic, Portuguese and Latin American studies some idea of the main events that affected the continent over the last two hundred years. It does not assume any prior knowledge of the subject on the part of the reader. It is first and foremost an introduction to modern Latin American history. Given that most modern languages courses are driven by the study of literature, I have noted those Latin American literary texts and films that are most commonly studied at university in order to highlight those cases where history and literature/cinema are closely related. A selection of historical documents in Spanish is also included at the end of each chapter, together with essay titles, as a starting point for discussion. I have added new questions in this edition and replaced the inserted documents of the original chapter six with excerpts from speeches by Morales and Chávez. One of the aims of this book is to encourage students to read more on the subject, and to discover for themselves the more complex details of the history of Latin America, which, owing to constraints of space, cannot be fully explored in the following pages.

# Acknowledgements

I could not have written this book without the help of a number of individuals and institutions. I am indebted to Tamsin Smith for having pushed me into writing this second edition and to Bianca Knights for her first-class editorial work. My colleagues in the Spanish Department at St Andrews deserve a mention for their unwavering support. The same goes to my SP1030 students, whose enjoyment of my course on modern Latin America has been so encouraging. I also thank the Latin Americanists who live in the vicinity (Mario Aguilar, Mark Harris, Eleni Kefala, Tristan Platt, Gustavo San Román and Crawford Spence) for their collegiality and willingness to discuss their findings with me. I am particularly grateful to Rebecca Earle, James Dunkerley, Paul Henderson, Peter Lambert, Rachel Sieder and Iain Stewart, all of whom read and commented on some of the chapters while they were being written. Their views and insights were extremely helpful, although I hasten to add that any mistakes that survived their analytical eyes are mine and not theirs. I must also thank Michael Hironymous, at the Nettie Lee Benson Latin American Collection, University of Texas at Austin, for having tracked down the pictures contained herein of Simón Bolívar, Benito Juárez and a group of Mexican revolutionaries. I am grateful to the Nettie Lee Benson Collection for having allowed the reproduction of these images. I thank the Hulton Getty Archive for allowing me to reproduce the picture of Evita Perón, the Fundación Rigoberta Menchú Tum for permitting the use of a picture of *doña* Rigoberta, and the British Academy for awarding me the grant that covered the cost of reproduction of the images presented in this volume. Last, but not least, I must thank my family. My mother, Rosa María Laffitte and my parents-in-law, Peter and Susan Wilkes, have backed me all along. I remain grateful to my father, W.S. Fowler, for the way he encouraged me when he was alive. Caroline and our children, Tom, Ed and Flo have all supported me (as well as *soportado*) during the time it took to write the first and second editions of this book. It is to Caroline that I dedicate it again. To quote Pablo Neruda: '*En ti los ríos cantan y mi alma en ellos huye/ como tú lo desees y hacia donde tú quieras./ Márcame mi camino en tu arco de esperanza/ y soltaré en delirio mi bandada de flechas*'.

# Chronology of main events

| | MEXICO, CENTRAL AMERICA AND THE CARIBBEAN | SOUTH AMERICA |
|---|---|---|
| **THE END OF THE COLONIAL PERIOD** | **1762** British occupy Havana<br>**1764** Captaincy-General of Cuba is created<br>**1767** Jesuits expelled from Spain and its colonies | |
| | | **1776** Viceroyalty of Río de la Plata is created<br>**1777** Captaincy-General of Venezuela is created<br>**1778** Captaincy-General of Chile is created<br>**1780–81** Tupac Amaru II's revolt in Peru<br>**1780** Comunero revolt in Socorro (Colombia)<br>**1781–82** Tupac Katari's revolt in Bolivia<br>**1783–87** Intendencies created throughout Spanish America<br>**1788–89** Minas Gerais conspiracy in Brazil |
| | **1791** Haitian Revolution<br>**1797** British seize Trinidad, Tobago, and St Lucia | |
| **THE STRUGGLE FOR INDEPENDENCE (1800–1825)** | **1803** US purchase Louisiana<br>**1804** Independence of Haiti | |
| | | **1806** British invasion of Buenos Aires<br>**1807** British invasion of Montevideo and Buenos Aires; Portuguese Court transfers to Brazil<br>**1809** Revolts in La Paz and Quito |
| | **1810** Revolt in Dolores (Mexico) | **1810** Revolts in Caracas, Buenos Aires, Santiago and Bogotá; Independence of Buenos Aires |
| | **1811** Hidalgo is executed | **1811** Revolt in Banda Oriental; Battles of Paraguarí and Tacuarí; Independence of Paraguay<br>**1813** Bolívar decrees *Guerra a muerte* |

**1814** Constitution of Apatzingán
**1815** Morelos is executed

**1814** Battle of Rancagua
**1814–15** Pumacahua's revolt
**1815** Artigas takes Provincia Oriental
**1816** Dr Francia becomes Dictator of Paraguay (1816–40)
**1816–20** Brazilian invasion of Uruguay

**1817** Mina's Expedition

**1817** Battle of Chacabuco
**1818** Battles of Cancha Rayada, Maipú, Semen; Independence of Chile

**1819** US purchase Florida

**1819** Battles of Casanare, Boyacá

**1821** Independence of Mexico and Central America

**1821** Battle of Carabobo; Independence of Venezuela and Colombia

**1822** Mexican Empire is forged
**1822–44** Haitian occupation of Santo Domingo

**1822** Battles of Bomboná and Pichincha; Independence of Ecuador; Independence of Brazil; Gran Colombia includes Venezuela, Colombia and Ecuador

**1823** Mexican Empire ends; Formation of United Provinces of Central America

**1823** Battle of Puerto Cabello; Bolívar arrives in Peru; Slavery is abolished (Chile)

**1824** Slavery is abolished (Central America)

**1824** Battles of Junín and Ayacucho; Independence of Peru
**1825** Battle of Tumusla; Independence of Bolivia

**THE EARLY NATIONAL PERIOD (1825–1850)**

**1824–35** First Federal Republic (Mexico)

**1825–28** Argentine–Brazilian War
**1826** Slavery is abolished (Bolivia)

**1827–29** Civil War in Central America

**1827** Battles of Juncal and Ituzaingó
**1828** Independence of Uruguay

**1829–39** Liberal factions rule Central America under Francisco Morazán
**1829** Spanish invasion of Tampico; Slavery is abolished (Mexico)

**1829** Rosas takes Buenos Aires

**1830** Ecuador and Venezuela separate from Colombia
**1830** Páez elected President of Venezuela for the first time
**1831** Pedro I abdicates
**1831–41** Regency (Brazil)

**1832** Federalist Civil War in Mexico
**1833** Santa Anna elected President of Mexico for the first time

**1833** Portales' Constitution (Chile); Rosas leads Campaign of the Desert; Britain seizes Las Malvinas

**1835–46** First Central Republic (Mexico)
**1835–36** Texan revolt

**1835–52** Rosas, Dictator of Argentine Federation
**1835–45** Rio Grande do Sul revolt
**1835–39** Santa Cruz forges Peruvian–Bolivian Confederation

**1836** Independence of Texas

**1836–39** War between Chile and Peruvian–Bolivian Confederation

**1837** Mita revolt (Guatemala)
**1838** French blockade of Veracruz; Costa Rica and Nicaragua break away from Central American Confederation

**1840–41** French blockade of Buenos Aires
**1841** Pedro II becomes Emperor (Brazil) (1841–89)

**1844** Independence of Santo Domingo from Haiti
**1845** US annexation of Texas
**1846–48** Mexican–American War

**1846** Slavery is abolished (Uruguay)

**1847** Guatemala, Honduras and El Salvador break away from Confederation
**1847–52** Caste War in Yucatán
**1848** British intervention in Mosquito Coast

**THE EARLY NEOCOLONIAL PERIOD (1850–1880)**

**1849–61** Liberal–conservative civil wars (Colombia)

**1850** Clayton–Bulwer Treaty

**1850** Slavery is abolished (Colombia)
**1852** Slavery is abolished (Ecuador)

**1853** US purchase La Mesilla

**1853** Slavery is abolished (Argentina, except Buenos Aires)

**1854–55** Revolution of Ayutla (Mexico)
**1855–56** William Walker's intervention in Nicaragua
**1858–61** Civil War of *La Reforma* (Mexico)
**1859** Britain returns Bay Islands to Honduras; Belize becomes British Honduras

**1854** Slavery is abolished (Peru and Venezuela)

**1860–75** Gabriel García Moreno rules Ecuador

**1861–65** Santo Domingo becomes a Spanish colony again

**1861–80** Liberals in power in Colombia

**1861–91** Liberals govern Chile

**1862–68** Mitre presides in Argentina

**1862–67** French intervention in Mexico

**1864–70** War of the Triple Alliance (Paraguayan War)

**1865** The Dominican Republic is formed

**1865–6** Spanish invasion of Chincha Islands

**1867** Liberal triumph in Mexico

**1868–74** Sarmiento presides in Argentina

**1868–78** Ten Year War (Cuba)

**1870** Tomás Guardia rises to power in Costa Rica (1870–82)

**1870** Guzmán Blanco (Venezuela, 1870–88); Slavery is abolished (Paraguay)

**1871** Liberal forces end conservative rule in Guatemala, El Salvador and Honduras

**1872** Slavery is abolished (Puerto Rico)

**1879–83** Argentine War of the Desert

**1879–83** War of the Pacific

**1879** Battles of Iquique and Cape Angamos

**1881** Battles of Chorrillos and Miraflores

**THE MATURE NEOCOLONIAL PERIOD (1880–1930)**

**1882–84** Ulíses Heureaux (Dominican Republic)

**1886** Slavery is abolished (Cuba)

**1886–91** José Manuel Balmaceda (Chile)

**1887–99** Heureaux returns to power (Dominican Republic)

**1888** Slavery is abolished (Brazil)

**1889–1930** First Republic of Brazil

**1890** Grace Contract (Peru)

**1891** Civil War (Chile)

**1891–1920** 'Parliamentary Republic' (Chile)

**1893–95** Rio Grande do Sul revolt

**1893–96** Canudos revolt

**1895–98** Cuban War of Independence

**1895** Liberal Revolution in Ecuador
**1895–1919** 'Aristocratic Republic' (Peru)

**1898** Hispano-Cuban–American War
**1898–1952** US occupation of Puerto Rico
**1898–1902** US occupation of Cuba

**1899–1901** War of a Thousand Days (Colombia)
**1903** Independence of Panama
**1903–7** Batlle y Ordóñez presides in Uruguay
**1905** *Semana Roja* (Santiago)

**1906** Río Blanco strike and massacre (Mexico)
**1907** Cananea strike and massacre (Mexico)

**1907** Iquique strike and massacre
**1908–35** Juan Vicente Gómez (Venezuela)

**1910–20** Mexican Revolution

**1911–15** Batlle y Ordóñez returns to power in Uruguay

**1912–33** US occupation of Nicaragua
**1914** Panama Canal opens; US attack Veracruz
**1915–34** US occupation of Haiti
**1916** US intervention in Mexico
**1916–24** US occupation of Dominican Republic

**1915** Puno revolt (Peru)

**1919** Massive strike and massacre in Lima; *Semana trágica* (Buenos Aires)
**1923** Uncía strike and massacre (Bolivia)

**1927–33** Sandino leads insurrection against US occupation forces (Nicaragua)

**THE DEPRESSION AND THE SECOND WORLD WAR (1930–1945)**

**1930–61** Trujillo, Dictator of Dominican Republic
**1931–44** Maximiliano Hernández Martínez, Dictator of El Salvador; Jorge Ubico, Dictator of Guatemala
**1932–48** Tiburcio Carías Andino, Dictator of Honduras
**1934–40** Lázaro Cárdenas, President of Mexico

**1930–45** Getulio Vargas rules Brazil

**1932** Women included in suffrage (Brazil)
**1932–35** Chaco War
**1934** Women included in suffrage (Chile)

**1934–44** Fulgencio Batista rules Cuba

**1934–35** José María Velasco Ibarra rises to power for the first time (Ecuador)

**1937–56** Anastasio Somoza, Dictator of Nicaragua
**1938** Oil is nationalised in Mexico

**THE COLD WAR (1945–1989)**

**1941** Ecuador–Peru War
**1946–55** Perón in power, Argentina
**1947** Women included in suffrage (Argentina)
**1948** *Bogotazo* riots (Colombia); *La Violencia* begins

**1950–54** Jacobo Arbenz governs Guatemala
**1952–59** Batista returns to power (Cuba)
**1952** Referendum leads to Puerto Rico becoming a free and sovereign state of the USA
**1953** Women included in suffrage (Mexico)
**1953–58** Figueres, President of Costa Rica

**1952** Bolivian Revolution; Women included in suffrage (Bolivia)

**1954–89** Stroessner, Dictator of Paraguay
**1955** Women included in suffrage (Peru)

**1956–59** Cuban Revolution
**1957–71** François Duvalier, Dictator of Haiti
**1961** Bay of Pigs invasion
**1962** Cuban missile crisis

**1964–85** Military junta in Brazil

**1966–78** Balaguer, ruler of Dominican Republic

**1967** Che Guevara is killed in Bolivia
**1968–75** Juan Velasco Alvarado (Peru)

**1968–89** Military rule (Panama)
**1969** Football (Soccer) War
**1971–86** Jean-Claude Duvalier, Dictator of Haiti

**1973–84** Military junta (Uruguay)
**1973–90** Pinochet, Dictator of Chile
**1976–83** Military junta (Argentina)

**1979** *Sandinista* Revolution (Nicaragua)

**THE AGE OF NEOLIBERALISM (1980–)**

**1981–87** *Contra* War in Nicaragua

**1982** Falklands War
**1983–85** Democracy restored in Argentina, Uruguay and Brazil
**1988** Pinochet loses plebiscite in Chile
**1989** Coup deposes Stroessner in Paraguay; *Caracazo* riots in Venezuela
**1990** Democracy restored in Chile

**1994** *Zapatista* revolt erupts in Chiapas (Mexico)

**1995** Ecuador–Peru War

**1996** Peace Treaty ends 36-year civil war (Guatemala)

**1998** Hugo Chávez elected President of Venezuela
**1999** Socialist electoral victory in Chile

**2000** PRI lose elections in Mexico for the first time

**2000** Hugo Chávez is re-elected; Alejandro Toledo wins elections in Peru
**2002** Chávez survives coup
**2002** Luiz Inacio Lula da Silva wins elections in Brazil (re-elected in 2006)
**2003** Néstor Kirchner wins elections in Argentina
**2005** Tabaré Vázquez wins elections in Uruguay
**2006** Michelle Bachelet wins elections in Chile; Evo Morales wins elections in Bolivia; Alan García wins elections in Peru; Rafael Correa wins elections in Ecuador; Álvaro Uribe is re-elected in Colombia and Chávez is re-elected for the third time in Venezuela
**2006** Morales forces shift in ownership of Bolivian gas fields

**2006** Felipe Calderón wins Mexican elections despite allegations of fraud; Daniel Ortega wins elections in Nicaragua

**2007** Chávez pulls Venezuela out of IMF and World Bank – and loses referendum to reform Constitution

Map of Latin America, 2000

# Prologue

## Many Latin Americas

On 22 June 1986, in the quarter-finals of the World Cup in Mexico City, England lost to Argentina 1–2. The match became notorious due to the two goals scored by Diego Maradona. The first was much talked about because he knocked the ball in over the English goalkeeper with his hand – and the referee allowed it. The second became famous because it was probably one of the most spectacular goals ever scored in soccer history. Maradona managed to take the ball with him from one end of the pitch to the other, dribbling past every single player who tried to stop him, eventually shooting it effortlessly past the goalkeeper once he reached England's area. Argentina went on to win the World Cup, beating Germany 3–2 in the final. For the British media and, in particular, the English press, Argentina's victory was almost inevitable, since they were considered to be virtually the home team. Since the World Cup was being held in a Latin American country, the assumption was that Argentina would benefit from the support of the locals, even if these were Mexicans and not Argentineans. Interestingly, this line of thought was not extended to the match England lost to Argentina in St Etienne, in the 1998 World Cup held in France. The fact that England was a European team playing in a European country was not perceived to be an advantage in the same way that it was for a Latin American team playing in a Latin American country. There was no sense that the French would cheer on England for the sake of

Europe. Not even British nationality meant that you wanted England to win. In Scotland, on that balmy evening of 30 June, most Scots cheered when David Beckham was sent off, and celebrated the defeat of Glenn Hoddle's side. What becomes evident from all this is that most British soccer commentators did not believe that there was a strong enough sense of Europeanness to make the English side feel that they were on home turf when they met Argentina in St Etienne. What also becomes clear is that, in contrast, they were convinced there was such a thing as a strong Latin American bond that could override different national identities when Argentina played England in Mexico. It should come as no surprise that this assumption was far from accurate. A high proportion of Mexicans (who tell numerous jokes about Argentineans) wanted Argentina to lose in 1986. Across the River Plate, mirroring the sentiments of the Scots towards England, dozens of Uruguayans watched their television sets, cursing the referee who allowed Maradona's first goal. To emphasise this point more strikingly, in Paraguay, the day Argentina faced Romania in Los Angeles in the 1994 World Cup, numerous banners went up in Asunción, announcing that the Paraguayans were hoping Romania would win. On the following day, after Romania beat Argentina 3–2, the Paraguayans filled the streets of the capital with more banners, which said 'Thank you, Romania!' In other words, Latin America is as much a united and monolithic entity as Europe is. Or, to put it differently, Latin America is as much a heterogeneous, divided, fractured and plural construct as Europe is.

We are dealing with the peoples of North America (Mexicans do not take kindly to being called South or Central American), the Caribbean, Central America and South America. Moreover, over the last two centuries the different countries of Latin America have been subdivided or grouped together under other categories that go beyond the strictly geographical. The term *Spanish America* has been used to refer to those countries that belonged to Spain prior to their respective wars of independence. This excludes those countries that were either Portuguese (Brazil), French (Haiti, French Guyana), British (Bahamas, Barbados, Belize, Guyana, Jamaica, Trinidad and Tobago) or Dutch (Suriname). Since Brazil was the only Portuguese colony in the continent, the term *Portuguese America* is seldom used. The term that has been used, in Spanish, to describe former Spanish–Portuguese America is that of *Iberoamérica* (Iberian America). However, *Iberian America* or *Ibero America* are not terms that have been often used in English. Therefore we tend to use that of *Latin America* to refer to these countries. It was the French who came up with the term *Latin America* in the late 1850s, to define that part of the American continent (from Alaska down to Cape Horn – what the Kuna Indians described as *Abya Yala*) that was not predominantly Anglo-Saxon, including all Spanish-speaking countries, Brazil and French-speaking Haiti. Although some attention will be given to former British and Dutch colonies, this book almost inevitably centres on *Latin America* in its original sense.

The sizes of these countries range from the expanse of Brazil (which occupies 8,511,965 square kilometres and is bigger than the whole of Europe, from Ireland to the Russian Federation) to the smallness of Haiti. With populations that range from almost 180 million in the former to 10 million in the latter, the differences that distinguish their social, economic and historical contexts cannot be emphasised enough. The distances that separate capitals such as Mexico City in North America from Buenos Aires in South America cannot be ignored either. It is quicker to fly from London to Mexico City than it is to fly from Mexico City to Buenos Aires. The landscapes that differentiate one country from another could not be more startling. The snowy peaks of the Andes that surround the highest capital in the world, La Paz, the Atacama Desert in Chile (the driest desert in the world), the 'English' countryside of the grasslands and gentle hills of Cuchilla Grande in Uruguay, the tropical rainforest of the Amazon, the sugar cane plantations of Cuba, are all contrasting landscapes that belong to the same continent. Even within one country alone, taking Mexico as an example, there are deserts, semi-deserts, tropical rainforests, alpine forests, grasslands and marshlands. In the autumn of 1999 it was possible to have floods in the states of Tabasco, Veracruz, Puebla and Mexico, and a drought in Chihuahua, Coahuila, Sinaloa, Sonora and Durango, the likes of which had never been experienced before.

The origins of the peoples of these twenty countries are equally disparate and varied. The strong Amerindian presence in Mexico, Central America, Ecuador, Peru and Bolivia contrasts with the African influence in the Caribbean (including Colombia and Venezuela) and Brazil, where a long history of slavery resulted in a race altogether different to that of the western hemisphere of the continent. To this day, in Mexico alone, there are fifty-six different indigenous ethnic groups, all of which speak different languages. And while the *mestizaje* (the fusion of Spaniards and Indians) which led to the emergence of a mixed race of Spanish–Indian descent came to characterise the populations of Mexico (75 per cent), Central America (62 per cent), Colombia (50 per cent), Venezuela (70 per cent) and Chile (70 per cent), in Southern Cone countries, such as Uruguay and Argentina, a nineteenth-century policy of extermination (not too dissimilar to the one the Anglo-Saxons employed in the United States with regard to the Native Americans), paired with a vast influx of Italian immigrants, resulted in a predominantly Caucasian population with little, if any, trace of Amerindian descent, and a flurry of Italian surnames.

If we were to take music as an example of the diversity that characterises the different existing expressions of Latin Americanness, the point could not be more obvious. The haunting sound of the Andean panpipes, the passionate *tango* from Buenos Aires, the lively, carnivalesque *samba* of Rio de Janeiro and its more sensual and warm Brazilian relative the *bossanova*, the sexy rhythms of *salsa,* with its plethora of variations (*rumba, cumbia, merengue, lambada*) depending on whether it is Cuban, Colombian, from the Dominican Republic or Brazilian, the frantic strumming of the Venezuelan *charango*, the trumpet fanfare of the Mexican *mariachis*, the Central American sound of the *marimba*, the Cuban *bolero*, the Mexican *corrido*, the western-style *rancheras,* are **all** equally representative of Latin America.

In the same way that we tend to view European novelists as representatives of the cultures of their own particular countries rather than as exponents of a continental approach to literature, Latin Americans are equally aware of the different national backgrounds of their most famous authors. It could be argued that John Fowles, Juan Goytisolo and Alain Robbe-Grillet share parallel approaches to writing, and that read alongside each other they might offer a European vision of the world which, set in a shared historical context, transcends their national differences. Nevertheless, for most Europeans, Fowles could only be English, Goytisolo, Spanish and Robbe-Grillet, French. The same is the case with Latin American writers. Although most literature courses that focus on Latin America throw writers such as Gabriel García Márquez, Mario Vargas Llosa and Carlos Fuentes together within their analytical parameters, for the majority of Latin Americans, García Márquez could only be Colombian, Vargas Llosa, Peruvian and Fuentes, Mexican. They might all write in Spanish and they may share a parallel approach to writing, but the different cultures they represent, obvious to a Latin American, cannot be ignored.

Moreover, within each Latin American country, there remains a strong sense of identity within the different communities that inhabit them, which means that even the notion of being Colombian, Peruvian or Mexican is a controversial and contested one. Since the early 1980s, different indigenous movements in countries such as Mexico, Ecuador and Bolivia have become increasingly active in their rejection of what they have come to see as the imposition of a *mestizo* interpretation of their national identity. The demands of the *Ejército Zapatista de Liberación Nacional* (Zapatista Army of National Liberation) in Mexico represent a forceful rejection of the current imposed united sense of patriotism that does not accept the plurality and diversity of the country's indigenous cultures. Bolivia's indigenous president Evo Morales' recent statement that the suffering of his country's indigenous peoples can be equated with that of the black population of South Africa under apartheid eloquently highlights the extent to which racism has marred race relations in Latin America (see Exhibit 6.1). Even beyond the problems arising from the racial and ethnic tensions that characterise those countries where a strong Amerindian presence has survived over five hundred years of European interference, *mestizos* sustain different views on who they are, regardless of whether they are all Venezuelan or Colombian. In a novel such as García Márquez's *Cien años de soledad* (1967), for the family of the Buendías, based in the imaginary lowlands village of Macondo, the worst thing about the character of Fernanda, who marries Aureliano Segundo, is that she comes from Bogotá, in the highlands. She is a *cachaca*. The passions that are aroused when a soccer team such as América (Mexico City) plays against Chivas (Guadalajara) exemplify only too well how *chilangos* (people from Mexico City) and *tapatíos* (people from Jalisco) believe they belong to different and even opposed communities, despite their shared nationality. Pelé (probably the greatest footballer of all time), Chief Raoni (Chief of the Megkronoti tribe from the Amazon basin who, through worldwide tours with rock musician Sting, drew international attention to the rainforests and their inhabitants) and Astrud Gilberto (the *bossanova* singer who became famous with her rendition of *Ipanema* in 1964), to name three famous Brazilians of recent times, might all belong to the same country, but it is obvious that what each of them represents offers a very different understanding of what it means to be Brazilian.

Furthermore, although the Spanish language could be seen as providing a unifying element in at least eighteen Latin American countries, it would be wrong to assume that there is such a thing as a standard Latin American Spanish, as opposed to the Spanish spoken in Spain. A parallel situation can be found with the English language. Evidently, the English spoken at a gathering of people from the United Kingdom, Ireland, Canada, the United States, Australia, New Zealand and South Africa is not so different as to make it impossible for them to understand each other. This does not mean, however, that their use of the language, regarding vocabulary and accent as well as certain grammatical points, is identical. The only unifying feature of so-called Latin American Spanish is that Spanish Americans, whether they are from Costa Rica, Chile or Uruguay, do not use the lisping Spanish *ceceo*. In other words, all Spanish Americans *sesean*. However, beyond this common feature, the Spanish spoken in Cuba, for instance, is as different from the Spanish spoken in Argentina as the English spoken in England is different from that spoken in Jamaica. As an example, Argentineans, Uruguayans and Paraguayans do not use *tú* (you) when employing the informal second person singular. Instead they say *vos* and, in doing so, conjugate the verbs in the second person singular in an entirely different way to the rest of the Spanish American community (with the exception of certain rural areas of Guatemala, Nicaragua and Venezuela). What for an Ecuadorian would be *tú comes, tú quieres, tú piensas*, for a Uruguayan would be *vos comés, vos querés, vos pensás* (you eat, you want, you think). There are nouns that are completely different depending on where you are in Latin America. A straightforward object such as a bus may be described as a *camión, pesero, combi, colectivo, trolebús, omnibús, micro, autobús* and *guagua*. In Mexico it might be preferable to avoid stating that you intend to *coger* the bus (as you would do in Spain), unless you do not mind people thinking that you intend to have sexual intercourse with the vehicle. Similarly, it is best not to christen your daughter *Concha* or *Conchita* (a particularly popular name in Spain and Mexico) in Argentina, for that would amount to naming her after the most intimate part of a woman's anatomy.

Of course, most of these countries *do* have something in common which differentiates them from the United States and Canada. Although it is important to stress the plurality and diversity of Latin America, the countries this book will focus on are united by their shared experience of Iberian conquest and colonisation. Following Christopher Columbus's first voyage across the Atlantic, in 1492, until the early nineteenth century, the different Amerindian peoples of what would later be known as Latin America, from the Aztecs to the Incas, were forced to become part of the vast Spanish and Portuguese empires. For better or worse, three hundred years of colonial rule have resulted in a people who, in their majority, speak either Spanish or Portuguese, are Catholic in their faith, and whose ties to Spain and Portugal remain a fundamental part of their culture to this day. Moreover, with some obvious exceptions, most Latin American countries fought their wars of independence at the same time, experienced parallel conflicts during the early national period, became export-economies at the end of the nineteenth century, found themselves overtaken by bloody revolutions and brutal dictatorships for the greater part of the twentieth century, and came to follow kindred paths towards democratisation, almost in unison, as the new millennium was born, in the midst of an emergent globalised vision of the world and a contested neoliberal economic framework.

For the purpose of this book, it will be the more general and common historical features that characterised the continent's development over the last two hundred years which will be outlined. The aim of *Latin America since 1780* is to offer a continental-based narrative which stresses the historical parameters its countries have in common, while allowing space for specific national contexts to be highlighted. An in-depth account of the numerous governments, presidents and movements that appeared in every single Latin American country would result in a vast and unwieldy book. The main thrust of this narrative is to show in broad terms, while noting the exceptions, how countries as far apart as Mexico and Argentina followed similar paths (albeit with variations) from the end of the eighteenth to the beginning of the twenty-first century. The danger remains that, in pursuing a global vision of the continent's modern history, the striking differences of Latin America's complex mosaic of diverse and plural identities and experiences will be sacrificed. Broad generalisations can be deeply misleading and inaccurate. While it has been my endeavour to avoid falling into the traps that the process of simplification places in the path of any historian attempting to condense over two hundred years of the history of twenty different countries into not more than 200 printed pages, it is almost inevitable that there will be passages in the text that do not do justice to the extraordinary contrasts that have characterised the recent past of Latin America's multiple, diverse and heterogeneous peoples and contexts. However similar some of the historical contexts may appear, there is no such thing as Latin America, but many different, contrasting, divided and, at times, even opposed Latin Americas, none of which is necessarily more representative than the others.

## CHAPTER 1

## World context

On 31 December 1799, the western hemisphere was immersed in a period of upheaval. Since 1755 uprisings had erupted throughout Europe as modernity clashed with tradition. Between 1775 and 1783 the American War of Independence was fought. In 1789 the French Revolution began, leading to the abolition of the monarchy (1792) and Louis XVI's execution (1793). During the first decade of the nineteenth century the revolutionary whirlwind raged on. In Latin America the situation was no different. Although revolutions did not become widespread throughout Spanish America until 1810, revolts in Peru (1780–81), Bolivia (1781–82), Colombia (1781) and Brazil (1788–89), without forgetting the Haitian Revolution (1791), exploded in tandem with those that rampaged elsewhere. A conflagration of issues had led to tensions running high. Building on the scientific knowledge of the seventeenth century, a novel faith in reason and progress emerged. This eighteenth-century faith, translated into the ideas of the Enlightenment, challenged long accepted

# The late colonial period and the wars of independence (1780–1825)

By 1800, fifty years of Bourbon reformism had led to major unrest in Spanish America. The French occupation of Spain, in 1808, resulted in a constitutional crisis which ultimately provoked the wars of independence. Likewise it inspired the Portuguese monarchy to transfer its court from Lisbon to Rio de Janeiro. After ten to fifteen years of brutal civil war in most of Spain's colonies, the Spanish monarchy lost control of its entire empire in continental America, succeeding only in holding on to Cuba and Puerto Rico. In 1822 Brazil became independent, with the Portuguese king's son, Emperor Dom Pedro I, serving as the new nation's monarch.

## The colonial experience

On 4 November 1780, in Tinta, Peru, a **mestizo** landowner called José Gabriel Condorcanqui started a revolt against the Spanish authorities. He claimed to be a direct descendant of the Incas and traditions and institutions, questioning authority, religion, privileges, church and monarchy. It also gave the European monarchies of the late eighteenth century the inspiration to centralise government and society, and to assault churches, corporations and guilds, aiming to improve society through direct bureaucratic intervention. Economic needs underlay the monarchies' attempts to control their kingdoms and colonies, raising unpopular taxes, as a global economy started to emerge. The European desire to control the African slave trade and the markets of India and East Asia resulted in this being not only a period of revolutions, but one of ongoing war. In a struggle for empire, Britain, France, Spain and the Netherlands fought each other throughout the century. With the rise to power of Napoleon Bonaparte, in 1799, these conflicts reached a climax. Between 1803 and 1814 Napoleon's empire spread throughout Europe, and his wars brought Russia, Prussia and Austria into the fray. While in Europe a relatively more peaceful period succeeded his defeat at Waterloo in 1815, in Latin America the revolution reached one of its bloodiest stages.

---

### mestizos

Racially mixed Spanish Americans of Spanish-Indian descent. The term **mestizaje**, deriving from *mestizo*, refers to the fusion of Spaniards and Indians.

---

### haciendas (estancias in the Southern Cone countries)

Large estates.

---

### creoles/criollos

White Spanish Americans of Spanish descent.

---

adopted the Inca name of Túpac Amaru II in direct reference to the last Inca noble, executed by the Spaniards. During the six months it took the Spaniards to quell the uprising, property was sacked, **haciendas** were destroyed, and there was a very high death toll. Túpac Amaru's forces did not restrict their attacks to Spaniards. **Creoles** and *mestizos* were also assaulted, giving his insurrection a strong ethnic and social dimension that deprived his movement of their support. The government in Lima sent a large military contingent that succeeded in defeating and capturing Túpac Amaru in May 1781. Túpac Amaru, his family and the other main leaders of the revolt were all executed, drawn and quartered, their limbs torn apart by horses.

Historians disagree over whether Túpac Amaru's revolt was an early bid for independence. Nevertheless, it is generally accepted that Túpac Amaru was rebelling against the abuses the Indian population was suffering at the hands of the Spaniards, demanding an end to the forced loans and taxes that had become common practice under the rule of Charles III (1759–88). The fact that Indian discontent had become extreme is undeniable. Although Túpac Amaru was defeated, his followers did not surrender and, under the leadership of the Aymara Indian Túpac Katari, went on to lay siege to La Paz. Their revolt did not end until January 1782, after an estimated 100,000 people had been killed. Divisions between the Aymaras and the Quechuas did not allow the Andean Indians to consolidate a united front against the Spaniards. The fear of a race war prevented the creoles from supporting a revolt they nonetheless sympathised with.

Although Túpac Amaru's revolt was a strictly Andean affair, it highlighted a number of issues that could be seen as representative of the tensions which were beginning to surface in Latin America at the time. There were growing disturbances in most of Spain's colonies after 1760, as a reaction to Charles III's reformism. Coinciding with Túpac Katari's revolt, from March to June 1781, another *mestizo*, José Antonio Galán, led the *comunero* revolt of Socorro, in Colombia. He mobilised between 15,000 and 20,000 Indians and *mestizos* who, in opposition to new tax demands and the usurpation of communal lands, routed the Spanish forces that were sent to suppress the uprising, and threatened to attack the capital of New Granada, Santa Fe de Bogotá. While the Peruvian revolts were crushed with particularly violent resolve, the Spanish authorities in Bogotá ended the *comunero* revolution initially through negotiation. Once the rebels disbanded, however, the Spanish authorities revoked their concessions, executed the leaders of the revolt and reimposed the taxes which had provoked the uprising.

What needs to be stressed is that in Spanish America there was an increasing sense among the population that, after 1760, Bourbon reformism was attacking the social bases and political values which had characterised the Spanish Empire for over two and a half centuries. Under the Habsburgs, Spain's policy towards its colonies could have been described almost as one of abandon. Centuries of inertia on the part of the monarchy had resulted in the colonies enjoying a high degree of autonomy. It was Charles III, a member of the Bourbon dynasty that had taken hold of Spain's destiny, replacing the Habsburgs in the wake of the Spanish War of Succession (1702–13), who changed all that. Determined to impose in Spain and its colonies his own brand of enlightened despotism, Charles III set about reforming his domains, resolved to encourage social and agricultural improvement while tightening his administration's control over the empire. The changes he promoted have come to be known as the Bourbon reforms.

It was under Charles III, and subsequently Charles IV (1788–1808), that the 'second conquest of America' took place. This was a bureaucratic conquest. New viceroyalties were created. The previous district officers of the Spanish Empire were replaced by intendants who set about closely supervising the American population. Government became far more centralised. While in 1750 the majority of existing administrators had been born and bred in the colonies, by 1780 over 72 per cent were newcomers from Spain. The fact that the creoles were discriminated against and that the majority of political posts went to Spaniards contributed to the heightening of tensions between Americans and Spaniards.

The majority of first-generation creoles were aware that they could not rise in the political hierarchy for the simple reason that, regardless of the fact that their parents might be Spanish, white and belonging to the elite, they had been born in the Americas. This awareness of discrimination would become a determining factor in motivating them to rise up in arms against Spain. Nevertheless, the leap they needed to take to progress from criticising the Spanish intendants to actually rebelling against them was not an easy one. They were bound to allegiance to the Spanish Crown due to the ethnic fabric of the cultures in which they lived. While they came to resent the Spaniards' interference in their affairs, they were terrified of the consequences of unleashing a revolution. The majority of the population, Indians, black slaves and even *mestizos*, might assault their properties and inspire a race war in which they could very easily be wiped out, belonging, as they did, to a rather exclusive minority. At the end of the eighteenth century, of an estimated total population of 17 million in Spanish America, only 3.2 million were whites, and of these 150,000 were Spanish. Most creoles wanted a free hand in the running of their provinces and thus opposed the pressures Bourbon Spanish domination represented. However, they would rather support the Spaniards than throw in their lot with revolutionaries like Túpac Amaru.

Bourbon economic policies also created upheaval in the colonies. It was Spain's need for greater revenues that inspired the bureaucratic expansion in the first place. Spain's involvement in the Seven Years War (1756–63), its war with Britain, renewed in 1779, its war with France in 1793 and its subsequent participation in the French Revolutionary and Napoleonic Wars, now serving the French (1796–1808), all meant that it became imperative for Spain to plunder the wealth of its colonies. Taxes were raised, monopolies were created, and trading laws were implemented, all of which were imposed to assist the Spanish economy while damaging the interests of the local elites in the colonies. As a result of this new controlled economy, ironically called *comercio libre* (free commerce), returns from America to Spain between 1778 and 1784 increased by 1,528 per cent! In addition, a mining boom at the end of the eighteenth century resulted in Spanish America yielding, in 1800, 90 per cent of the total world production of silver, the profits being spent on Spain's war efforts. By 1800 most creoles were under the impression that:

- their countries were being invaded by Spaniards, depriving them of all positions of political responsibility; and
- their wealth was being plundered in order to subsidise foreign wars in which they had no interest.

Spain's ongoing wars with Britain, which entailed the loss of Trinidad, Tobago and St Lucia in 1797, resulted in a further grievance for the people of Spanish America: the creation of standing armies in the colonies. The British occupation of Havana in 1762 sent a clear signal to Madrid that Spain needed to strengthen its defences. During the War of the Austrian Succession (1739–48), Britain had already attempted to seize some of Spain's colonies, attacking Cartagena in New Granada, Panama, and Guantánamo in Cuba, and stationing squadrons of warships in Jamaica and Antigua. The Havana debacle alerted Madrid that these attacks could prove successful for the British. In an attempt to protect its colonies, unprecedented numbers of Spanish officers and soldiers were sent out. However, given that most Peninsular troops were needed to fight the different wars in Europe, it became necessary to form colonial military units, enlisting members from the local populations. The arrival of Spanish officers exacerbated the grievances of the creoles by denying them the opportunity to attain the higher ranks in the army. The need to sustain the increased troops became another source of discontent, as it fell on the local communities to feed, house and pay for them. The means by which soldiers were levied affected not only the creoles, but also the majority of the population. In the long run, the formation of standing armies in the colonies not only created much discontent, it resulted in the arming and training of militias that would ultimately revolt against Madrid.

## Church–State relations

Church–State relations were to represent an equally important part of the Americans' eventual rejection of Spain. One of the main ideas proposed by the Enlightenment, adopted by Charles III, was that the Church's power and influence should be restricted. Religion and superstition must give way to the new scientific and philosophical ideas that dominated eighteenth-century France. The Church's influence was viewed as a major obstacle in mankind's pursuit of material and intellectual enlightenment. Therefore, the clergy were ousted from positions of political responsibility. A serious attempt was made to secularise education, a domain that had been the Church's monopoly until then. Ecclesiastical immunities and privileges (**fueros**), by which the clergy were not expected to pay taxes, were severely reduced. The need to raise revenue for the war efforts also meant that the Church's wealth and properties ceased to be treated as inviolable.

Needless to say, the Bourbon reforms met fierce opposition in Spain as well as in Spanish America. In the Spanish countryside, where traditional values had their greatest stronghold, these measures were perceived to be foreign and heretical. The Bourbons and their enlightened ministers were accused of being *afrancesados* (Frenchified). In Spanish America public resentment was even more acute. This was due to the ethnic composition of the clergy, paired with the profound religious fervour that characterised the Indian and *mestizo* population of America. For although the Church, as a whole, resented the assault the Bourbon reforms entailed, its hierarchy responded to the increased state pressure on its revenues by balancing its accounts to the detriment of its lower clergy. The higher clergy, all of whom were Spanish, ensured that their welfare was not affected, while they allowed the lower clergy (creoles and *mestizos*) to bear the brunt of the Church's depleted funds. A disgruntled creole and *mestizo* lower clergy discovered not only that their prospects of ascending in the ecclesiastical hierarchy were blocked by Peninsular dominance of the Church, but that their own personal and financial circumstances were profoundly affected by Bourbon fiscal demands.

At a deeper level, in a context whereby a new generation of Spanish bishops, appointed by the Crown, arrived in the colonies advocating a new understanding of the Church's role, the clash between traditional practices and those now espoused by certain members of the higher Peninsular clergy became deeply

> ### *fueros*
> Corporate rights and privileges dating from medieval Spain which the Church and the army retained until the mid nineteenth century.

unsettling. The bishops who arrived in the colonies after 1760 attacked popular religious manifestations and cults, arguing that these were examples of superstition that needed to be eradicated in the name of a more enlightened Church. In those countries where Roman Catholicism had come to integrate a wide range of Indian practices, these views challenged the very essence of Spanish American devotion. Long held autochthonous festivities, such as the Mexican Day of the Dead on All Saints, processions, pilgrimages, cults of 'Indian' saints and, in particular, of the Virgin Mary in her many manifestations, were suddenly considered to be fanatical by the higher Peninsular clergy.

The generation-long Bourbon assault on the Church had very serious repercussions in Spanish America. At one level, the lower clergy were being pushed into adopting a confrontational stance by the way they were being treated, both financially and morally. At another, it was precisely the parish priests who, through direct and daily contact with the suffering of their parishioners, were in a position to realise the extent to which Bourbon Spain was directly responsible for the social deprivation that had come to characterise the early 1800s. By the time the wars of independence began, a high proportion of leading revolutionaries were priests. It is significant that the revolts in which priests played a key role were characterised by their defence of a seemingly
✳ contradictory agenda, whereby what was at one level a reactionary clerical backlash against the main secularising tenets of the Enlightenment was also a radical movement against social injustice.

## The emergence of creole patriotism

One specific decree that was to have major repercussions in the collective imagination of Spanish America was the expulsion of the Jesuits in 1767. Over 2,500 Jesuits, most of them creoles, were forced to abandon their homelands. This measure deprived Spanish America of its most outstanding educators. The population regarded their forced, life-long exile as a vile example of Bourbon despotism. In the first instance, the dismay of the populace was expressed in a number of riots and minor uprisings. Thereafter, a great resentment was borne by the communities the Jesuits left behind.

It was these exiles who began the intellectual process of defining the particularity of the future nations they had been forced to leave. Ostracised in Europe, the creole Jesuits found themselves pining for their homelands. They took it upon themselves to refute the views generally accepted in Europe that the New World was an inferior continent. Offended by the writings of European philosophers and scientists, some of the exiled Jesuits wrote works of outstanding scholarship that defended their homelands' geographies and histories. Francisco Javier Clavigero, Juan Ignacio Molina and Juan de Velasco, to name but a few, initiated a process of national reappraisal that soon caught the imagination of Europe as well as the Americas. Almost immediately after the exiled Jesuits' works started to be circulated in America, a wide range of creole intellectuals went on to develop their rebuttal of European prejudices. Publications started to abound in the colonies, celebrating the wealth and beauty of their regions, referring to them as their mother countries.

With creole patriotism came a vigorous attempt to rescue the Indian past of the continent. Even in countries like Chile, where the pre-conquest Indian civilisations were not as sophisticated as those of Peru or Mexico and Central America, there was a move towards praising what they had achieved prior to the arrival of the conquistadors. It was in countries like Mexico, home to the Aztecs and the Mayas, that creole patriotism acquired a particularly strong **indigenista** streak. At a

> ### indigenista
> Literally, *Indianist*; refers, in this context, to patriotic creoles who idealised the pre-conquest indigenous cultures of their countries as an expression of their rejection of Spain and as a means to forge an emergent national identity. **Indigenismo** is the term given to their ideology.

political level this became a means to condemn everything Spain had brought to the Americas. They argued that the Spanish conquest of the Americas had resulted in three hundred years of oppression and that it was their duty to renew the struggle of the Aztecs where it had been left off. Needless to say, the creoles' *indigenismo* was strictly historical. They regarded their contemporary Indians with as much contempt as the Spaniards did. Nonetheless, however contradictory their emergent nationalism was, their condemnation of everything Spanish, and their affirmation of an emergent national identity that had its roots in pre-conquest America, became a very powerful creed once the wars of independence erupted.

Coinciding with this proliferation of creole writings, a leading Prussian scientist, Alexander Von Humboldt, visited and explored Venezuela, Colombia, Peru, Cuba and Mexico between 1799 and 1804. The books he wrote recounting his adventures, once he returned to Paris, were to become extremely influential. The fact that the writings of a European confirmed many of the views which had been defended by the creole intellectuals served to validate what the creoles already knew. However, perhaps more significantly, it was Humboldt who predicted that with independence the future prosperity of the different American nations would be extraordinary. Humboldt's writings, translated almost immediately into Spanish, led many creoles to believe that all that was needed for them to enjoy the abundant wealth of their regions was to become independent.

## Who revolted and why

By 1808 a conflagration of issues meant that Spanish America was on the verge of a revolutionary explosion. More than fifty years of Bourbon reforms had led to high creole, *mestizo*, Indian and slave discontent. Bourbon political, economic, military and religious policies had succeeded in alienating the majority of the colonial population. The American War of Independence (1775–83) had become a source of inspiration for many creoles. The French Revolution (1789) had been equally, if not more influential in spreading beliefs that exalted the need for equality, liberty and fraternity.

Those countries where there was a high population of black slaves were also reaching breaking point. One of the immediate effects the French Revolution had in the Caribbean was to inspire the mulattoes and free blacks of the French colony,

SPANISH SOUTH AMERICA AFTER
BOURBON REFORMS, *c.*1800

Cartagena

Caracas • Cumaná

CAPTAINCY GENERAL
OF VENEZUELA
1777

• Bogotá

VICEROYALTY
• Popayán
OF NEW GRANADA
•Quito
1717 AND 1739

Guayaquil

I. TRUJILLO 1784

Trujillo

I. TARMA 1784

I. LIMA 1783

VICEROYALTY
OF PERU
1542

Lima

I. HUANCAVELICA
1784
I. HUAMANGA 1784
I. CUZCO 1784

• Cuzco

P. MOJOS

I. PUNO 1783  Arequipa

I. AREQUIPA 1784

La Paz

I. COCHABAMBA 1783

I. LA PAZ 1784
I. CHARCAS 1783

P. CHIQUITOS

I. PARAGUAY 1783

I. POTOSÍ 1783

*Pacific Ocean*

VICEROYALTY
• Salta   Asunción
I. SALTA 1783
Tucumán

P.
MISIONES

Corrientes

OF RIO DE LA PLATA

*Atlantic Ocean*

I. SANTIAGO

I. CÓRDOBA
1783

Santiago •

P. MONTEVIDEO

CAPTAINCY-GENERAL

Concepción

Buenos Aires •

Montevideo

OF CHILE

1776

I. CONCEPCIÓN

I. BUENOS AIRES 1783

1778

P. THE MALVINAS ISLANDS

• Viceregal Capital
I. = INTENDENCY OF
P. = PROVINCE OF

Map of South America, 1800

Saint-Domingue, to press their claims for equality. The rich sugar cane planters on the island demanded colonial autonomy and refused to accept the French National Assembly's decision of May 1791 to grant comparable rights to the free people of colour. It was while Saint-Domingue's elites wrangled over their response to the French government's decrees that over 100,000 slaves revolted on the Plaine du Nord part of the island, in August 1791. The slaves burnt the cane fields and went on a rampage, killing whites. By 1794, in spite of the interference of a French expeditionary force, it was clear that white supremacy in the colony was over. The white elites requested the help of the British and the Spanish (who retained their part of the island, present-day Dominican Republic, until it became a French colony temporarily, 1801–09). However, British troops abandoned the island in 1798, defeated by what had become a formidable army of former slaves under the leadership of François-Domingue Toussaint Louverture, a former slave himself. On consolidating their victory, Toussaint Louverture renounced the bid for independence as long as Revolutionary France granted the island special laws, including the abolition of slavery. Napoleon Bonaparte, France's new ruler (1799–1814, 1815), rejected Toussaint Louverture's demands and sent a further expeditionary force. Although Toussaint Louverture was captured and died in prison in France in 1803, the French army was unable to overcome the blacks' resistance. At the start of 1804, one of Toussaint Louverture's lieutenants, Jean-Jacques Dessalines, claimed victory and declared Saint-Domingue independent under the old Indian name of Haiti. Dessalines was crowned Emperor Jacques I soon after and a policy of exterminating the remaining whites was implemented. Alejo Carpentier's novel, *El siglo de las luces* (1962), set between the Haitian Revolution of 1791 and the popular rising in Madrid of 2 May 1808, is a masterful depiction of the turmoil of these years.

While the Haitian Revolution terrified planters throughout the Caribbean, in the southern states of the United States, in Venezuela, Colombia and Brazil, it became an inspiration for the black slaves, who started to become involved in more frequent revolts. However, while all these issues meant that Spanish America was close to being consumed by revolutionary activity, a spark was needed to set the colonies on fire. This spark came from Spain. In December 1807 Napoleon gave the order for the military occupation of the Peninsula. On 19 March 1808, following the mutiny of La Granja, Charles IV abdicated in favour of his son Ferdinand VII, who, in turn, left Madrid in the hands of the French in April, to meet Napoleon at Bayonne. On 5 May, only three days after the people of Madrid took up arms in a popular uprising against the invaders, Ferdinand relinquished his claim to the Spanish throne. Napoleon had his brother crowned King Joseph I of Spain, precipitating what is known in Spain as the War of Independence (1808–13).

It was the French usurpation of the Spanish throne that unleashed the constitutional crisis which led to the outbreak of the wars of independence in Spanish America. With Ferdinand VII held captive in France, once news of the seizure of Madrid reached the Americas it became evident that the colonies had been left without a monarch they could obey. They could not take their orders from Joseph I, since he was a usurper, and it was not clear whether they should obey the Spanish rebel juntas that were formed in

**peninsulares**

Neutral term that was used to describe Spaniards. Pejorative terms that were used include: **gachupines**, **maturrangos**, **godos** and **chapetones**.

the Peninsula, since these had awarded themselves rights which had not been granted by the king. As long as the king was a prisoner of the French, power was, by necessity, devolved to the people. Throughout the summer of 1808, the different viceregal and municipal authorities found themselves having to decide who was to be responsible for the day-to-day running of their regional administrations. As long as Ferdinand VII was in France, it was clear that they would have to run the show themselves. This, of course, is where the problems began. Many creoles realised that the time had come to seize the day. Most Spaniards posted in the colonies, aware that the next step from allowing the creoles in would probably be independence, resisted the creoles' attempts to become involved in the political administration of the colonies, and sought guidance from the rebel juntas in Spain. The power struggle between creoles and **peninsulares** fast reached breaking point. Within two years of the French occupation of Spain, the political situation of most of Spanish America had descended into a state of brutal civil war. Between 1809 and 1810, creole rebellions led to the capture of numerous cities and governments. The Spaniards retaliated and all hell broke loose.

Between 1808 and 1825, most of Spanish America was ravaged by war. Control of the main cities changed hands as the development of the wars favoured either the royalist or the patriot armies. Developments in Spain further complicated matters, creating divisions within both the royalist and the patriot forces. In 1812, the rebel junta in Cádiz drafted what was one of the most progressive constitutions of the period. It guaranteed a wide range of individual and collective rights. And while it established that Spain was a monarchy, it granted power to its legislative body, the *Cortes* (parliament) rather than to its executive branch, the king. It assaulted the rights and properties of both Church and nobility, and it established that the representatives in the *Cortes* would be elected partly by universal male suffrage. With the liberals controlling Cádiz and representing the legitimate government of Spain, responses in the colonies to the 1812 Constitution were fraught with contradictions. When the Constitution began to be implemented in Spanish America in 1813, many liberal creoles preferred to remain attached to Spain rather than support independence movements which, in some cases, appeared to be led by reactionary clerical traditionalists. For many Spanish administrators, in contrast, the implementation of the Constitution was viewed as a blow to their attempts to crush the revolts, since it enabled the population at large, **castas** and creoles alike, to elect their representatives in the *Cortes*. Once Ferdinand VII returned to power and revoked the Constitution, in 1814, the Spanish forces in the colonies became divided between those who were liberals and those who

**castas**

Term used to describe all people who were racially mixed.

were absolutists. Their divisions became further exacerbated in 1820, when a liberal revolt in Spain succeeded in forcing the monarch to impose the 1812 charter all over again, only to overthrow it once more in 1823.

The wars of independence were a complex affair. It was not an easy case of creoles fighting Spaniards. Creoles fought against Spaniards, against each other, against Indians, against *castas*, and against blacks. Divided between unitarians/centralists and federalists, defenders of free market economics and protectionist policies, abolitionists and slave traders, republicans and monarchists, absolutists and constitutionalists, anti-clerical radicals and pro-clerical traditionalists, the creole elites were only united by a fragile desire for independence. This desire, moreover, remained hesitant in many cases, faced as they were with the threat of social dissolution and a race war in which they were numerically inferior. The Indians' response to the wars was equally varied and difficult to categorise. In certain provinces where it became evident that the war was a power struggle between whites in which there was little for them to gain, their stance was one of notorious apathy. In other areas, Indians participated with vigour, sometimes fighting for the Spaniards, sometimes against. The *castas*, whether they were *mestizos* or mulattoes, fought for both sides, depending on where they were from and what their particular context was. The black slaves, when they revolted, as was the case in Venezuela, took it upon themselves to attack all whites, regardless of whether they were patriots or royalists. In most cases, local issues were key to motivating them to take one side or another. Ancient rivalries between and within local communities meant that different families and villages used the pretext of the wars to settle old grudges. They joined the patriots or the royalists in response to the side their local rivals adopted, regardless of whether they believed in grand and abstract terms such as *independence*. People fought for their regions, their districts, their village-based clans, for themselves. Notions such as Mexico or Colombia were not even commonly used by the high-ranking officers of the patriot-insurgent armies, let alone by the illiterate majority forced to fight for one cause or the other. The wars were characterised by murders, looting, pillage and rape. Banditry proliferated. It became common for people to change sides from patriot to royalist and back again, depending on circumstances, on who had the upper hand, on what favoured their regional or personal interests. Regional rivalries also meant that as the emergent nations came into being, conflicts between them abounded. Buenos Aires' attempts to control Montevideo, Asunción and La Paz meant that future Uruguayans, Paraguayans and Bolivians found themselves fighting the Argentineans with as much resolve as they fought the Spaniards.

The constitutional crisis of 1808 resulted in a mosaic of parallel, yet not altogether identical, contexts in the colonies. The power vacuum that resulted from the French occupation of Spain provided the instability necessary for the discontent caused by fifty years of Bourbon reformism to erupt into violence. However, independence did not come easily. Between ten and fifteen years of war were fought before Spain's control of its colonies in continental America was brought to an end. The fact that the Spaniards were a minority no doubt meant that winning the wars would prove almost impossible. Of the 40,000 Spanish troops that were dispatched to the colonies between 1811 and 1818, the majority died of tropical diseases. However, due credit must be awarded to the military genius of those creole generals who ensured that independence was achieved: Simón Bolívar (1783–1830), José de San Martín (1778–1850), Francisco de Paula Santander (1792–1865) and Antonio José de Sucre (1795–1830).

## Mexico's war of independence

In terms of its origins, the Mexican War of Independence (1810–21) bore greater resemblance to Túpac Amaru's revolt than it did to the independence movements that spread throughout the rest of Spanish America post-1808. On 16 September 1810, in Dolores, the creole priest Miguel Hidalgo y Costilla summoned his parishioners to church and inspired them to revolt against Spanish domination. The revolt was initially supported by creoles, who soon withdrew their support as Hidalgo's spontaneous army of 50,000 assaulted and ransacked properties large and small, regardless of whether they belonged to creoles or *gachupines*, killing anybody who stood in their way. The army, almost in its entirety, remained loyal to Spain, despite its predominantly creole and *mestizo* make-up, and after December 1810 initiated a successful campaign of counterinsurgency against Hidalgo's forces. Hidalgo retreated to Guadalajara, where he became, as well as *generalísimo* (general of generals), *Su Alteza Serenísima* (His Serene Highness). Hidalgo was captured, however, and subsequently executed on 30 June 1811. Nevertheless, the insurgency remained strong without Hidalgo. Another priest, José María Morelos, took over the leadership of the revolution, while guerrilla armies, led by regional chieftains, surfaced throughout the colony. It was Morelos who gave the revolution a clearer ideological direction, as well as a more disciplined approach to the military organisation of the patriot forces. He supported the creation of a rebel congress, based in Chilpancingo, which went on to draft the 1814 Constitution of Apatzingán, inspired by his *Sentiments of the Nation* (see Exhibit 1.1). However, Morelos was also captured and executed, on 22 December 1815.

Following Morelos' death, the insurgency lost both its strength and its momentum. From a total of 80,000 insurgents, there remained, by 1816, no more than 8,000 poorly armed rebels in the field, and these were divided and scattered over the vast territories of the country. Although Francisco Javier Mina, a Spanish liberal who joined the insurgents on arrival in Mexico, led the 1817 expedition that gave the revolution some respite, he was taken prisoner after a few months of fighting and was executed on 11 November that year. The years from 1810 to 1815 were the years of greatest revolutionary activity in Mexico. From 1816 to 1821, the War of Independence was characterised by constant yet minor skirmishes that in no way resembled the large military campaigns of the previous years. Nonetheless, guerrilla warfare proved effective in the long run, as it became clear to the creole high-ranking officers in the royalist army that peace would not be restored until Mexico became independent. It was this realisation, paired with the impact of events in Spain on the colonies, in the wake of the restoration of the 1812 Constitution in 1820, that led these creole officers to finally turn their backs on Madrid and join forces with the insurgents.

On 24 February 1821, Colonel Agustín de Iturbide, one of the colonial government's more dedicated creole officers, rebelled against Spain and proclaimed Mexico's independence with his Plan of Iguala. With the promise of Three Guarantees – that Mexico would be independent, that Roman Catholicism would be the official religion, and that all Spaniards could continue to live unharmed in Mexico – the war soon came to an end. Iturbide succeeded in bringing old insurgents and old royalists together, although they opted to unite for very different reasons. Independence was formally attained on 27 September 1821, when the Army of the Three Guarantees marched into Mexico City. Iturbide proclaimed himself Emperor Agustín I on 18 May 1822.

It was in response to the events in Mexico that Central America achieved independence from Spain in 1821. Prior to 1820, no unified independence movement had surfaced in Central America. It was only after news of the Plan of Iguala reached Central America that, on 15 September 1821, the authorities in Guatemala City issued their own declaration of independence. The other cities in the region followed suit and were initially integrated into Iturbide's Mexican Empire (1821–23). Once Iturbide abdicated (19 March 1823), the five provinces of Guatemala, El Salvador, Honduras, Nicaragua and Costa Rica (the elites of Chiapas opted to remain part of Mexico) reaffirmed their independence in their joint declaration of 1 July 1823, whereby they became the United Provinces of Central America.

## The independence of the River Plate provinces

The Viceroyalty of the River Plate encompassed present-day Argentina, Uruguay, Paraguay and Bolivia (after 1776), with its administrative capital in Buenos Aires. Its own wars of independence were different from the rest due to the impact on the area of a British expeditionary force, prior to the 1808 constitutional crisis. On 27 June 1806, as part of the war Britain was fighting against France and Spain, British troops took Buenos Aires. The Spanish viceroy, together with the majority of the Spanish elites, abandoned the port and took refuge in their country estates. It was left up to the creoles and the lower classes of the port to confront the invaders. This they did with a vengeance, defeating the British on 12 August 1806, taking the British commander and 1,200 troops prisoner.

When a second British expeditionary force was defeated in Buenos Aires, after they had succeeded in taking Montevideo in 1807, it became patently clear to the Argentinean creoles that it was they, and not the Spanish, who had defended their community from the invaders. When the Spaniards attempted to restore the old order they found that the creoles in Buenos Aires, in military control of the provincial capital, were not prepared to let go of it. Therefore, when news arrived of the French occupation of Spain, Buenos Aires was already controlled by the creole elites. However, it was not until 18–19 May 1810 that the creoles in Buenos Aires, feeling that there was a need to exert greater power over their province, staged the May Revolution that brought about, in effect, the independence of Argentina. Thereafter, from 1810 to 1821, the conflicts that affected the region were mainly fought by creoles against each other. The social dimensions that characterised the war in Mexico and the racial dimensions that characterised it in Peru, Ecuador, Colombia and Venezuela, were absent in the River Plate. The different economic interests of Buenos Aires and the interior led to clashes over the policies that were pursued: free market or protectionist. The federalism of the provinces led to continuous revolts against the centralism of Buenos Aires. Within Buenos Aires itself, creole divisions resulted in the government changing hands on five occasions between 1810 and 1819. In 1820 the government changed hands on average once a fortnight, and it was only after Bernardino Rivadavia came to power in July 1821 that Argentina achieved some form of stability.

Montevideo, which remained deeply royalist in 1808, in part out of its own desire for emancipation from Buenos Aires, rejected the May 1810 revolution from the outset. However, for the Uruguayan creoles it became evident that supporting Spanish rule purely to avoid dependence on Buenos Aires was too damaging a policy to pursue. José Gervasio Artigas, a *gaucho* creole renowned for his enlightened views, used the support of Buenos Aires to revolutionise his homeland. When, in February 1811, the Spanish viceroy in Montevideo declared war on Buenos Aires, the independence movement of the Banda Oriental was ignited. On 26 February 1811, a *gaucho* army was formed in the south-west corner of the province and pronounced the *grito de Asencio*. Artigas, with a small Argentinean force, moved into Uruguay, defeated the Spaniards at the battle of Las Piedras and came close to taking Montevideo. Faced with the prospect of defeat, the viceroy allowed a Portuguese army from Brazil to come to his rescue. Fearing that the Portuguese might use their presence in Uruguay to annex the province for Brazil, the authorities in Buenos Aires signed a treaty with Montevideo (20 October 1811) whereby Buenos Aires accepted Spanish control of the Banda Oriental as long as the Portuguese withdrew their forces.

Betrayed, Artigas led a heroic exodus of more than 4,000 Uruguayans out of the Banda Oriental into the wilderness, announcing that the people from the Banda Oriental would never be subordinated to either Spain or Buenos Aires. Once the Portuguese evacuated the province, nonetheless, an uneasy alliance was formed between Artigas and the Buenos Aires junta, which led to a joint siege of Montevideo in 1813. This alliance soon crumbled after Artigas issued his *Instrucciones* (see Exhibit 1.2), in which he demanded the independence of the United Provinces of the River Plate from Spain, while awarding independent sovereignty to the Banda Oriental. The authorities in Buenos Aires declared him an outlaw and dispatched a new expeditionary army to Montevideo in June 1814. After a further year of war, in February 1815, the Argentineans finally evacuated Montevideo and Artigas became the ruler of the Provincia Oriental.

However, Uruguay did not achieve complete independence until 27 August 1828. Although Artigas ruled the Banda Oriental with noteworthy agrarian radicalism, his plans were thwarted in August 1816 when the Portuguese invaded the province. Between 1816 and 1820, Artigas led the war against the Portuguese, only to find himself eventually defeated, seeking refuge in Paraguay, where he died thirty years later. Uruguay became a province of Brazil in July 1821, only achieving its own sovereign status after the Argentine–Brazilian War (1825–28) came to an end.

Asunción also rejected Buenos Aires' authority. However, unlike Montevideo, its support for Spain did not last as long. The May 1810 Revolution in Buenos Aires served as the catalyst that provoked the independence movement of the region. The Paraguayan elites responded to the Buenos Aires junta by stating that they would remain loyal to Spain while maintaining fraternal relations with the port. However, when Buenos Aires sent General Manuel Belgrano to impose its control over the province, around 5,000 Paraguayans rose up in arms to defend their autonomy, and defeated the Argentineans at the battles of Paraguarí (9 January 1811) and Tacuarí (9 March 1811). The Spanish authorities in Asunción played a small part in the conflict and, after Belgrano retreated, the creoles took over the provincial capital in the revolution of 14 May 1811. On 17 May 1811, Paraguay declared its independence from Spain and Buenos Aires. A creole junta was formed, and after two years of attempted liberal government allowed Dr José Gaspar Rodríguez de Francia to become 'Supreme Dictator of the Republic' in 1814. On 1 June 1816, Dr Francia was further appointed 'Perpetual Dictator' for the rest of his life, and went on to serve as *El Supremo* until 1840.

## José de San Martín's campaign in the South

While Buenos Aires was unsuccessful in its attempts to control Paraguay, Bolivia and Uruguay, it was in many respects responsible for the liberation of Chile. José de San Martín, an Argentinean from Misiones who had fought in the Spanish War of Independence, returned to Buenos Aires in 1812 with the clear intention of joining the revolution and leading it from Argentina, over the Andes, to Chile, Peru, Bolivia and Ecuador. For San Martín it became evident that as long as Peru was controlled by the royalists, the independence of South America would be in jeopardy. Given that the three military expeditions Buenos Aires had dispatched to control La Paz had all ended in failure, San Martín came up with the idea of reaching Lima by heading first west to Chile and then north along the Pacific coast.

On 9 January 1817, with an army of 5,000, San Martín set his plan in motion. The timing of his expedition was crucial in determining its success. After seven years of conflict in Chile, whereby the creole control of Santiago had come and gone, leading to the imposition of a particularly oppressive Spanish-dominated regime, most Chileans were ready to join a liberating army. The key leader of Chilean independence, Bernardo O'Higgins Riquelme, who had been defeated at the battle of Rancagua (1–2 October 1814) and subsequently forced into exile in Mendoza, joined forces with San Martín. In what must have represented one of the most extraordinary feats of the wars of independence, San Martín's army crossed the Andes in two separate sections, managing to regroup on the other side at the appointed time. On the plains of Chacabuco, Argentinean and Chilean soldiers defeated the royalist forces (12 February 1817) and went on to capture Santiago. On 12 February 1818, O'Higgins proclaimed the independence of Chile from Spain and Argentina. However, the royalists made one last bid to reconquer Santiago. Although San Martín was defeated at the battle of Cancha Rayada (19 March 1818), he managed to reconcentrate his forces and strike a definitive blow against the Spanish forces in the battle of Maipú (5 April 1818). Chile consolidated its independence. O'Higgins became the head of the Chilean government and San Martín set about orchestrating the next stage of his plan: the liberation of Peru.

On 25 August 1820, San Martín's expedition, consisting of 4,500 Chilean troops and a large contingent of British mercenaries who had joined the Latin American revolutions following the end of the Napoleonic Wars, set sail from Valparaíso. They landed at Pisco and remained there for six weeks while San Martín waited for the Peruvians to join his liberating army. This did not happen. The memory of Túpac Amaru's revolt had

Simón Bolívar

played a key role in determining the Peruvian creoles' ambiguity over the issue of independence. A second major Indian uprising (1814–15), led this time by Mateo
Pumacahua, meant that the creoles had become even more reluctant to reject Spanish
rule than before. The end result was that between 29 December 1820, when the town
hall of Trujillo launched its proclamation of independence, and January 1826, when the
last Spanish stronghold in Callao capitulated, the government of Peru changed hands
with alarming frequency. Lima was taken by San Martín and Spaniards alike; the
Peruvian creoles changed sides on a number of occasions; and, in the end, it was left to
**Simón Bolívar**, who arrived in Peru on 1 September 1823, to see independence consolidated after a further three years of war. San Martín, in his despair, after meeting Bolívar
in Guayaquil (present-day Ecuador) in 1822, decided to abandon Peru. He left the field
clear for Bolívar and retired to Europe, where he died in 1850.

## Simón Bolívar's campaign in the North

Simón Bolívar was a highly educated aristocratic creole from Caracas who had travelled
extensively in Europe prior to the constitutional crisis of 1808. Well versed in enlightened philosophy, thanks to the teachings of his mentor, Simón Rodríguez, and committed to the ideals of independence from an early age, his decision to join the revolution
in Venezuela came naturally. Following the creole revolt of 19 April 1810 in Caracas,
Bolívar organised the return of Francisco de Miranda from his exile in London to lead the
new Venezuelan government. Miranda was a revolutionary who had fought against the

British in the American War of Independence, and who had ever since been promoting the liberation of Spanish America in Paris and London. Together they inspired the creole elites to proclaim the independence of Venezuela on 5 July 1811. The First Venezuelan Republic came into being, and Miranda became its dictator in 1812. However, Caracas fell to the Spaniards on 25 July, Miranda was taken prisoner to Spain, where he died in 1816, and Bolívar escaped to New Granada.

From 1812 to 1823, Venezuela and New Granada were ravaged by war. The Spanish forces, enlarged after Ferdinand VII dispatched an expeditionary army of 10,000 men to the colony in 1815, were notoriously brutal in their effort to crush the rebels. Bolívar responded to their reign of terror with his 15 June 1813 proclamation of *Guerra a Muerte* (war to the death), whereby any Spaniard who refused to join the patriot forces would be punished by death before a firing squad. He led a Colombian expedition which succeeded in retaking Caracas on 6 August 1813, only to be forced into exile once more, in September 1814, after the royalists gained the upper hand again. In New Granada, Bolívar took Bogotá, on 9 December 1814, and from there he went to Jamaica, where he wrote his famous *Carta de Jamaica* (Jamaica Letter) (6 September 1815), outlining his political beliefs. He visited Haiti, obtained weapons and men, with the support of the Haitian president Alexandre Pétion (1807–18), and in May 1816 led another expedition to Venezuela which was also repelled. Finally, in December 1816, Bolívar's long, yet ultimately successful, campaign to liberate Venezuela began with a second Haitian expedition that brought him to Guayana and from there to the Apure plains.

## Simón Bolívar (1783–1830)

Born in Caracas into a wealthy family, Bolívar benefited from an enlightened education and the opportunity to travel extensively. As well as becoming a revolutionary, a military leader and a politician, he was a man of ideas and a gifted writer. His ideology transcended class and national interests in the way that he strove to achieve the liberation of all peoples (including slaves) and countries in Spanish America. More than anyone else, he was responsible for the liberation of Venezuela, Colombia, Ecuador, Peru and Bolivia. However, although he succeeded in bringing about the independence of five countries, he failed to achieve his aim of establishing a continental federation of Spanish American nations. As time went by, his hopes, enthusiasm and generous liberalism started to falter as the situation in the countries he had liberated degenerated into violence and anarchy. By 1830, not even five years after he had led the independence movements of northern South America, he had become an unpopular figure. His attempts to forge strong central governments were perceived to be dictatorial and despotic. He died on his way to exile, afflicted with tuberculosis, despairing of Spanish America's ability ever to see progress and stability established.

Supported by José Antonio Páez and Francisco de Paula Santander, the patriot forces started to force the retreat of the royalists between 1818 and 1819. With Bogotá once more under Spanish control after May 1816, Bolívar, following a similar strategy to

### Antonio José de Sucre (1795–1830)

Born in Venezuela, Sucre became Bolívar's most trusted commander. He fought for independence in Venezuela and New Granada, and became one of the main leaders of the patriot armies in the campaigns that developed in Quito, Peru and Upper Peru. Responsible for the liberation of Upper Peru, he became the first President of Bolivia (1826–28), where he tried to forge an enlightened system of government. His assassination in Colombia in 1830 represented a particularly bitter blow to Bolívar, who considered him to be one of the greatest liberators of Spanish America, as well as his most loyal friend.

San Martín, conceived of the idea of crossing the Andes to conquer Venezuela by reconquering New Granada first. On 27 May 1819, Bolívar and Santander crossed the mighty *cordillera*, reaching the other side of the mountains at the village of Socha on 5 July. From then on the Liberator's victories gathered momentum. He defeated the royalists at the crucial battle of Boyacá (7 August 1819) and went on to take Bogotá. With Colombia liberated, he left Santander in charge of the new country and moved into Venezuela in September, leading a long campaign against the Spaniards that culminated in the final confrontation of Carabobo (24 June 1821). On 29 June 1821, Bolívar liberated Caracas, and the independence of Gran Colombia (incorporating Venezuela and Colombia, as he decreed would happen on 17 December 1819) was consolidated. Although 5,200 royalist forces held on to Puerto Cabello until they were finally defeated by Páez on 10 November 1823, Spanish supremacy in Venezuela was over.

With Venezuela and Colombia in patriot hands (Spanish resistance in Colombia was ultimately crushed in the battle of Bomboná on 7 April 1822), Bolívar set about liberating Ecuador. This he did after his close friend and aide **Antonio José de Sucre** defeated the Spaniards at the battle of Pichincha (24 May 1822). Sucre liberated Quito the following day, and on 16 June 1822 Bolívar entered the provincial capital, only to press on towards Guayaquil, which he formally incorporated into Gran Colombia on 13 July 1822. It was less than a fortnight after this event that Bolívar met with San Martín, on 27 July, and agreed to proceed with his campaign in Peru.

On 1 September 1823, he arrived in Lima. Crippled by illness, he was forced to remain in Pativilca, a village north of the capital, while creole divisions led to the Spanish reoccupation of Lima (12 February 1824). Once recovered, he established himself in Trujillo and, together with Sucre, set about organising a new army. By April 1824, this army was 8,000-strong and ready for action. Benefiting from divisions in the royalist camp, Bolívar and Sucre led the victorious battle of Junín (6 August 1824). Thereafter, Bolívar left Sucre to harass the last major royalist army in the Andes, while he set about taking Lima, which he did in December. The final major and decisive battle of the wars of independence took place high up in the Andes, in Ayacucho, on 8 December 1824. Led by Sucre, the patriot forces routed the royalists, and on 9 December the Spanish high command offered its unconditional surrender. Although one Spanish stronghold held on, in Callao, until 23 January 1826, the independence of Peru was now consolidated. In the meantime, in Upper

Peru, the brief monarchy the Spaniard Pedro Antonio de Olañeta tried to impose collapsed after the battle of Tumusla (1 April 1825). On 6 August 1825, under the supervision of Sucre, a newly formed assembly declared the independence of this new nation, stating that it would have as its name Bolívar (subsequently Bolivia), in honour of the great Liberator. Although countless poems and songs have been written celebrating the feats of the warriors of independence, the fourth *Canto* in Pablo Neruda's epic poem on the history of Latin America, *Canto general* (1950), remains probably the most memorable of them all. Neruda's stirring ode to Bolívar, *Un canto para Bolívar*, belongs, however, to his combative book of poems *Tercera Residencia* (1935–45).

The only indisputable statement that can be made regarding the end of the wars of independence is that by 1825 Spain was no longer in control of its former colonies in continental America. However, while it was clear who had lost the wars of independence, it was less evident who had won. In most countries it was the creoles who succeeded in rising to power. Nevertheless, since the creoles were deeply divided over a whole range of economic interests and political ideals, the onset of independence did not lead to a period of obvious emancipation. For many *castas*, Indians and black slaves, little had changed. To make matters worse, ten to fifteen years of war had resulted in the almost complete destruction of those industries that once had been so profitable for the Spanish monarchy.

## The independence of Brazil

Although there were many similarities between late eighteenth-century Brazil and Spanish America, there were a number of significant differences. The three most obvious differences revolved around:

- The ethnic composition of the population;
- The nature of the colony's economy; and
- The way in which Portugal governed Brazil.

Regarding the population, there were very few *mestizos* (*mamelucos* or *caboclos*) in the main towns and cities of Brazil. Power, both political and financial, rested with a population made up of Portuguese settlers and Brazilians of Portuguese ancestry. The majority of the colonial population (2.3 million in 1800), excluding the numerous tribes that inhabited the Amazon, were therefore black slaves, imported from Portugal's colonies in Africa. This meant, particularly after the Haitian Revolution (1791), that the threat of a black revolt made the white population – Portuguese and Brazilians – natural allies.

The nature of Brazil's economy further contributed to unifying the interests of the white population. While Spain conquered an Indian empire, Portugal transformed Brazil into a sugar plantation. From the outset, Brazil's economic development was linked to European and African markets. By the mid eighteenth century, Brazil had a thriving export economy, with strong ties to Portugal and, by default, to Britain, which resulted in the emergence and consolidation of a wealthy land-owning class of plantation owners who shared common interests, regardless of whether they were Portuguese or Brazilian.

The manner in which Portugal sought to control Brazil proved to be equally important in consolidating a fairly united Portuguese–Brazilian elite in the colony, whose relations were markedly harmonious in contrast to creole–Spanish relations in Spanish America. The Brazilian economy was a shared enterprise. Brazil's bureaucracy was minimal. Although taxes were levied, they were collected by local farmers. Although the judicial system was reformed, the legal profession was made up of Brazilians who had studied in Portugal and then returned to the colony to serve as magistrates. Power and administration were, in essence, devolved to the landowners in the colony, held together by four captaincies (Minas Gerais, Bahia, Pernambuco and Rio de Janeiro), in which white Brazilians played as much part as the Portuguese. The Portuguese Crown protected its Brazilian planters and gold miners. It did not attack the interests of the Brazilian elites. Under the rule of King José I (1750–77), inspired by the enlightened mercantilist policies of the Portuguese minister of state, the Marquis of Pombal (Sebastião José de Carvalho e Melo), a series of policies further increased the participation of the white Brazilians in the economy.

It is significant that the only noteworthy Brazilian movement for independence, the Minas Gerais conspiracy of 1788–89, led by Joaquim José da Silva Xavier (popularly known as *Tiradentes* – the teeth-puller), coincided with a period in which a number of Pombal's reforms were reversed under the reign of Queen Maria I (1777–95). However, his protégés and followers succeeded in returning to power, and reverted Portugal's policies towards Brazil to what they had been under Pombal, avoiding a potentially explosive situation. The policy towards Brazil of Pombal, who died in 1782, and his disciples was one of accommodation.

In the aftermath of the Haitian Revolution, moreover, the Brazilian economy boomed, no longer undermined by competition from Saint-Domingue. The elites soon abandoned any liberal ideals they might have held, aware that it was fundamental that a slave-led revolution should not erupt in their provinces. By the early 1800s, the great majority of Brazil's elites saw the monarchy as a stabilising force, and did not believe that independence from Portugal would result in any significant benefits. By 1808, the situation in Brazil, despite the existence of slave discontent, expressed in the slave revolts of Rio de Janeiro (1794), Bahia (1798, 1807) and Pernambuco (1801), was in no way as explosive as that in most parts of Spanish America.

Events were to conspire to ensure that in Brazil independence would be achieved without a revolution. When, in August 1807, Napoleon issued the Portuguese monarchy the ultimatum whereby it either declared war on Britain or faced a French invasion, the entire Portuguese court was transferred to Brazil. On 30 November 1807, escorted by British warships, the prince regent, his court and over 8,000 Portuguese ministers, politicians, officers, bishops, noblemen and merchants set sail from Lisbon in what must have been an extraordinary flotilla of vessels and warships. This vast expedition arrived in the Bay of All Saints and set about recreating the Portuguese State in Brazil. The Portuguese court resided in Brazil from 1808 until 1821.

It was during these years that the seeds of independence were planted. The prince regent, who became King João VI in 1816, after the queen died, instigated a number of reforms during his Brazilian stay that empowered the Brazilian elites to the extent that they became partners rather than subjects of their Portuguese brethren. On 28 January 1808, he abolished the Portuguese monopoly on Brazil's trade. In April, freedom of manufacturing and industry was declared. In October, the Bank of Brazil was created. Rio de Janeiro replaced Lisbon as the main distribution centre for the exports of Portugal's Asian empire. Free trade led to Brazil's economic independence from Portugal and the development of closer ties with Britain than it had enjoyed with Portugal in the past. In 1815 he decreed that Brazil was no longer a colony, but a kingdom in its own right. By 1821, Brazil, albeit with a Portuguese monarch at its head, was a kingdom on a par with Portugal. It had an independent treasury, court system and bureaucracy. Its thriving economy was controlled by Brazilians.

Although one major revolt, in Pernambuco in 1817, occurred during the monarchy's stay, Brazil's landowners sided with the Crown. It was not until 1820, when revolts in Lisbon and Oporto demanded the convocation of the *Cortes* and the return of the king, that the need for independence surfaced. King João VI returned to Lisbon in April 1821, and left Prince Dom Pedro in Brazil to serve as regent. The *Cortes* that was convoked, albeit committed to liberal ideals, was determined to dismantle the entire bureaucratic infrastructure that Dom João had created during his time in Brazil. They pressed for the reversal of most of the king's Brazilian's decrees, hoping to regain control of the colony. By 1821 this was an impossible objective.

The Brazilian elites were not prepared to surrender their political autonomy and the benefits of free trade. Nevertheless, they were afraid of the immediate consequences of independence. Instability would be a recipe for disaster. As long as order prevailed, slave revolts would be kept at bay. The dilemma they might have faced, of seeking independence while hoping to avoid the dangers they perceived to be an inherent part of republican government, never became an issue. It was the prince regent, Dom Pedro, who took the lead, and with the support of the Brazilian planters, bureaucrats and businessmen, he declared the independence of Brazil in his *Grito de Ipiranga* on 7 September 1822, becoming Emperor Dom Pedro I of Brazil (1822–31). Although some Portuguese troops attempted to resist independence, by 1824 the entire country was under Dom Pedro's control. Brazil was a monarchy until the reign of Emperor Dom Pedro II (1840–89) came to an end sixty-seven years later.

## The case of Cuba

In the Spanish colonies in the Caribbean, namely Cuba, Puerto Rico and Santo Domingo, the impact of the Haitian Revolution on the collective imagination of the creoles was such that the urge for independence was paralysed by their fear of a parallel slave revolution in their own backyard. Outnumbered as they were by the black population, creoles and Spaniards found themselves forming a fairly united front, which entailed continuing loyalty to Spain during the 1808 crisis and increasingly heavy-handed treatment of the slaves. Moreover, the repressive nature of the islands' administrations

(Santo Domingo was recaptured by the Spaniards in 1809) was accompanied by a ruthless and effective clampdown on anybody and anything that might have inspired subversive activities. Revolutionary publications from France and Haiti were banned. Masonic organisations, which had become the clandestine forum for enlightened individuals to plot against absolutist and clerical practices since the end of the eighteenth century, were persecuted. While a minority of enlightened creoles were opposed to the Bourbon fiscal policies and the liberal agenda of the 1812 *Cortes*, the restoration of absolutism in 1814 pacified their unrest. Pursuing a deliberate policy to ensure that the Cuban creoles remained loyal to Spain, the Crown granted them a number of key concessions. The Crown's tobacco monopoly was abolished, allowing the creole elites to finally reap the profits of this thriving industry. Moreover, the economic prosperity of Cuba and Puerto Rico reached unprecedented heights following the Haitian Revolution. Given that the production and sale of sugar and coffee had been undermined previously by the competition posed by Saint-Domingue, the destruction that the Haitian Revolution wrought on its plantations resulted in a significant expansion of these industries in Cuba and Puerto Rico.

While the control of Santo Domingo was constantly jeopardised by invasions from neighbouring Haiti, Cuba and Puerto Rico remained Spanish colonies until 1898. In the Spanish Caribbean, fear of a slave uprising, the beginning of a period of economic expansion and the granting of important concessions to the islands' creole elites resulted in a context altogether different from that of continental Spanish America. Needless to say, there were constant slave revolts, and a number of Masonic conspiracies that embraced abolitionist ideals were organised, although none of them succeeded in overthrowing the colonial regimes. Those slaves who escaped went on to become known as *cimarrones*, forming hidden communities known as *palenques* (*quilombos* or *mocambos* in Brazil) in the depths of the islands' jungles. Those who were caught were invariably killed, their heads stuck on pikes at the entrances of the **ingenios** to deter others from following their example, as depicted in Tomás Gutiérrez Alea's film, *La última cena* (1977).

Once the wars of independence drew to a close, the new emergent nations were faced with the extraordinary task of having to define the political systems by which they would be governed. In most cases, this process was made all the more difficult because the main sources of their prosperity had been destroyed by the war. The three-hundred-year-old links to Spain and Portugal were now broken. The make-up of colonial government had been destroyed. However, the deeply rooted foundations of colonial society were to linger on. For many Indians, blacks and *castas*, little had changed. One ruling class had replaced another. Notions such as liberty, fraternity and equality were far from being achieved. Political independence was not the end, but the beginning of a long and tortuous series of cycles which were to characterise the following two hundred years and which continue to characterise the present. In the minds of many, full social and economic independence remains to this day incomplete and unfulfilled.

> **ingenios**
> Sugar mills, sugar cane plantations.

## Exhibit 1.1: *Sentimientos de la Nación o puntos dados por Morelos para la constitución* (Mexico, 1813)

1. Que la América es libre e independiente de España y de toda otra Nación, Gobierno o Monarquía, y que así se sancione, dando al mundo las razones.
2. Que la Religión Católica sea la única, sin tolerancia de otra.
3. Que todos sus ministros se sustenten de todos y solos los diezmos y primicias, y el pueblo no tenga que pagar más obvenciones que las de su devoción y ofrenda.
4. Que el dogma sea sostenido por la jerarquía de la Iglesia, que son el Papa, los Obispos y los Curas…
5. La Soberanía dimana inmediatamente del Pueblo, el que sólo quiere depositarla en sus representantes dividiendo los poderes de ella en Legislativo, Ejecutivo y Judiciario, eligiendo las Provincias sus vocales, y éstos a los demás, que deben ser sujetos sabios y de probidad.
6. …
7. …
8. …
9. Que los empleos los obtengan sólo los americanos.
10. Que no se admitan extranjeros, si no son artesanos capaces de instruir y libres de toda sospecha.
11. Que la patria no será del todo libre y nuestra, mientras no se reforme el gobierno, abatiendo el tiránico, sustituyendo el liberal y echando fuera de nuestro suelo al enemigo español que tanto se ha declarado contra esta Nación.
12. Que como la buena ley es superior a todo hombre, las que dice nuestro Congreso deben ser tales que obliguen a constancia y patriotismo, moderen la opulencia y la indigencia, y de tal suerte se aumente el jornal del pobre, que mejore sus costumbres, aleje la ignorancia, la rapiña y el hurto.
13. Que las leyes generales comprendan a todos, sin excepción de cuerpos privilegiados, y que éstos sólo lo sean en cuanto al uso de su ministerio.
14. Que para dictar una ley se discuta en el Congreso, y decida a pluralidad de votos.
15. Que la esclavitud se proscriba para siempre, y lo mismo la distinción de castas, quedando todos iguales, y sólo distinguirá a un americano del otro, el vicio y la virtud.
16. Que nuestros puertos se franqueen a las naciones extranjeras amigas, pero que éstas no se internen al reino por más amigas que sean, y sólo haya puertos señalados para el efecto, prohibiendo el desembarco en todos los demás señalando el 10% u otra gabela a sus mercancías.
17. Que a cada uno se le guarden las propiedades y respetos en su casa como en un asilo sagrado señalando penas a los infractores.
18. Que en la nueva legislación no se admitirá la tortura.
19. Que en la misma se establezca por la ley Constitucional la celebración del día 12 de diciembre en todos los pueblos, dedicado a la patrona de nuestra libertad, María Santísima de Guadalupe, encargando a todos los pueblos, la devoción mensual.
20. …
21. …
22. Que se quite la infinidad de tributos, pechos e imposiciones que más agobian, y se señale a cada individuo un cinco por ciento en sus ganancias, u otra carga igual ligera, que no oprima tanto, como la alcabala, el estanco, el tributo y otros, pues con esta corta contribución, y la buena administración de los bienes confiscados al enemigo, podrá llevarse el peso de la guerra y honorarios de empleados.
23. Que igualmente se solemnice el día 16 de septiembre todos los años, como el día aniversario en que se levantó la voz de la independencia…

*Source:* Ernesto de la Torre, *La independencia de México* (Madrid: Mapfre, 1992), pp. 250–51.

## Exhibit 1.2: *Instrucciones que se dieron a los diputados de la provincia oriental para el desempeño de su misión ante la asamblea constituyente de Buenos Aires. Delante de Montevideo, 13 de abril de 1813* (Uruguay, 1813)

Primeramente pedirá la declaración de la independencia absoluta de estas colonias, que ellas están absueltas de toda obligación de fidelidad a la corona de España, y familia de los Borbones, y que toda conexión política entre ellas y el estado de España, es, y debe ser totalmente disuelta.

Art. 2   No admitirá otro sistema que el de confederación para el pacto recíproco con las provincias que formen nuestro estado.

Art. 3   Promoverá la libertad civil y religiosa en toda su extensión imaginable.

Art. 4   Como el objeto y fin del gobierno debe ser conservar la igualdad, libertad y seguridad de los ciudadanos y de los pueblos, cada provincia formará su gobierno bajo estas bases, a más del gobierno supremo de la nación.

Art. 5   Así éste como aquél se dividirán en poder legislativo, ejecutivo y judicial.

Art. 6   Estos tres resortes jamás podrán estar unidos entre sí, y serán independientes en sus facultades.

Art. 7   El gobierno supremo entenderá solamente en los negocios generales del estado. El resto es peculiar al gobierno de cada provincia.

Art. 8   El territorio que ocupan estos pueblos de la costa oriental del Uruguay hasta la fortaleza de Santa Teresa, forma una sola provincia, denominada: LA PROVINCIA ORIENTAL.

Art. 9   Que los siete pueblos de Misiones, los de Batoví, Santa Tecla, San Rafael y Tacuarembó, que hoy ocupan injustamente los portugueses, y a su tiempo deben reclamarse, serán en todo tiempo territorio de esta provincia.

Art. 10   Que esta provincia por la presente entra separadamente en una firme liga de amistad con cada una de las otras, para su defensa común, seguridad de su libertad, y para su mutua y general felicidad, obligándose a asistir a cada una de las otras contra toda violencia o ataques hechos sobre ellas, o sobre alguna de ellas, por motivo de religión, soberanía, tráfico, o algún otro pretexto, cualquiera que sea.

Art. 11   Que esta provincia retiene su soberanía, libertad e independencia, todo poder, jurisdicción y derecho que no es delegado expresamente por la confederación a las Provincias Unidas juntas en congreso.

Art. 12   Que el puerto de Maldonado sea libre para todos los buques que concurran a la introducción de efectos y exportación de frutos, poniéndose la correspondiente aduana en aquel pueblo…

Art. 13   Que el puerto de Colonia sea igualmente habilitado en los términos prescritos en el artículo anterior.

Art. 14   Que ninguna tasa o derecho se imponga sobre artículos exportados de una provincia a otra; ni que ninguna preferencia se dé por cualquiera regulación de comercio o renta a los puertos de una provincia sobre los de otra; ni los barcos destinados de esta provincia a otra serán obligados a entrar, a anclar, o pagar derechos de otra.

Art. 15   No permita se haga ley para esta provincia…, sobre multas y confiscaciones que se aplicaban antes al rey, y sobre territorios de éste, mientras ella no forma su reglamento…

Art. 16    Que esta provincia tendrá su constitución territorial; y que ella tiene el derecho de sancionar la general de las Provincias Unidas que forme la Asamblea Constituyente.

Art. 17    Que esta provincia tiene derecho para levantar los regimientos que necesite, nombrar los oficiales de compañía, reglar la milicia de ella para la seguridad de su libertad, por lo que no podrá violarse el derecho de los pueblos para guardar y tener armas.

Art. 18    El despotismo militar será precisamente aniquilado con trabas constitucionales que aseguren inviolable la soberanía de los pueblos.

Art. 19    Que precisa e indispensable sea fuera de Buenos Aires donde resida el sitio del gobierno de las Provincias Unidas.

Art. 20    La constitución garantirá a las Provincias Unidas una forma de gobierno republicana, y que asegure a cada una de ellas de las violencias domésticas, usurpaciones de sus derechos, libertad y seguridad de su soberanía, que con la fuerza armada intente alguna de ellas sofocar los principios proclamados. Y asimismo prestará toda su atención, honor, fidelidad y religiosidad, a todo cuanto crea, o juzgue necesario, para preservar a esta provincia las ventajas de la libertad, y mantener un gobierno libre, de piedad, justicia, moderación e industria.

*Source:* Washington Reyes Abadie, *Artigas y el federalismo en el Río de la Plata, Vol. 2: 1810–1820* (Montevideo: Ediciones de la Banda Oriental, 1987), pp. 306–7.

# Topics for discussion in class

- Which articles in Exhibit 1.1 strike you as being pro-clerical and reactionary?

- Which strike you as being particularly radical?

- To what extent are the economic grievances that resulted from Bourbon fiscal measures apparent in Exhibits 1.1 and 1.2?

- What political system does Morelos recommend be established in Mexico?

- Which articles in Exhibit 1.2 strike you as being particularly radical?

- What political system does Artigas recommend be established in Uruguay and the River Plate?

- To what extent is Artigas' federalism a disguised form of secessionism with regard to Uruguay's relation to Argentina and the other provinces of the River Plate?

- What are the main differences and similarities between Exhibits 1.1 and 1.2?

# Topics for essays and presentations

Making use of the recommended texts (see Further reading, p. 161) and/or others that may be available to you in your local library, write an essay/give a seminar presentation on **one** of the following topics.

1  'The origins of the war of independence (*c.*1810–*c.*1825) must be traced back to the impact the Bourbon reforms had in the region.' Discuss with relation to *one* case study.

2  Compare the experience of the wars of independence in Mexico and Venezuela.

3  'Bolívar may have died fearing that he had "ploughed the sea". In the end, though, history has remembered Simón Bolívar as a great man' (John Chasteen). Do you agree with history's verdict? Discuss.

4  'Independence was a powerful yet finite force, which tore through Spanish America like a great storm, sweeping away the lines of attachment to Spain and the fabric of colonial government, but leaving intact the deeply rooted bases of colonial society. The Mexican peasants saw it as the same rider on a new mule, a political revolution in which one ruling class displaced another' (John Lynch). Discuss.

## CHAPTER 2

# Early national period (1825–1850)

**Following the achievement of independence, the political class that came to power throughout Latin America attempted to establish the foundations on which their newly formed nations would develop and prosper. However, their dreams of imposing long-lasting liberal constitutions that could create stable and orderly societies wherein humanity's condition could improve proved impossible to attain. The early national period was characterised by civil war. *Caudillismo* became rife and dictatorships common. In some cases the newly formed nations were dismembered. By 1850, after approximately thirty years of independent life, the situation of the new countries was anything but encouraging.**

## The age of proposals

In the aftermath of independence, Spanish America's formidable resources had been devastated by ten to fifteen years of war. Most of the silver mines in Mexico and Peru had been destroyed. With Spain and its European allies refusing to acknowledge the emergent nations' independence, trade floundered for over a decade, with Britain, the United States and the other Latin American countries serving as the only nations prepared to enter into commercial treaties with the newly formed governments. Once trade relations

## World context

The first half of the nineteenth century witnessed the spread of the Industrial Revolution in a number of European countries and in the north-east of the United States. Modern factories, steam engines, engineering plants and ironworks mushroomed. Rivers were made navigable, canals were built, railways started to be laid down, steamships were constructed. Where there were coalfields industrial growth was unstoppable. Increased industrialisation in these countries also made them more powerful. It was the European industrial powers that thrust out into the world in what was the beginning of an age of expanding imperialism. Industrialisation gave Britain a commercial edge, exporting surplus manufactured goods, textiles in particular, at a rate that the non-industrialised world could not compete with. It also gave Britain military power. Colonies were established in parts of India and South Africa. In tandem, France invaded Algeria (1830), Spain acquired Ceuta on the Moroccan coast (1830), and the Russian Empire spread into northern Asia as far as Persia, Afghanistan, India and China. The Americans started to conquer the west and the Australians began to explore the great inland plains. Within Europe, following the defeat of Napoleon (1815), these were years of relative peace. The only major conflicts were those whereby Greece and Belgium achieved their independence in 1830, the former from Turkey, the latter from Holland.

did start to flourish, the import of cheap, factory-made European products, namely British textiles, crippled Latin American craft industries. This was to create a chronic balance-of-trade crisis. The tendency of the first independent administrations to abolish the unpopular taxes of the colony further depleted the governments' funds. In contrast, enormous sums of money were spent in covering the expenses of the triumphant patriot armies that expected to be showered with promotions and land concessions. The revolutions of independence did not bring about the significant redistribution of land and income that might have led to a much-needed growth of internal markets and productive forces. The large *haciendas* remained in the possession of a select number of landowners, a situation that resulted in economic stagnation.

The sheer size of the new nations, paired with their geographical and climatic diversity, also proved problematic. Communications were poor. For trade and industry to prosper, roads would have to be built, rivers would have to become navigable, and mountains, jungles and deserts would have to be overcome. The natural resources of Latin America could not be fully exploited until there was an effective means of transporting them to the outside world. The lack of roads also meant that news from the capitals travelled slowly, and when it reached the distant rural provinces it did not necessarily mean much. Behind vast mountain ranges, hidden in the depths of the jungle or lost in the pampas, names of faraway presidents and abstract concepts such as 'nationhood' bore little significance in the everyday lives of the majority. The burning issues that divided the political class in the congresses and Masonic gatherings of the main cities were virtually incomprehensible to the average **campesinos** and Indians of the countryside.

### caudillos
Leaders, strongmen, regional (and subsequently national) chieftains. **Caudillismo** is the term used to describe the phenomenon whereby the *caudillos* gained political prominence.

### campesinos
Peasants.

It would be another thirty years before a general sense of belonging to the newly formed nations started to develop. The wars of independence had never been a clear-cut conflict between nationals and Spaniards. Independence as a goal had meant many different things. For the slaves, it meant emancipation and equality before the law, dreams that were generally postponed once the Spanish forces withdrew. For the creole elites, independence represented political power, but it was not clear even to them whose destiny they were fated to rule. For the Buenos Aires creoles, their early understanding of the

Map of Latin America, 1830

boundaries of their country included Uruguay, Paraguay and Bolivia. Simón Bolívar did not even think in terms of countries and sustained a continental vision whereby he hoped Spanish America would become a world power one day, governed as a united Pan-American whole. For most Indians, independence meant very little. One ruling class had displaced another, but little else had changed.

Regardless of who had risen to power in the 1820s, the task of governing the new nations was going to present insurmountable problems. How could any government ensure that its laws, decrees and reforms were implemented throughout the country? The nature of the population posed a particularly difficult challenge to overcome when it came to the exercise of government. The majority were illiterate and uneducated. In extensive areas of Mexico, Central America, Ecuador, Peru and Bolivia people did not even speak Spanish. They did not embrace the notion that they belonged to a new country. For generations they had owed their allegiance to the mythical king of Spain and had taken their orders from the local chieftains, mayors and landowners. They could not tell from outside the capital whether one presidential candidate was more worthy than another, or whether the nation, whatever that was, would benefit more if it was governed by one creole clique rather than another. Although in the first constitutions that were drafted, following in the steps of the Cádiz 1812 charter, there was an attempt to include the majority of the male population in the political life of the emergent nations, it was not long before suffrage was restricted to property-owning citizens. It became evident to the liberal creole intelligentsia that most people were too poor, too ignorant or too far removed from events to fully understand what they perceived to be the major issues of the day. The emergent political class reached the conclusion that the majority needed to be guided by the educated and prosperous few. Once the population as a whole had been educated and had acquired enough property to become responsible citizens, it would be possible, they reasoned, to aspire to a truly representative political system. In the meantime, political participation should be restricted to an enlightened minority.

As if the penury of the new governments, the awful communications of their countries, and an impoverished population with strong regional and ethnic affinities were not enough to make any political system fail from the outset, ten to fifteen years of war had resulted in a significant militarisation of society. There was now a military class whose most prominent high-ranking officers were unwilling to subject themselves to the orders of civilian politicians. After a decade in which some of them had been fully in charge of the regions in which they had operated, they were naturally averse to relinquishing the power they had become accustomed to exercising. Military uprisings became frequent. High-ranking officers led one revolt after another against different regional and national governments. They led their revolutions in order to overthrow a government to prevent it from pursuing policies that undermined their personal and regional interests, and to acquire accelerated promotions and bountiful rewards when the enterprise was successful. It is worth noting that although many rebellious military chieftains were more than willing to lead or second a revolt, they were, in most cases, invited to intervene by those civilian politicians who had failed to defeat their antagonists through elections. They became the arbiters of their nations' destinies as, time and again, the civilian political class reached a dead end.

And while most of the recently formed nations were rapidly consumed by revolutions and instability, which served to deter foreign capitalists from investing in the region, powers such as Spain, France, Britain and the United States harassed the newly independent countries, blockading their ports and invading them. Spain, which did not recognise the independence of its former colonies until the late 1830s, attempted to reconquer Mexico in 1829, sending an expedition to Tampico, repelled by the incipient *caudillo* **Antonio López de Santa Anna**. France blockaded the Atlantic coast of Mexico and Buenos Aires, bombarding Veracruz in the process, between 1838 and 1841. Britain seized Las Malvinas (the Falkland Islands) in 1833 and went on to blockade and attack Nicaragua throughout the 1840s. The United States annexed half of Mexico's national territory, including the present-day states of Texas, New Mexico, Arizona, Colorado, Nevada, Utah and California, following the Mexican–American War (1846–48).

It is perhaps not surprising that the early national period has been repeatedly portrayed as a bleak period in which *caudillos*, **pronunciamientos**, chaos, penury, instability, civil war, loss and dictatorship were the most characteristic features of the political landscape. In numerous Latin American countries this is a period that has been deliberately forgotten. There is no denying that numerous regional chieftains (*caudillos*) – at times **hacendados**, at times high-ranking officers, in most cases both – came to dominate the political arena of former Spanish America. Santa Anna in Mexico, Rafael Carrera in Guatemala, José Antonio Páez in Venezuela, Andrés Santa Cruz in Peru and Bolivia, José Gaspar Rodríguez de Francia in Paraguay, Fructuoso Rivera in Uruguay and Juan Manuel de Rosas in

### Antonio López de Santa Anna (1794–1876)

Born in Xalapa, in the province of Veracruz, Santa Anna joined the royalist army as a cadet in 1810. Like so many creole officers he embraced the cause of independence following the proclamation of the 1821 Plan of Iguala, and he was mainly responsible for liberating his home province. Once independence was achieved, he led four revolts (1822, 1823, 1828 and 1832) before becoming President of the Republic. Thereafter he was President on six different occasions (1833–35, 1839, 1841–43, 1843-44, 1846–47 and 1853–55), preferring to retire to his *haciendas* in Veracruz whenever he had the chance. His military victories included repudiating a Spanish and a French invasion (1829 and 1838 respectively) and slaughtering the Texan rebels at the Alamo (1836). His defeats included the battle of San Jacinto (1836), after which Texas became independent, and the Mexican–American War (1846–48), whereby Mexico lost half of its national territory. Often branded a traitor and a cynical turncoat, Santa Anna's political views in fact evolved from upholding a liberal agenda to a conservative one as the different constitutions failed to give Mexico a stable political system. Exiled following his 1853–55 dictatorship, Santa Anna tried unsuccessfully to return to Mexico on two occasions before he was allowed back in 1874. Having been one of the most influential *caudillos* in Mexico at the height of his career, he died impoverished and forgotten in Mexico City.

**pronunciamiento**

Often translated as 'revolt', the *pronunciamiento* was a written protest signed by a high-ranking officer, often drafted as a list of grievances or demands that could result in an armed rebellion if the government did not attend to them.

**hacendados**

*Hacienda* landowners.
**Estancieros** is the term used in the Southern Cone.

Argentina are all names that are difficult to avoid when studying these years. However, a closer look at this period shows how misleading it remains to oversimplify its political context, stating that it was nothing other than an age of *caudillos*.

The explosion of constitutional and political ideals that came with independence deserves more attention. An extensive range of ideological proposals were conjured up in a determined quest to find a legitimate constitutional framework that would offer the new nations a representative political system that could guarantee order and stability while providing for the improvement of humanity's condition in the region. Constitutionalism became such a force in its own right that, with the notable exceptions of Dr Francia in Paraguay and Rosas in Argentina, none of the aforementioned *caudillos* was able to rule without having to liaise, at some point, with their respective congresses. Even in these exceptional cases, it was Congress that granted them absolute power. Chile, following the advent of Diego Portales' 1833 Constitution, became the one Spanish American country that established a long-lasting representative system. The intensity that characterised the political debate, and the energy that went into finding solutions to the numerous problems encountered by the emergent political class, all meant that this was as much an age of proposals, of political inquiry and experimentation, as it was one of revolts and dictatorship.

Constitution writing became a continental obsession. Between 1817 and 1850, over 40 different constitutions were implemented in Latin America. The emergent political class was determined to impose political systems that were, to a greater or lesser extent, representative. Overall they pursued enlightened goals which generally favoured elections, equality before the law, freedom of speech, educational reform and industrialisation. Most of them believed in weakening the role of the executive (president, monarch or *caudillo*) while strengthening that of the legislature (Congress), in order to prevent despotism from rearing its ugly head.

However, modernity clashed with tradition. Abstract theories, inspired by the great thinkers of the Enlightenment, and foreign models (such as the 1787 US Constitution) stumbled on a reality that could not be transformed overnight. It was impossible to overcome customs, traditions and beliefs handed down over centuries by Indians and colonials from one day to the next. The ardent individualism of mainstream liberal philosophy clashed with the long established corporate practices upheld by Indian communities, *mestizo campesinos* who worked in communal lands, and powerful institutions such as the Church and the army, whose brotherhoods continued to benefit from exclusive privileges such as the *fueros*. All attempts to secularise society, providing the people with a basic education not controlled by the Church, floundered against opposition from the traditional sectors of society, which were the majority. The radical reforms that proliferated throughout Latin America in the hopeful 1820s were almost immediately met by popular revolts and military uprisings. According to the nineteenth-century Argentinean politician and writer Domingo Sarmiento, it was a conflict between civilisation and barbarism. It was a conflict between the civilised, enlightened few whose aim was to reform their countries and drag them out of the middle ages into modernity, and the barbarism of a rural, ignorant majority who did not understand what was best for them and their nation. Sarmiento's *Facundo. Civilización y barbarie* (1845), written before he became president of Argentina (1868–74), was to become one of the most influential texts in nineteenth-century Latin America.

However, the civilised, enlightened few proved to be deeply divided over the political models they wished to impose. There were those who believed that it would be impossible to create a republican system when their nation had been governed by a monarchy for so long. Others believed that you could not start a monarchy from scratch, since few would feel any ancestral sense of obedience to a newly appointed king. Most felt that the republican system was the most progressive of all, using the United States as their role model. And yet they could not agree as to whether it should be a federal or a central republic. They argued over whether Congress should be made up of one chamber or two, whether elections should be direct or indirect, whether representation should be proportional or not, whether Catholicism should be protected by the state or not, whether they should pursue free market economics or adopt protectionist measures.

The pace at which reforms should be implemented turned out to be equally divisive. While the ideology of radical and moderate liberals was almost identical, they could not agree over the speed with which they should change the colonial legacies of their respective societies. The radicals advocated breaking with the past, starting anew, destroying the old order so as to create their new utopia. Independence represented a new dawn where anything was possible. The moderates, in contrast, argued that society was not ready for such drastic changes. You needed to prepare the ground first. The moderates adopted a gradualist approach that led the radicals to accuse them of being reactionary.

As the first national decades went by, it became clear that whatever the adopted ideology, all constitutional experiments appeared to be doomed to failure. It made no difference whether they were centralist or federalist, pro-clerical or anticlerical, radical or traditionalist. The high hopes of the 1820s degenerated into the disillusion of the 1830s, and, in a country like Mexico, the despair of the 1840s. The ideals of the generation of independence came to be replaced by more pragmatical views and a cynical approach to politics. Simón Bolívar went from hope to despair, ahead of the rest, as the decade of the 1820s unfolded. His generous liberal beliefs were eroded as the new states he created disintegrated into chaos. While he never quite abandoned his strong faith in constitutionalism, the charters he drafted (1817, 1821 and 1826) became increasingly dictatorial as time went by. He became disenchanted with the behaviour of the congresses and came to the conclusion that a strong executive was essential. By the time he wrote the 1826 Constitution of Peru and Bolivia, he was defending the creation of a dictator for life. The nature of the countries' population, their lack of political experience, and the propensity of their congresses to tie 'the hands and even the heads of its men of state' meant that 'no form of government is so weak as the democratic'. They were 'far from emulating the happy times of Athens and Rome'; they could not compare themselves 'in any way to anything European'. Given that their race was 'of the most unwholesome sort', they were not in a position to 'place laws above heroes and principles above men'. If they attempted to do so, they would witness again 'the beautiful ideal of a Haiti and see a breed of new Robespierres become the worthy magistrates of this fearful liberty'. In brief, 'our America can only be ruled through a well-managed, shrewd despotism'. At the end of his life, beautifully portrayed in Gabriel García Márquez's *El general en su laberinto* (1989), Bolívar wrote the often-quoted and anguished letter in which he stated, in no uncertain terms, that America was ungovernable and that those who served the revolution 'ploughed the sea' (see Exhibit 2.1).

With the passing of time, dictatorship would become the only realistic means by which the political class believed their countries could be governed. Nonetheless, the political class remained persuaded that if despotism were to prevail, it should be enlightened. A decade of writing constitutions resulted in a widespread belief that whatever government was imposed, it must be based on some constitutional legitimacy. Only Rosas in Argentina and Dr Francia in Paraguay would succeed in imposing their will without any need to account to Congress for their actions. While it is true that dictatorial governments became a common feature in Latin America during the early national period, most of them felt the need to justify their measures in constitutional terms. Perhaps more significantly, with the exceptions of Rosas and Dr Francia, constitutionalism became strong enough to prevent the creation of the kind of long-lasting and resilient absolutist totalitarian regimes that surfaced in the twentieth century. And yet, not even the most authoritarian governments of the period were able to impose the ever elusive order and stability the creole political class pined for. In some extreme cases, such as in Mexico in 1840, there was a faction which came to the conclusion that not even a benevolent dictatorship could work, and that it was imperative that a European prince was placed at the head of their country (see Exhibit 2.2).

## Caudillos

It was towards the end of the 1820s, as the unrealistic expectations that inspired the first constitutional experiments were subverted by the hostile reaction their reforms provoked, that most of Spanish America witnessed the rise of the *caudillo*. The majority of successful *caudillos*, with the notable exception of Dr Francia, were high-ranking officers. At the time of their rise to power, most of them had already gained the admiration of the masses for their heroic feats in the army. Santa Anna, **Páez**, Santa Cruz and Rivera's heroic status was based on their military record during the wars of independence. In the cases of Rosas and Carrera, although they did not participate in the wars of independence, they acquired a mythical status for the way in which they led the revolts that brought an end to the unpopular governments of the day.

Their popularity was further increased by their populist conduct. Santa Anna frequented cockfights where he mingled with the masses and gained their admiration as a man of the people. Páez and Santa Cruz were *mestizos* whose careers in the military had allowed them to leap up the social hierarchy in a way that no other profession would have made possible. Their careers in themselves demonstrated that with independence you no longer had to be a member of the creole elite to aspire to occupying the National Palace. Carrera was an Indian-looking **ladino** of an even poorer background, who was adored for being a 'true' representative of the oppressed masses. Deeply popular with the Indians of Guatemala and supported by the Church, Carrera became *El rey de los indios* (King of the Indians), *el hijo de Dios* (Son of God) and *nuestro Señor* (Our Lord). Although in some cases their claims to be 'one of the people' were questionable, these men nonetheless succeeded in presenting themselves as representatives of the people. The propaganda of the Rosas regime promoted the idea that there were no longer any class distinctions in Argentina. They were all federalists, regardless of whether they were black, white, rich or poor. The country values of the *gauchos* were celebrated, while the European pretensions of the enlightened elite of Buenos Aires were condemned as foreign and unpatriotic. Dr Francia demonstrated his fervent anti-Spanish beliefs by forbidding all Spaniards from marrying creoles. They were only allowed to marry Indians, blacks or *castas*.

Frequent parades, *fiestas*, ceremonial masses, dances and cockfights in honour of the *caudillos*, celebrating memorable dates from their past, birthdays and saints' days, marriages, arrivals and departures, all contributed to giving them a messianic fame that was almost impossible to undermine. Statues of them were erected. Streets, squares and theatres were named after them. These personality cults were further spiced with the numerous anecdotes that abounded about their sexual prowess, their courage and their indisputable manliness. Most *caudillos* fathered numerous children, both legitimate and illegitimate, had countless mistresses as well as long-suffering wives, enjoyed gambling and drinking, and were physically

### José Antonio Páez (1790–1873)

Páez was a *mestizo* horseman of humble origins from the Venezuelan Apure plains (*llanos*). He proved himself a natural leader of the *llaneros* in the War of Independence (1810–22) and a particularly useful ally for Simón Bolívar to have in the region. Although their relationship was notoriously uneasy, together they inflicted a number of key defeats on the royalist forces. Following independence, Páez became the providential man who led the 1826 secessionist revolt of Valencia that eventually brought about the 1830 separation of Venezuela from Gran Colombia. Thereafter he was Venezuela's constitutionally elected president on three occasions (1830–35, 1838–43 and 1846–47), establishing a dictatorship in 1861–63. Starting from nothing, he became one of the wealthiest landowners of Venezuela. Despite the popularity he enjoyed in the 1830s and 1840s, he was exiled to the United States in 1863, where he died ten years later.

### ladino

Central American version of *mestizo*.

**patrón**

The boss, landowner, employer.

strong and energetic. They were also described by their contemporaries as being irresistibly charismatic.

However, there was more to the *caudillos'* success in the early national period than their commanding personalities, their populist measures and their heroic past. The *caudillos* often rose to national power on the back of the power they had acquired in their respective provinces. They were the strongmen of their homelands before they aspired to taking on national politics. They dominated their home provinces either because of the prominence they had achieved there during the wars of independence or because they belonged to families who owned the largest *haciendas* in the area. Thus they were backed repeatedly by their provinces, using their peons as their soldiers when they were not already in charge of a military division. They were able to profit at a national level from the patron–client relationship they had established in their home provinces. This is what is known as the politics of patronage and clientelism.

The *caudillo* obtained the undying support of his region by ensuring that their support was rewarded. At a regional level this meant employment, land concessions and the benefits of having a **patrón** who would not let the national government's decrees harm local interests. Once the regional *caudillo* became a national one, preferential treatment would continue to be bestowed on his original bailiwick. Nevertheless, the patron–client network of a national *caudillo* expanded and incorporated a wider range of interested parties. Influential landowners, businessmen, high-ranking officers and bishops would throw in their lot with a rebellious *caudillo* in exchange for benefits to be reaped once he came to power. The most resilient *caudillos* were those who most generously rewarded their clientele.

The end result of this was that most *caudillos* did little to change the societies they came to govern. The rich *hacendados* became richer as their *haciendas* expanded with the approval of the leader they had assisted in his rise to power. Nepotism and cronyism became rife. In spite of all the populist rhetoric, the majority of *caudillos* pursued policies that favoured elite interests. Their cultural affinity with the masses did not amount to social solidarity. The masses needed to be pacified, educated and controlled, and while they did not display sufficient political maturity, it was essential that they were not included in the electoral process. The populism of the *caudillos* was emphasised precisely so that the masses felt included in the political process, even though their right to vote was in most cases taken away from them. Power remained in the hands of the creole elites.

For the creole elites, sharing power with *caudillos,* who were at times unpredictable and volatile, and who in certain cases belonged to a lower social class, was tolerable once it became apparent that they were the only men capable of instilling law and order. With the increase of poverty that came with independence, crime became rampant. Bandits roamed the highways, and the streets of the main cities became dangerous places to frequent at night. The fear of social dissolution was the one thing that united the elites, regardless of their political convictions. For them, the *caudillos* became the means of guaranteeing law and order. Their populism quelled the discontent of the popular classes. Their tendency to support military measures to deal with crime and revolutionary activities appeared to be the most effective means of protecting the lives and properties of the creole elites. Most

> **hombres de bien**
> Refers to upper-class men who often formed the political class.

*caudillos* introduced brutal and repressive measures with which to keep the danger of popular riots at bay. The underground prisons of Dr Francia became as notorious as Rosas' paramilitaries, known as *la mazorca* (i.e. *más horca*, more hanging). The press was censored. Political opponents were either exiled or executed. In some exceptional cases, the control the *caudillos* exercised over their countries was indeed remarkable. As depicted in Augusto Roa Bastos' extraordinary novel, *Yo el Supremo* (1974), Dr Francia was able to isolate Paraguay from the rest of the world, forbidding anybody to leave or enter the republic without his personal consent between 1822 and 1840.

Nevertheless, most *caudillos* paid lip service to the political codes established in their respective constitutions. Most of them failed, in fact, to establish long-lasting personalist rules, even though the historiography has tended to label this period as one of dictatorships. They pressurised their congresses to award them exceptional powers. At times they even closed down congress. However, the common trend was one in which they ruled despotically for temporary spells while a constituent assembly drafted a new constitution, or for the time it took the different political factions to overcome the crisis that had led them to invite the intervention of the *caudillo* in question. Few were the *caudillos* who attempted to rule their countries on a permanent basis.

The *caudillos'* rise to prominence in the early national period was due, in general terms, to the following factors. They were famous before they rose to power because of their heroic feats in the army. The massive publicity they received kept them in the public mind as warriors of Napoleonic stature. The personality cults, perpetuated in *fiestas* and ceremonies, further enhanced their popular status. A tendency to put on populist performances allowed them to appear in the eyes of the majority as their true representatives. Their opportunism enabled them to know when the mood of the country was opposed to the rampant reformism of a particular government. They generously rewarded those who supported them and established successful patronage–clientelistic networks with the more influential sectors of society. Their despotic inclinations represented a promise of stability, a halt to what the **hombres de bien** feared most – social dissolution. They also used the federalist–centralist divide to suit their own interests.

## Federalists and centralists

The question as to whether the new nations should be governed within a federalist or a centralist system was one of the most complex issues to be resolved. The vast size of most of the countries, their climatic diversity, and the isolation of the provinces brought about by distance, mountains, jungles and deserts represented a monumental challenge to anybody who intended to govern the independent countries. The terrain, paired with the legacies of a colonial period whereby the politics of immense territories had been administered by a small number of widely scattered viceregal authorities, meant that the very action of defining the parameters of the emergent nations would be problematic. The attempts that were made in Buenos Aires, Bogotá and Guatemala City to base the new nations on a parallel model all failed during the early national period, with the gradual secession of Uruguay, Paraguay, Bolivia, Venezuela, Ecuador, Nicaragua, Honduras, Costa Rica and El Salvador from their envisaged unions. The struggle led by regional elites against the centralising tendencies of the national governments became one of the hallmarks of this period.

For the centralists, centralism was a natural step since it did not involve dismantling entirely the administrative structures of the colony. It was a liberal system since it was the one that had been adopted in the Cádiz 1812 Constitution. It gave the national government the power to rule over the vast territories of the republic in a way that could keep the centrifugal forces of the provinces under control. Centralism was tidy. It did not entail entering into disputes over the different responsibilities national and provincial governments claimed to be their own. To allow the provinces autonomous governments with the power to raise their own taxes, militias and jurisdiction was a recipe for disaster. It meant weakening the national government at a time when the threat of foreign intervention from Spain, Britain, France and the United States demanded the creation of a strong and united administrative body. Federalism was, in their opinion, the first step towards secessionism. A federalist system was also seen as a cradle for *caudillos*. In order to prevent the chieftains and strongmen of the provinces from influencing national politics, a strong centralist government was perceived to be essential.

For the federalists, the very nature of the territories of the new nations meant that only a federalist system could work. The pressing matters of the provinces required prompt responses, something that a national government in a faraway capital could never deliver. The marked geographical differences of the regions also meant that their problems were different, requiring different legislative measures that a centralist government which treated everybody the same could not deal with. Federalism did not mean secessionism. By respecting the local needs of the provinces, devolving power to them and granting them state sovereignty, their people would be more than willing to support a national government that respected their particularity, their need for self-determination. They believed in unity, but not uniformity. Centralism, in contrast, led to secessionism, since it provoked the provinces into seeking their own independence from a national government that was not prepared to attend to their very concrete and local needs. Federalism was a liberal system since it was the one that had been adopted in the 1787 US Constitution. A centralist system was also seen as one that favoured the emergence of despotic *caudillos*. With a federalist system, however authoritarian a president might be, he would be unable to impose his will in the different states of the republic, if their regional governments voted against his dictatorial measures.

However, beyond the realm of ideas, a pragmatical approach to politics resulted in a context whereby the regional elites were not necessarily consistent in their support of a centralist or a federalist agenda. Many centralists became federalists, and vice versa, as different governments with different interests rose and fell from power. Most regional elites paid more attention to their particular interests than the demands of any specific ideology. It made sense, for instance, to support a centralist system if you were a radical liberal at the time of Rivadavia's presidency, even if you were living in remote San Juan, when the local *caudillo* was the tyrannical federalist *gaucho*, Juan Facundo Quiroga.

Most *caudillos* were both federalists and centralists at different junctures, depending on whether they were in power or not. Rosas came to power as the leading *caudillo* of the federalists. At the head of the provincial *estancieros,* who resented the centralism of the liberal elites of Buenos Aires, Rosas took the capital on 3 November 1829 and transformed Argentina into a confederation. Nevertheless, in spite of the *rosista* propaganda, with its repeated slogans, 'Long live the Argentine Confederation. Death to the Savage Unitarians', the Rosas model was, in essence, a centralist one. Once Rosas was in power, it was not in his interest to defend a federalist system whereby the provinces could disobey his orders. He had regional *caudillos* such as Quiroga, who had initially supported him, assassinated, once it became clear that they wanted to dominate their respective regions. And he ensured, through patronage, coercion and populism, that the *gaucho* provinces remained supportive of his measures. Two key literary texts on the Rosas era are José Mármol's romantic novel-cum-political thriller *Amalia* (1851) and Esteban Echeverría's short story *El matadero* (1871), in which the Rosas regime is equated with a slaughterhouse.

## Church–State relations

While the federalist–centralist divide was the main cause of the thousands of revolts that spread throughout Latin America during the early national period, Church–State relations became the other burning issue. The enlightened justifications for the Bourbon assault on the Church were quickly taken up by the emergent liberal political class of the early national period. For most Latin American liberals it became evident that in order to forge a progressive and modern society the power of the Church would have to be curtailed. It was imperative that education was secularised. It was essential that the state had control of all of the affairs of the country and that the Church's sphere of influence was reduced to spiritual matters. Ecclesiastical privileges, such as the *fueros,* had to be abolished so that all individuals would be equal before the law. The obligatory tithe that everybody paid to support the Church needed to be eradicated.

However, beyond the ideological reasons adopted by radical liberals to justify their assault on the Church, the dire straits of the young republics heightened the need to expropriate, nationalise and auction Church properties, as well as to levy forced taxes and loans on the Church. By the mid 1830s, it was not only the radicals who were trying to force the Church to subsidise the state, but also most governments, whether they were liberal or traditionalist. In Mexico, the assault on the Church was led by the more radical wing of the liberal movement, notably in 1833–34 and 1846–47, on those occasions when the vice president, Valentín Gómez Farías, acted as the executive during Santa Anna's absence. However, while in the mid 1830s and the mid 1840s revolts prevented the radicals' reforms from being implemented, Santa Anna succeeded in extracting large loans from the Church by promising to leave the Church's *fueros* untouched. In Guatemala, while the assault on the Church was more effective than in

Mexico, the reaction it provoked was also more violent. Between 1829 and 1837, the anticlerical liberals, led by Francisco Morazán (1831–39), went beyond seizing Church funds and confiscating Church property, by exiling antiliberal priests, censoring ecclesiastical correspondence, authorising civil marriage, legalising divorce and removing education from clerical supervision. However, the Church fought back. Following Carrera's rise to prominence in 1840, Morazán's liberal programme was dismantled. Roman Catholicism became once more the official religion of the state; education was re-established under Church auspices; the Church regained its *fueros*, was given back a high proportion of its confiscated property and was relieved of paying the taxes the liberals had imposed on it. In return for these measures, Carrera benefited from the financial (as well as moral) support of the Church.

It was only in those countries where the hold of the Church had either never been complete under the colony, or had been severely weakened during the wars of independence, that anticlerical reforms were implemented without causing the kind of backlash that was experienced elsewhere. In Colombia and Venezuela there were extensive areas that had not been thoroughly catechised. As a result, Church domination of rural life was not significant, in comparison to Mexico, Guatemala and Argentina. Therefore Páez paid little attention to Church demands and was even able to expel the archbishop of Caracas in 1835 without unleashing a popular revolt. General Francisco de Paula Santander, in Colombia, was equally cool towards the Church, and found that he did not need to pursue policies that appealed to clerical opinion. In Bolivia, the war of independence greatly weakened the role of the Church. Under the government of Antonio José de Sucre (1825–28), the Church in Bolivia lost control of a vast range of properties that were expropriated by the state. The resulting strengthening of up-and-coming landowners and merchants who profited from Sucre's radical attack on the Church prevented it from gathering the necessary power to fight back.

Whether assaulted by a frontal attack from radical liberal administrations, or forced into allowing the state to increase its influence over ecclesiastical affairs as part of the price of retaining some of its privileges, the Church continued to lose its power in Latin America during the early national period. This by no means signifies that the Church ceased to be a particularly influential institution in the aftermath of independence. Nevertheless, as the first national decades went by, the Church did lose ground to the state. The most indicative sign of this revolved around the exercise of the *patronato*. With the Vatican unwilling to recognise the independence of the new Spanish American republics until the late 1830s, one government after another, regardless of whether it was pro- or anticlerical, found a way to assume responsibility for selecting and appointing the priests, bishops and archbishops of their respective countries. The right to do this (the so-called *patronato*) thus ceased to be one of the Pope's prerogatives and became a right of the states of the newly formed nations.

## The Brazilian empire

The experience of the early national period in Brazil, while quite different to that of most Spanish American republics, still involved a number of similarities. In political terms, the main difference stemmed from the fact that independence had been achieved without significant bloodshed and that Emperor Pedro I belonged to a well-established and respected royal household. Unlike Emperors Jacques I (1804–06) and Henri I (1808–20) in Haiti, or Agustín I (1822–23) in Mexico, Pedro I was the natural heir to the throne and not a revolutionary who had had himself crowned. His political legitimacy was respected; he represented both independence and continuity. He was perceived to be the safest bet when it came to guaranteeing order and stability in a country where slave discontent posed a major threat to the white elites, regardless of whether they were Portuguese or Brazilian. However, many of the problems that soon surfaced in independent Brazil bore great similarities to those that afflicted former Spanish America.

Constitutionalism was strong in Brazil too. The 1823 Constituent Assembly's attempt to draft a constitution that limited the power of the executive mirrored parallel efforts throughout the continent. Pedro I's response, dissolving the Assembly and replacing it with a handpicked commission to deliver a constitution more to his liking, was also typical. Although the subsequent 1824 Constitution created a constitutional monarchy rather than a republic, it echoed Bolívar's and anticipated Portales' constitutional proposals, whereby the executive was granted extraordinary powers. Nonetheless, it was a constitutional monarchy and not an absolutist one. There was a parliament with two chambers, and although the senate was made up of members chosen by the monarch, an elected chamber of deputies did exist as elsewhere (albeit voted in by a very limited male suffrage).

Pedro I also developed patronage–clientelistic networks, whereby important interest groups gained political and economic ascendancy in exchange for their support of the regime. The emperor also benefited from the support of the Church by establishing Catholicism as the religion of the state. And like most traditionalist contemporary rulers in Latin America, he protected the Church at a price, retaining the right of patronage (*Padroado Real*) in ecclesiastical appointments, and obtaining financial support in exchange when in need.

Similarly, many of the problems that were soon to shake the stability of independent Brazil were common ones. The federalist–centralist divide was as acute in Brazil as elsewhere. There were major federalist/secessionist revolts in Pernambuco (1824), Pará (1835–36), Rio Grande do Sul (1835–45), Bahia (1837) and Maranhão (1838). The white elites were equally divided. The emperor's tendency to favour Portuguese rather than Brazilian interests fractured the fragile unity that had kept the elites together throughout the 1810s. The more radical liberals found themselves calling for the creation of a republic. The moderates advocated a gradualist approach. The traditionalists demanded closer ties with Lisbon. Their divisions grew as the Argentine–Brazilian War (1825–28) raged on in Uruguay, resulting in a destabilising loss of men, money and, eventually, prestige. The final loss of Uruguay in 1828 brought discredit on Pedro I. The economic disarray provoked by the war resulted in high inflation. The resentment felt towards Portuguese merchants increased, and in March 1831 riots broke out in Rio de Janeiro. The so-called *Noites das Garrafadas* (Nights of Breaking Glass) confirmed to Pedro I that he could no longer control Brazil, and he abdicated on 7 April 1831, returned to Portugal and left his five-year-old son behind as his successor.

The experience of the Regency (1831–40) was no different to that of Brazil's neighbouring countries. Uprisings and revolts spread throughout the country. Attempts to deal with the grievances against Pedro I, such as federalising the political system and abolishing his Council of State in the 1834 Additional Act, did not improve the situation. The elites' divisions became more accentuated, and Brazil came very close to dissolving into a constellation of independent republics.

It was not until it became evident to the Brazilian elites, after nine years of dramatic upheaval, that it was only a matter of time before the large slave population would take advantage of their divisions, that a consensus was reached. The liberal and traditionalist elites of Rio de Janeiro, São Paulo and Minas Gerais put aside their differences and allowed the fifteen-year-old prince to be crowned in 1841. By 1844, the comparative chaos of the previous decade was a thing of the past, and a long period of noted stability followed under Pedro II (1841–89).

The fundamental aspect of Brazilian society that differentiated it from that of the rest of Spanish America was the large population of African slaves who inhabited the new nation. Until 1830, when the British navy started to enforce the prohibition of the slave trade, African slaves were imported into Brazil at a rate of 50,000 a year. Although the Anglo-Brazilian Treaty of 1826 specified that the slave trade would end in Brazil by 1829, slavery was not actually abolished until 13 May 1888. In the rest of Latin America, with the exception of Spain's remaining colonies in the Caribbean, Cuba and Puerto Rico, and the isolated case of Paraguay, slavery was abolished by the mid 1850s. The speed with which slavery was outlawed in the different countries illustrates – with the exception of Haiti, where the slave population succeeded in taking hold of the island – the extent to which their economies relied on forced labour. It was in those countries where the need for slaves was less pressing, and where, by default, the black population did not pose a major threat to the white elites, that slavery was abolished earlier than elsewhere: Chile (1823), Central America (1824), Bolivia (1826) and Mexico (1829).

In Brazil, in spite of the violent disputes that divided the white elites during the Regency, a consensus was achieved, something which had proved impossible for the majority of *hombres de bien* in Spanish America. While clearly the fear of social dissolution was never absent from their minds, they were not, as was the case with their counterparts in Brazil, threatened by the very real danger of a huge slave uprising. The elites' common fear of a slave revolution, and their common dependency on forced labour, meant that, in the end, they were able to forge a certain kind of class unity. This allowed them, after 1841, to consolidate a more stable and orderly form of government than those which their counterparts in Spanish America were able to establish.

## The United Provinces of Central America

In contrast, the case of the United Provinces of Central America serves as the obvious example of how, in a region where the elites were not threatened by a large slave population, their inability to reach a consensus led to dismemberment as well as a constant state of civil war. Civil conflict exploded from as early as 1827. Although the liberals won that civil war, by 1837 their control of the confederation had become tenuous in the wake of Carrera's indigenous, Church-backed Mita revolt. It is worth stating that although the liberals controlled the federal government (1829–40), transferring the capital from Guatemala City to San Salvador in 1834, they did not necessarily control the state governments that surfaced in the different provinces. Civil conflict became frequent as one province or another attempted to interfere in the affairs of their neighbouring regions. In this context, turmoil among rival *caudillos* proved devastating. In addition, wide-scale Indian discontent became another key destabilising factor.

In April 1838 Costa Rica and Nicaragua broke away from the confederation. In essence, 1838 marked the end of the confederation. Guatemalan interference in Honduras and El Salvador meant that the three nations remained loosely and formally united for another nine years, until Guatemala declared its own independence in 1847. This unity was only maintained, however, after Guatemalan troops repeatedly intervened in Honduras and El Salvador, with Carrera ensuring that *caudillos* who were supportive of his regime occupied the presidencies of their respective countries. Moreover, internal conflicts within the provinces led to further instability. In Nicaragua, the rivalry between the cities of León and Granada, controlled by opposing political factions, resulted in further outbreaks of violence. Only Costa Rica experienced relative peace and stability following its separation from the United Provinces in 1838. In Nicaragua, Guatemala and Honduras, there was the additional problem of foreign intervention.

Britain, which had controlled Belize since the early seventeenth century, and imposed a protectorate on the Mosquito Coast over the Miskito Indians of Honduras and Nicaragua since 1678, took the Bay Islands in 1821. Making the most of the ongoing state of turmoil in Central America, the British Crown used the 1830s and 1840s to extend its control on the Mosquito Coast, claiming it as one of the United Kingdom's colonies. In 1848, allegedly invited to intervene by the 'king' of the Miskito Indians, British troops went as far as seizing San Juan del Norte, on the Nicaragua–Costa Rica border, renaming it Greytown. As will be seen in the following chapter, the problems that arose from British interventionism came to a head in the late 1850s.

## The Chilean Constitution of 1833

The great exception was Chile. It was the only large republic to establish a long-lasting constitutional government with solid foundations. The resilient 1833 Constitution was the work of Diego Portales, a powerful merchant from Valparaíso. Unlike the majority of Latin American constitutions, Portales' Constitution empowered the executive, giving Chile a strong presidentialist tradition. The president was allowed to serve for two consecutive five-year terms of office, but no more, and enjoyed extensive powers over the judiciary and public administration. Nonetheless, a Congress was created which could check on the executive and deny assent to his budgetary and military policies, and this, in turn, was made up of elected members. Suffrage was typically limited to males whose income was of a certain level, and who could read and write. It was a centralist constitution that put an end to the federalist experiments of the 1820s, and it was sympathetic towards the Church, allowing it to retain its privileges.

The Portalian system encapsulated many of the aims that were pursued by a significant number of Latin American *caudillos*. It defended the Church. It favoured the interests of the landed classes. It allowed for the kind of strong government that elites throughout the continent were hoping their *caudillos* would consolidate. But there was a difference. The Portalian system, by its very constitutional nature, prevented *caudillos* from rocking the boat, from perpetuating themselves in power or from pursuing megalomaniac policies. The powerful men of the period, General Joaquín Prieto (1831–41) and General Manuel Bulnes (1841–51), were each able to rule for ten years, allowed as they were to be re-elected, but not for ever. More significantly, a consensus was reached among the elites that resulted in them supporting the Constitution.

Inevitably, the Portalian system was maintained by a series of extra-constitutional measures. A dramatic purge of notorious liberal officers in the army in the early 1830s curbed the threat of a radical revolution. Elections were generally manipulated so that the favoured candidate would win. Repression, although not used to the same degree as in Argentina or Paraguay, was employed for the following three decades, with the arbitrary arrest and exile of troublemakers. However, this alone does not explain the success of the 1833 charter. After all, most *caudillos* exiled members of the opposition, fixed elections (in those cases where they took place) and employed repressive measures. This did not stop rival *caudillos* from revolting or popular uprisings from erupting.

The stability enjoyed by the Portalian system can be understood by appreciating the distinctive nature of Chile and its population during the early national period. Although Chile's territory was extensive, the Central Valley around Santiago was where the majority of the population was based. The usual problems that stemmed from poor communications did not affect the majority of Chileans in the same way that they did elsewhere. With most economic activities taking place around Santiago, creole landowners and merchants developed much tighter ties than in other Latin American countries. The resulting absence of the kind of regional elite rivalry that inspired the numerous federalist/secessionist revolts in Mexico, Brazil and Central America was equally important in guaranteeing stability. The Chilean landowning class, sharing common interests, was more inclined to find a consensus, since they all benefited, to a greater or lesser degree, from the same economic policies.

The composition of the population also meant that the ethnic tensions that were so important elsewhere did not feature as prominently in Chilean society. The majority of the population, lower classes included, were either white or *mestizo*. The only Indian community of any significance was the Araucanian Indians, and they were allowed to live to the south of the Bío-bío River as a separate republic. The caste wars that affected Mexico in the late 1840s, or the Indian rebellions that brought Carrera to power in Guatemala, could not have occurred in Chile, where the Indian population was so marginal. Likewise the black population was almost non-existent. This accounts for the abolition of slavery in 1823, but it also means that Chile did not have a society like that of Venezuela or Colombia, where racial tensions ran high. Almost inevitably, once a stable government was put in place, the situation in Chile went from strength to strength. Stability attracted foreign investment, which, in turn, resulted in a strong economy. Chile's victory over the Peruvian–Bolivian Confederation in the 1836–39 war further boosted national pride and led to an economic boom, whereby Valparaíso became the leading South American port on the Pacific and Chile the chief producer of copper in the world.

## Major international wars (1825–1848)

During the early national period only two major wars were fought between Latin American nations. These were the Argentine–Brazilian War (1825–28) and the war between Chile and the Peruvian–Bolivian Confederation (1836–39). The third major war was between Mexico and the United States (1846–48). In 1844, following the fall of President Jean Pierre Boyer (1818–43), and coinciding with the outbreak of conflict that ensued in Haiti, a military coup in Santo Domingo sealed the independence of the Dominican Republic. However, neither the occupation of Santo Domingo in 1822 nor the 1844 independence movement constituted a war as such, given that both the Haitian annexation and the loss of the Spanish-speaking part of the island took place without significant bloodshed.

The Argentine–Brazilian War (1825–28) represented the first war fought between newly independent nations in Latin America. The Banda Oriental had, since 1818, been occupied by Portuguese–Brazilian forces, becoming the Cisplatine Province of Brazil. With Artigas exiled, and subsequently trapped in Paraguay as a result of Dr Francia's 1822 law of isolation, it took seven years for his Uruguayan comrades-in-arms to organise a second bid for independence. This they did in April 1825, when the so-called Heroic Thirty-Three *Orientales* launched an invasion from the Argentinean border to liberate Uruguay. The Brazilian court responded by declaring war on Argentina in December 1825. For the next two and a half years, Brazilian and Argentinean forces engaged in battle, while the Uruguayan forces found themselves fighting the Brazilians in an uncomfortable alliance with the Buenos Aires government. By the spring of 1828, in spite of Fructuoso Rivera's successful campaign in Misiones, the Uruguayans' control of the north of Montevideo and the Argentine victories at the battles of Juncal and Ituzaingó (February 1827), Brazil was still in control of most of the towns in the Banda Oriental. With both Brazil and Argentina having exhausted their military resources, and it remaining unclear who had the upper hand, British demands for negotiation were finally listened to. It was through pressure and mediation by Britain, inspired to seek an end to the war after its commercial interests in the region had been badly affected by the conflict, that Argentina and Brazil accepted the terms of the 27 August 1828 peace treaty. Thereafter Uruguay became a 'buffer country', with all the problems which that entailed.

The war between Peru, Bolivia and Chile (1836–39) was provoked by the creation of the Peruvian–Bolivian Confederation. Since independence, both Peru and Bolivia had undergone the common upheavals of the period, experiencing a series of short-lived constitutional experiments and governments. However, by the early 1830s, while Peru continued to be afflicted by ongoing revolts and instability, Bolivia had found a certain degree of stability under the benevolent and constitutional dictatorship of Andrés Santa Cruz (1829–39). Santa Cruz, whose political career had already involved briefly governing Peru, from 1826 to 1827, made the most of Peru's decline into chaos by taking Lima in 1835. Although there was some hostility towards a supposed Bolivian takeover of Peru, most Peruvian elites welcomed the prospect of peace, order and stability that had become associated with Santa Cruz's style of government. The Confederation created by Santa Cruz, recognised by Britain, the United States and France, was virulently condemned by Brazil, Argentina and Chile, whose governments feared the effect such a concentration of power could have in South America. Brazil, however, was not in a position to dispatch troops to the area. Rosas' Argentina made a feeble attempt to do so, but his troops were repulsed without difficulty. It was Chile, whose very proximity to the Confederation meant that it was the country most threatened by Bolivian expansionism, that made the strongest bid to bring down Santa Cruz. In 1836 Chile declared war on the Peruvian–Bolivian Confederation and sent two large expeditionary forces to Peru. The first was successfully repelled in 1837. The second, led by General Manuel Bulnes, succeeded in taking Lima and defeating Santa Cruz's forces at the battle of Yungay (January 1839). Yungay brought the war to an end with the subsequent exile of Santa Cruz to France, and the end of the Peruvian–Bolivian Confederation.

The Mexican–American War deserves closer attention due to its importance not only in terms of Mexican history, but also because of what it represented for Latin America as a whole. From a Mexican perspective, its outcome represented the traumatic loss of half of Mexico's national territory. From a Latin American perspective, it signalled the beginning of what most Latin Americans define as US imperialism.

The origins of US interventionism in Latin America date back to 1823, when President James Monroe stated that 'the American continents, by the free and independent condition which they have assumed and maintained, are henceforth not to be considered as subjects for colonisation by any European powers'. Monroe argued that it was the obligation of the United States to assist any American country whose sovereignty was threatened by European imperialism. Although what became the Monroe Doctrine was initially conceived as the means to prevent countries such as Britain, France and Spain from interfering in the politics of the Americas, it was not long before it was used to justify US interference in the region.

However, while the Monroe Doctrine was to be used as the principal explanation for US interventionism in Latin America in the twentieth century, it was not employed as a pretext for the Mexican–American War. Nevertheless, it was there as a philosophy that granted the United States the role of protector of the Americas. In other words, if the situation in any Latin American country was deemed as being detrimental to US interests or allegedly destabilising for the continent at large, the Monroe Doctrine gave the USA the right to intervene as the self-proclaimed guarantor of 'freedom' in the western hemisphere. Needless to say, a concept such as that of manifest destiny could not have surfaced without there first having been a Monroe Doctrine.

Manifest destiny was the term used in 1845 by a New York journalist, John L. O'Sullivan, to describe the fated, moral obligation of the United States to expand its domains and influence throughout the continent. It justified the conquest of the west, establishing 'the moral dignity and salvation of man', over the 'savage' Native Americans. It gave the USA the divine right to extend 'liberal democracy' and 'freedom' south of the border. It justified US expansionism in religious terms, dismantling any ethical arguments standing in the way of their hopes of annexing the rich, fertile and gold-ridden northern provinces of Mexico.

The US desire to annex provinces such as Texas, Arizona and California dated from the early nineteenth century. Following the purchase of Louisiana from France in 1803, and that of Florida from Spain in 1819, the next step was the acquisition of Texas. With independence, the newly formed Mexican governments refused to sell any of their national territory. Nevertheless, an extremely liberal law of colonisation, paired with the fact that distance prevented the Mexican government from controlling the influx of Anglo-American settlers who came to occupy Texas, resulted in a situation whereby there were nine Americans for every Mexican in the region by 1828. The realisation that this could eventually result in the loss of Texas to the United States led Anastasio Bustamante's administration (1830–32) to issue the law of 6 April 1830, which forbade US citizens from emigrating to Texas. It was a law that was impossible to enforce because of the state of communications at the time. The aversion towards the Mexican government felt by most American Texans (who objected to becoming Catholics, abiding by Mexican law, learning Spanish, etc.) was further exacerbated by the 1829 abolition of slavery. As long as the 1824 Federal Constitution was in place, however, slavery was allowed to continue under Texan law. It was the overthrow of federalism in 1835 that finally inspired the Texans to revolt, given that a centralist state would enforce the abolition of slavery throughout the republic. Initially, Texas became the independent Lone Star Republic, after Santa Anna's troops suffered a humiliating defeat at the battle of San Jacinto, only a month and a half after the *caudillo* had led the notorious victory of the Alamo in 1836. By 1845 Texas had been annexed by the United States. With the Mexicans feeling outraged by the annexation, since they had never recognised Texan independence, and a fever of expansionism gripping the United States, war was inevitable. On 25 April 1846, Mexican forces opened fire on US troops mobilised to the Río Bravo (within Mexican territory) and war was declared.

The Mexican–American War lasted for seventeen months. It took three US invasion forces to take Mexico City. Of the 104,556 men who were dispatched to Mexico, 13,768 died, representing the highest death rate in any war fought by the United States up to the present. Abraham Lincoln opposed the war, since he thought it worked in the interests of the slave-dependent southern states of the Union. The end result was the 2 February 1848 Treaty of Guadalupe, whereby Mexico lost half of its territory to the United States. Thereafter, US influence in Latin America would grow to encompass the whole of the southern western hemisphere.

Independence did not result in an age of peace, prosperity and stability. For most Latin American countries, the early national period was characterised by turmoil. The emergent political class, creoles in their majority, experimented with a plethora of constitutional systems, few of which survived the passing of time. Instability, penury,

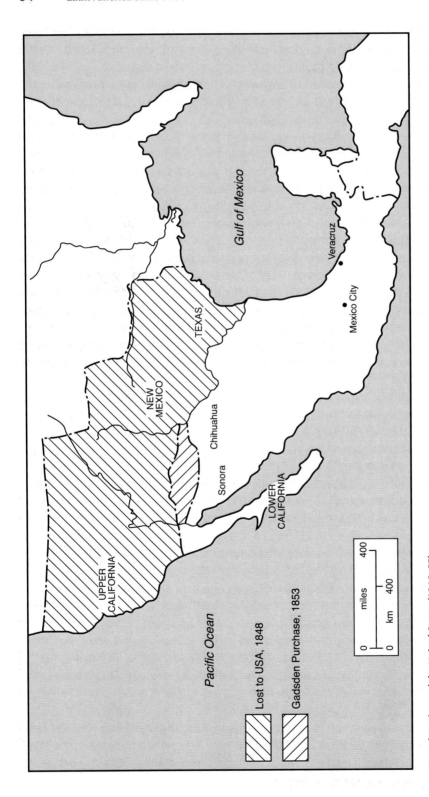

Map of Mexico and the United States (1846–53)

civil conflict and revolutions became common features throughout the continent. Progressive reforms clashed with traditional practices. For the most part, the elites were unable to reach a consensus. Poor communications prevented commerce from flourishing and made the exercise of government almost impossible. Regional differences, both cultural and economic, resulted in a continuous struggle between federalists and centralists. In some cases, these led to the dismemberment of the newly formed republics. For the majority, little changed. One ruling class had replaced another, but there was no redistribution of land. The rise of the *caudillo* throughout Spanish America resulted in a common trend towards authoritarian regimes, whereby certain elites prospered at the expense of a majority that was kept out of politics through populist gestures and a restricted suffrage. Sometimes, dictatorship became the only means of achieving order and stability. By the end of the 1840s, the concept of nationhood was still far from being accepted. Most Latin American countries were still far from becoming nation states. In most cases, they were no more than a conglomeration of provincial fiefdoms, tenuously linked together by an unstable national government that increasingly became the servant of a particular *caudillo*. For the generation of independence it was a dark period, during which they had moved from the high hopes of the 1820s to the despair of the 1840s without finding the means of forging a long-lasting constitutional system. The time had come for a new generation, born either during or just after the wars of independence, to take the reins of power and attempt to redress the failures of their parents.

## Exhibit 2.1: Excerpts from a letter written by Simón Bolívar to Juan José Flores (Barranquilla 9 November 1830)

Mi querido general:

...Vd. sabe que yo he mandado 20 años y de ellos no he sacado más que pocos resultados ciertos: 1) La América es ingobernable para nosotros. 2) El que sirve una revolución ara en el mar. 3) La única cosa que se puede hacer en América es emigrar. 4) Este país caerá infaliblemente en manos de la multitud desenfrenada, para después pasar a tiranuelos casi imperceptibles, de todos colores y razas. 5) Devorados por todos los crímenes y extinguidos por la ferocidad, los europeos no se dignarán conquistarnos. 6) Si fuera posible que una parte del mundo volviera al caos primitivo, éste sería el último período de la América.

La primera revolución francesa hizo degollar las Antillas y la segunda causará el mismo efecto en este vasto continente. La súbita reacción de la ideología exagerada va a llenarnos de cuantos males nos faltaban o más bien los va a completar. Vd. verá que todo el mundo va a entregarse al torrente de la demagogia y ¡desgraciados de los pueblos! y ¡desgraciados de los gobiernos!...

Este país ha sufrido una Gran Revolución, y marcha sobre un terreno volcánico... Todo el pueblo, la iglesia y el ejército son afectos al nuevo orden de cosas, no faltan sin embargo asesinos, traidores, facciosos y descontentos, cuyo número puede subir a algunos centenares. Desgraciadamente, entre nosotros no pueden nada las masas, algunos ánimos fuertes lo hacen todo y la multitud sigue la audacia sin examinar la justicia o el crimen de los caudillos, mas los abandonan luego al punto que otros más aleves los sorprenden. Esta es la opinión pública y la fuerza nacional de nuestra América...

*Source:* Manuel Pérez Vila (ed.), *Simón Bolívar, Doctrina del libertador* (Los Ruices: Biblioteca Ayacucho, 1976), pp. 321–6.

## Exhibit 2.2: Excerpts from José María Gutiérrez Estrada's pamphlet, *Carta dirigida al Excelentísimo Señor Presidente de la República sobre la necesidad de buscar en una convención el posible remedio de los males que aquejan a la república; y opiniones del autor acerca del mismo asunto, por J.M. Gutiérrez Estrada* (Mexico City: Imp. de I. Cumplido, 1840)

Exmo. Señor:

...[E]l amor a mi país y mi gratitud a V.E., me mueven a exponerle mis ideas..., con respecto a la presente situación de la república... Después de una dolorosa experiencia iy tan reciente y tan incontestable! atribuir exclusivamente nuestras desgracias a la constitución de [1]836, y esperar su inmediato y completo remedio únicamente del restablecimiento de la de [1]824, sería una grata ilusión, que harto nos pesa no poder abrigar a los que sintiendo grabados hondamente en nuestros pechos los males de la patria, estamos convencidos de que una constitución por sabia que sea, es un documento muerto si no hay hombres que sepan, quieran y puedan poner en práctica sus benéficas disposiciones... [D]esgraciadamente no tenemos esa clase de hombres, expresión viva y fiel de una sociedad en todos aspectos más adelantada... Por esta razón, y porque no hay que esperar salud, sino de la generación venidera, si acaso tuviera escuelas en que aprender, ninguna fe tengo en lo que existe, ni en cuanto pueda hacer la generación presente... De cuantos modos, pues, puede ser una república, la hemos experimentado; democrática, oligárquica, militar, demagógica y anárquica; de manera que todos los partidos a su vez, y siempre con detrimento de la felicidad y del honor del país, han probado el sistema republicano bajo todas las formas posibles... [S]e ha trocado todo en ruina, desolación, pobreza, matanzas por iras civiles, y en fin, en oprobioso descrédito... Disértese cuanto se quiera sobre las ventajas de la República donde pueda establecerse, y nadie las proclamará más cordialmente que yo; ni tampoco lamentará con más sinceridad que México no pueda ser por ahora, ese país privilegiado: pero la triste experiencia de lo que ese sistema ha sido para nosotros, parece que nos autoriza ya a hacer en nuestra patria un ensayo de verdadera monarquía en la persona de un príncipe extranjero... [L]os más acérrimos partidarios de la República, son los primeros en confesar que ésta no se ha consolidado entre nosotros, porque todo en México es monárquico... [L]a forma monárquica (con un soberano de estirpe real) sería más acomodada al carácter, las costumbres y las tradiciones de un pueblo que desde su fundación fue gobernado monárquicamente... Por eso, repito, que me parece llegado ya el momento en que la nación dirija su vista hacia el principio de una monarquía democrática, como el único medio de ver renacer entre nosotros la paz que tan ardientemente anhelamos... No descubro tampoco otro modo de salvar nuestra nacionalidad inminentemente amenazada por la raza anglo-sajona, que trasladada a este continente, se apareja a invadirlo todo... Si no variamos de conducta, quizá no pasarán veinte años sin que veamos tremolar la bandera de las estrellas norteamericanas en nuestro Palacio Nacional; y sin que se vea celebrar en la espléndida Catedral de México el oficio protestante.

# Topics for discussion in class

■ Of the six points Bolívar lists in Exhibit 2.1, which strike you as being an accurate interpretation of the failings of the early national period?

■ Beyond the metaphors and dramatic language of Exhibit 2.1, what are the factors that Bolívar considered contributed to preventing independent America from prospering?

■ In Exhibit 2.2, what reasons does Gutiérrez Estrada give for the failure of the republican system in Mexico?

■ Why does he believe it is important that a monarchy is established in Mexico with a European prince at its head?

■ What are the main differences and similarities between Exhibits 2.1 and 2.2?

# Topics for essays and presentations

Making use of the recommended texts (see Further reading, p. 161) and/or others that may be available to you in your local library, write an essay/give a seminar presentation on **one** of the following topics.

1 With reference to *at least one* specific case study, provide an interpretation of the factors that contributed to the longevity and resilience of *caudillo* rule in Spanish America during the early national period.

2 Analyse the importance or lack thereof of constitutionalist thought during the first half of the nineteenth century in a Latin American country of your choice.

3 Outline and discuss the relevance of the federalist–centralist divide in Latin America during the early national period.

4 'Civil war has become emblematic of nineteenth-century Latin America' (Rebecca Earle). Discuss with reference to the experience of Mexico, Colombia or Peru during the early national period.

## CHAPTER 3

# The rise of the neocolonial order (1850–1880)

The years 1850–80 marked a key watershed in the history of Latin America. At an economic level, it was during these years that most Latin American countries were thrust into the global market. The discovery of gold in California opened up the trade of the Pacific to the world. A revolution in communications technology drastically transformed the continent. Most Latin American economies came to rely on the export of primary products in exchange for the import of manufactured goods from industrialised Europe and the United States. The *haciendas* expanded and an increasingly powerful oligarchy was formed. The new economic dependency forged initially between Latin America and Britain, and later the United States, marked the emergence of a neocolonial order. However, these changes did not come about easily. Two decades of major unrest preceded the triumph of a conservative form of liberalism. By 1880 most of those colonial legacies that had survived independence had been destroyed.

## World context

The numerous revolutions that erupted in Europe in 1848 marked the beginning of the end of the old order. Industrialisation resulted in the growth of a middle class that felt dissatisfied with absolutism and the restrictions on political and economic activity that prevailed. The mid-century liberal revolts were led and fought by the bourgeoisie. Although the 1848 explosion did not lead to the changes the revolutionaries had hoped for, by the 1860s most European states did come round to implementing liberal constitutions, guaranteeing representative government while opening up the economy. The triumph of a conservative or moderated brand of liberalism gave way to a period in which progress became the main goal of the new ruling class, within a framework that enabled capitalist economic activity to develop. A second wave of industrialisation came about, leading to growing prosperity, temporarily dampening the discontent of the working classes. Education also started to expand, encompassing a large proportion of the

## The watershed

The years 1850 to 1880 represented a key water-shed in the history of the Americas. In Spanish population. Building on this increasing wealth and stability, European imperialism extended to Africa, Asia and the Far East in the last decades of the nineteenth century, while the Ottoman Empire entered a period of decline. Italy and Germany were unified, and the United States, in the wake of its Civil War (1861–65), established the foundations on which would develop one of the world's most powerful nations in the twentieth century.

America they came to mark the end of those colonial legacies that had survived the early national period. In the United States, a particularly sanguinary civil war (1861–65) brought the Southern Confederacy, with its slavery, its agriculture-based economy and its traditionalist aspirations, under the yoke of northern liberal industrial domination. In Cuba, the Ten Year War (1868–78) came close to bringing about the island's independence. In Canada, following sixteen unstable years (1851–67), a new federal regime was inaugurated which led to Alexander Mackenzie's liberal administration (1872–78). The women's movement started to gather momentum in the wake of the Seneca Falls 1848 'Declaration of Sentiments', which stated that 'It is the duty of the women of this country [USA] to secure for themselves their sacred right to the elective franchise.' Karl Marx published *The Communist Manifesto* (1848), *The Eighteenth Brumaire of Louis Bonaparte* (1851) and the first volume of *Capital* (1867). They were three decades which gave way to the emergence of a new order that would last until the 1930s.

What is referred to in the historiography as the oligarchical or neocolonial periods had their origins during these years. A new generation, born either during or after the struggle for independence, came of age and, either inspired or terrified by the 1848 Revolution in France, replaced the former generation in the corridors of power. As one cycle came to an end, another began. The despair of the generation that had witnessed the dreams of the hopeful 1820s dissolve during the subsequent three decades of constitutional failures was replaced by the hope of a young emergent political class.

For this mid-century generation, independence was no longer a contested issue. It was taken for granted. They did not remember the colonial experience and were less inclined to accept those colonial legacies that were still in place. In the wake of the 1848 popular uprisings in Europe, the liberal factions were also predisposed to take on the traditionalist governments of the day with renewed vigour. While the previous generation had come round to supporting the imposition of dictatorships (or governments with strong executives) as the only realistic remedy to the problems they had faced in power, the mid-century generation was confident that the time had come for a major liberal revolution. The traditionalist sectors, now more formally integrated into a more clearly defined conservative movement, fought hard to prevent the mid-century liberals from ousting them from power.

In Mexico it took two particularly bloody civil wars (1854–55 and 1858–61), and the defeat of the French-imposed Habsburg Emperor Maximilian I (1864–67), for a new liberal order to emerge triumphant. In Guatemala, Carrera's death in 1865 marked the end of an era. The liberal reaction that ensued was both dramatic and unstoppable.

Once Justo Rufino Barrios rose to power (1871–85), like his counterpart in Mexico, Benito Juárez, he led a fierce attack on the Church that crippled its influence in the region, making its recovery impossible in subsequent years. In El Salvador and Honduras, events followed a parallel course, with the end of conservative rule in 1871. In Costa Rica, it was Tomás Guardia who, either as president or as master of presidents (1870–82), led the way, in a country where, rather atypically, the regular army was abolished in the 1848 Constitution. In Venezuela, as in Mexico, it took over two decades of civil conflict before the liberals gained control of the country. Nevertheless, once they did, under the leadership of Antonio Guzmán Blanco (1870–88), there was no looking back. In Colombia, the conservative–liberal divide resulted in twelve years of political upheaval, until Tomás Cipriano de Mosquera, a former conservative turned radical liberal, took Bogotá in July 1861 and imposed twenty years of liberal rule (1861–80). In Chile, the triumph of the liberal party was brought about through elections (preceded by an armed liberal show of strength). Between 1861 and 1891, with the Chilean liberals in power, the Catholic Church lost its monopoly over religion and its *fueros,* as well as its control over education. Civil marriage was legalised, suffrage was opened up to encompass a wider spectrum of society, and Congress gained power. In Argentina, the fall of Rosas and his subsequent exile to England in 1852 allowed the liberals to recover the ground lost during his dictatorship. Nevertheless, a decade of acute instability transpired before they succeeded in controlling the region, first under Bartolomé Mitre (1862–68), and subsequently under Domingo Faustino Sarmiento (1868–74). Once Julio Roca became president in 1880, the liberal order became fully consolidated in Argentina. In Uruguay, where the liberal–conservative divide (*colorados* vs *blancos*) had resulted in a constant state of civil war for much of the early national period, the watershed came in 1870. As a direct result of the victory of the Triple Alliance (Argentina, Brazil and Uruguay) over Paraguay in the 1864–70 war, the *colorados* secured their control over Uruguay for the next twenty years. In Haiti, it was President Fabre Geffrard (1859–67) who set the foundations of a liberal government that would eventually gather momentum under the presidencies of Lysius Salomon (1879–88) and Florvil Hyppolite (1889–96). In Brazil, Pedro II (1841–89) avoided the tensions that surfaced elsewhere by ensuring that his ministers pursued a liberal course.

There were exceptions. In Nicaragua, after the liberals invited a US adventurer, William Walker, to assist them in their struggle, in 1855, the conservatives were able to fight back with nationalism on their side. Walker, in extraordinary circumstances, was elected president of Nicaragua in 1856, after he successfully took Granada by force. Although he surrendered and returned to the USA a year later, he made two more attempts to invade Central America, and was executed in Honduras in 1860. From 1863 to 1893, the conservatives consolidated their control of the country. It would take the 1893 revolt for liberalism to triumph in the region. In Ecuador, Gabriel García Moreno, whose staunch conservatism became all the more extreme after he personally witnessed the 1848 uprisings in Europe, imposed an unusual theocratic state (1860–75), which remained in place, in spite of his assassination in 1875, until the liberals came to power in 1895. In Peru, although the liberal *caudillo* Ramón Castilla succeeded in stabilising the country's political situation (1845–51, 1854–62), he was unable to consolidate this early triumph for liberalism in the continent. The increasing corruption of the successive governments, and the power of both Church and the army, prevented Peru's first civilian liberal president, Manuel Pardo (1872–78), from implementing his ambitious reforms. The instability that ensued in the wake of Pardo's assassination, and the defeat Peru suffered in the War of the Pacific (1879–83) at the hands of the Chileans, meant that liberalism would only triumph once Andrés Cáceres came to power (1885–90). In Bolivia, the Liberals did not consolidate their control of the country until 1899, having first experienced thirty years of acute instability (1848–79), a major defeat in the War of the Pacific, and almost fifteen years of Conservative rule (1884–99). The generals who ruled between 1848 and 1879 (Manuel Belzu, Mariano Melgarejo and Hilarión Daza) were those described by the Bolivian writer Alcídes Arguedas as 'barbarous *caudillos*'. In Paraguay, even after Francisco Solano López's dictatorial presidency (1862–70) came to an end in the wake of the War of the Triple Alliance (1864–70), the conservatives managed to hang on to power, albeit occasionally sharing the presidency alternately with the liberals. And in the Dominican Republic, fear of Haiti proved too strong for any coherent liberal or conservative government to emerge during these years. Pedro Santana sought protection from Spain, and between 1861 and 1865 reverted Santo Domingo to its condition of colony. With this experiment having failed, José María Cabral (1866–67) turned towards the United States, in the hope that they might protect them instead. Although Buenaventura Báez (1868–82) won the following elections on a nationalist platform, it was he who subsequently went as far as proposing that the United States should annex the Republic. Ironically, it was the US senate's opposition to the annexation that prevented it from happening.

However, although the 1850–80 watershed resulted in the triumph of liberalism in Latin America, the nature of this liberalism needs to be qualified. In spite of the defeat of the conservatives, many of their proposals and defenders became assimilated by the liberal administrations that came to power in the latter half of the nineteenth century. If the traditionalist governments of the early national period could be described as having been relatively liberal in their orientation, it follows that the liberal governments of the neocolonial period bore many conservative traits. The years that transpired between 1850 and 1880 led to the end of the liberal conservatism of the first national decades and gave birth to the emergence of a conservative form of liberalism. In order to appreciate this, it is essential that we understand what the mid-century liberal–conservative divide was all about.

## Liberals and conservatives

Although most general histories of Latin America have tended to simplify nineteenth-century politics as a struggle between liberals and conservatives, such a divide did not surface consistently until the mid to late 1840s. During the first national decades, the main conflicting factions were not opposed to each other along clearly drawn, conservative–liberal lines. The ideologies adopted by most early nineteenth-century political movements in Latin America had their origins in the Enlightenment, Bourbon reformism and, ultimately, the liberal ideals of the Cádiz 1812 Constitution. The emergent political class was deeply divided, not between liberals and conservatives, but between federalists and centralists, monarchists and republicans, gradualists and radical reformers, pro-clericals and anticlericals. Until the mid 1840s, the struggle was between radical, moderate and traditionalist liberals, divided over whether the colonial legacies could be overturned overnight. It was only after politics became deeply polarised in the 1840s, after two decades of turmoil and civil strife, that more clearly defined parties were formed. The radical liberals appropriated the term Liberals for themselves and the traditionalist liberals evolved into Conservatives. The moderate liberals were to find such polarities difficult to live with, and in some countries, while at certain conflictive turning points they joined forces with the Liberals, at others they supported the Conservatives.

By 1850 most Conservatives believed in protecting traditional institutions such as the Church and the regular army. They were committed to retaining colonial legacies such as the *fueros,* and believed that Catholicism needed to be defended as one of the few elements remaining which could give the heterogeneous population of their respective countries a sense of national identity. Tolerating freedom of religious practice meant destroying one of the main cultural pillars of society. They were opposed to civil marriage, legalising divorce, giving similar rights to legitimate and illegitimate children, and undermining the moral influence of the Church. Fearful of social dissolution, and suspecting that the moral behaviour of the people had been in decline since independence, they supported strengthening the Church as a means of instilling a sense of God-fearing obedience and humility in the population.

The moral decadence they considered to be spreading like an illness had come hand in hand with acute instability, civil wars and a rampant crime rate. The need to instil a strong sense of law and order in their respective societies was viewed as a fundamental priority. The Conservatives were not only the party of morality, but also the party of order. This entailed a staunch defence of repression if need be, a commitment to eradicating crime through strengthening both army and police, and a hardened intolerance towards criminal and revolutionary activities. In the name of order, most Conservatives believed that the press should be censored and controlled, that suffrage should be restricted to the elites, and that it was imperative that the executive was strong. Although there were evident exceptions, most Latin American Conservatives became dedicated centralists, espousing the view that federalism weakened the position of the national government.

With their support of strong government came a belief that the state should be strengthened. The Conservatives advocated the formation of an interventionist state. They believed in implementing protectionist economic policies that could restrict the import of cheap, factory-made, foreign (and, in particular, European) products, while giving incentives to national industrialists. In Mexico, under the guidance of the Conservative ideologue Lucas Alamán and the industrialist Esteban de Antuñano, this entailed an attempt to develop a thriving national textile industry in Puebla in the 1840s. This brand of early Latin American nationalism also included a defence of the corporate institutions and community practices that had remained in place since colonial times. Beyond guaranteeing the survival of military and ecclesiastical *fueros*, it also meant respecting the communal lands of an extensive range of peasant and Indian communities. Unlike the Liberals, who broadly believed in breaking up communal lands, transforming their owners into individuals with small private properties, the Conservatives were averse to what, at the end of the twentieth century, became known as privatisation. While the Liberals defended the integration of the Indian population into society, forcing them to abandon their cultural practices and asking them to become Mexican or Guatemalan citizens, the Conservatives believed in continuing to allow them to live as separate corporate societies, alongside, albeit within, the national state. The Conservatives supported the preservation of the *repúblicas de Indios* (Indian Republics).

The Conservatives drew their ideology from what they considered to be the inherent pragmatism of their beliefs. For them, the most important lesson offered by three decades of constitutional failure and unrest was that there was nothing more damaging than abstract ideas. To attempt to reform society overnight, without taking into consideration its condition, customs and traditions, in the name of some foreign or esoteric form of idealism, was a recipe for disaster. Progress lay in understanding reality as it was (or, at least, as the Conservatives thought it was). It could be achieved as long as it was done slowly, gradually amending the existing structures. If you attempted to destroy the past and present order in an attempt to create an entirely new utopia, you would not only fail, but would inspire the kind of instability that had featured so prominently during the early national period.

The Liberal standpoint was quite different. Nevertheless, for the radical liberals of the late 1840s and early 1850s, state intervention was also an important part of their agenda. Needless to say, the triumphant liberals of the 1870s would eventually renounce such a belief, replacing it with one which, in favouring the rights of the individual, reduced the parameters of state influence. However, the mid-century reformers viewed state intervention as the only secure means of redistributing the land and wealth of their nations. It was imperative for them to encourage the expansion of the middle classes. In order to do so, the peasants needed incentives to prosper as individuals. For this to happen, it was important that they no longer worked on communal lands or as peons on *haciendas*, but that they acquired their own property. Once they could work on their own fields, it followed that they would work harder, given that they would not be labouring for the good of everybody and nobody, or as slaves of some unjust, absentee ***latifundista***. Having property of their own would make them more responsible, more ambitious. It would turn them into useful, as well as wealthier citizens. It was the state's obligation to break up the communal lands and the larger *haciendas* so that a new class of small landowners could emerge. This entailed expropriating the larger *haciendas* and, in theory, auctioning their fragmented lands to those peons who had worked them for so long without either owning them or having a say in the means of production.

> **latifundista**
> Large estate owner; ***latifundio***: large estate.

The Liberals were constitutionalists who believed in the need for representative government. In the 1850s and 1860s, they were virulently opposed to dictatorships and *caudillismo*. In theoretical terms, popular political participation was as important to them as ensuring that everybody was offered a basic education. As the inspired Mexican liberal Benito Juárez put it:

> As a son of the people I will not forget them. On the contrary, I will defend their rights. I will ensure that they are educated, that they grow and prosper, and that they forge their own destiny and abandon the path of chaos, of vices and of poverty to which they have been subjected by those men who claimed to be their friends and liberators, but whose actions proved they were their cruellest tyrants.

They stressed the need for elections, a strong legislative chamber and, in their majority, favoured a federalist system. They believed in replacing the conservative regular army with civilian-led militias. The quest for liberty entailed a defence of freedom of speech and freedom of religious belief. Progress and modernity demanded assaulting the more reactionary elements of society. The wealth of the Church and the more affluent landowners was there to be expropriated and redistributed. The power of the Church, like that of the army, needed to be dramatically curtailed. The guarantee of equality before the law meant the abolition of the *fueros* that protected members of the Church, army and specific Indian communities from being tried by civil courts. The time had come for all men (women's rights were not yet overtly on the agenda) to become integrated into society, with no institutional or racial exceptions. As for the economy, the Liberals, notwithstanding their noted support for state intervention, favoured free market policies. Evidently, the 1850–80 watershed was brought about by a major shift in the international economy. To a certain extent, the need to adapt to this shift, paired with a desire to expand and diversify the nations' stagnant economies, meant that free market economic policies became the only means by which the elites could survive in and benefit from the emergent world market.

In the long run, many of these beliefs would be moderated, particularly once the Liberals came to power. Most liberal rulers found themselves tampering with or finding the means to ignore the constitutions that were approved between the late 1840s and early 1870s, awarding themselves exceptional powers that enabled the executive to remain stronger than the legislatures. While suffrage was generally extended to encompass a wider proportion of male voters, elections were almost systematically fixed so that the emergent liberal *caudillos* could come to power or succeed in being re-elected. The need for stability and order also meant that by the end of the century, most liberal administrations favoured the use of censorship and repression. Most large landowners survived the initial bout of expropriations and went on to benefit from the break-up of Church properties and communal lands. The expected expansion of the middle classes did not really take off, as it was either the large landowners or foreign entrepreneurs who bought up the auctioned lands, and not the peasants who were meant to become small landholders in the process. The tensions that existed between the idealism of the mid-century liberals and the pragmatical approach to politics they adopted once in power can be sampled in Exhibit 3.2, in which Domingo Sarmiento outlines his liberal intentions on becoming President of Argentina in 1868.

The process whereby a Conservative thesis was challenged by a Liberal antithesis resulted in a Conservative–Liberal synthesis. Authoritarianism remained a characteristic trait of the governments that emerged in the 1870s. However, it was an authoritarianism that defended liberal rather than traditionalist policies vis-à-vis the role of the Church, corporate privileges and the economy. *Caudillismo* evolved to the extent that the strongmen of the late nineteenth century (Porfirio Díaz in Mexico (1876–1910), Justo Rufino Barrios in Guatemala (1873–85), Antonio Guzmán Blanco in Venezuela (1873–88), Rafael Núñez in Colombia (1882–94)) became, in the eyes of the elites and their European counterparts, energetic state builders, the architects of material progress. Unlike their predecessors, their autocratic style of government (adorned in constitutional garments) was focused on generating modernisation and development. The political system that surfaced was one that has been labelled by some historians as authoritarian developmentalism. Their networks of patronage were also far more sophisticated and varied. They did not view themselves as regional *caudillos,* but as national ones. They were also open to foreign influence, and openly encouraged foreign investment, foreign advice, European immigration and the active participation of foreigners in the building of railways, bridges, roads and canals. Their control of society became tighter, in part as a result of the consensus reached by the elites after approximately twenty years of unrest. The emergence of (and threat represented by) socialist, even communist and anarchist societies also helped the elites to find an accord whereby a conservative form of liberalism could unite them in ways that had been impossible before. Perhaps the most important contributory factor to the formation of long-lasting autocratic liberal governments was the impact of technology in the region, and the vested interests which the main European powers and the United States developed there as a result.

## The neocolonial order

The 1850–80 watershed was not just political, but also economic. The discovery of gold in California in 1848, paired with the growth of the economies of industrialised Europe, thrust Latin America into the world market. The gold rush transformed Mexico and Central America (including Panama in Colombia) into a busy trade route, as the isthmus offered the quickest route from Europe to the Pacific. Although by 1860 the USA had laid an estimated 49,288 kilometres of rail track (forty times that laid in Latin America at the time), the first trans-continental railroad was not completed until 1869. In other words, from 1848 to 1869, the fastest and easiest way to reach California was through Central America. This opened up the isolated Pacific coast to a much larger market. Transportation technology, trains and steam-boats, together with the arrival of the telegraph, revolutionised the continent, allowing most Latin American nations to cater to the frenzy of consumption that took the more powerful countries of Europe and the United States by storm. As can be seen in Exhibit 3.1, the Argentinean intellectual Juan Bautista Alberdi (1810–84) realised as early as 1852 that the invention of the train would transform Argentina, and by default Latin America, in a variety of essential ways. After 1870, money started to pour into Latin America, and its dormant, *hacienda*-based economies awakened with the subsequent development of export economies based on the sale of primary products to Europe in exchange for the import of surplus European manufactured goods. Produce such as bananas, coffee, sugar, guano, rubber, copper, nitrates, meat, wheat, cocoa and tobacco started to flow towards Europe and the United States at a breathtaking pace, while clothes, including *ponchos* made in Manchester, together with European machinery, inundated the Latin American markets.

This new economic situation led to a new dependency in Latin America. Britain, and subsequently the United States, replaced Spain and Portugal as the dominant partners in these emergent trade relations. It was this dependency that accounts for the historiographical application of the term neocolonial to describe the order that came into being between 1850 and 1880, and which remained in place until the 1930s. Britain was the dominant power during the early neocolonial period (1850–1914). However, with the exception of British intervention in Central America, its imperialism relied on economics and not on displays of military supremacy. Unlike the United States for most of the twentieth century, or France in the 1860s, Britain did not overtly interfere in Latin American politics. The colonial dependency Britain imposed on Latin America was exerted through economic pressure. British diplomats secured commercial treaties that were favourable to British interests, but which also catered to the private interests of an emergent Latin American oligarchy, which benefited, at least initially, from the consequent dramatic expansion of their *haciendas* and their profitable export agriculture. From 1860 onwards, the majority of monetary exchanges between Latin America and Europe were handled by British banks. It was London bankers who served as the financial agents of Latin American governments. They organised the numerous loans that undermined Latin America's independence, as most countries became deeply indebted to them. Being in a position to offer credit to those governments which were in financial duress, the British financiers could pressurise them into pursuing one policy or another without having to resort to military threats. Afflicted by an endemic need for cash, most governments, particularly once liberalism triumphed in the region, were more than ready to comply with British demands so that further loans could be raised.

From 1850 to 1880, Latin America grew steadily more dependent on British economic interests and demands. Numerous companies were founded in Britain in the 1870s, aimed at developing concessions and buying businesses in Latin America. By 1913, according to one estimate, British entrepreneurs were responsible for running seventy-seven railways, fifty-three utility companies, nine banks, thirty-six nitrate firms, eighty-five other mining companies, fifteen oil firms, and 112 other enterprises in industry, land and commerce. Economic life in Argentina, Brazil, Chile and Uruguay became entirely dependent on British investment. According to one US visitor who went to Valparaíso in Chile, in 1885:

> trade is practically controlled by Englishmen, all commercial transactions are calculated in pounds sterling, and the English language is almost exclusively spoken upon the street and in the shops. An English paper is printed there, English goods are almost exclusively sold and this city is nothing more than an English colony.

The one exception was Bolivia. Following the expulsion in 1852 of the British ambassador, John Lloyd, by General Belzu's government, diplomatic and trade relations between Bolivia and Britain were put on hold for almost fifty years. It was Bolivia's refusal to re-enter into negotiations with Britain that allegedly led Queen Victoria to order that Bolivia be erased from her maps.

It was in Central America that British imperialism found its most aggressive expression. However, this was mainly due to a breakdown in communications between the British consul in Central America, Frederick Chatfield, the superintendent of Belize, the Foreign Office and the Colonial Office, rather than a clearly defined imperial policy. It was Chatfield himself who interfered in Central American politics rather than the Foreign Office, whose civil servants were not entirely aware of the situation in the region. Between 1837 and 1852, British support of Carrera in Guatemala and the conservatives in the isthmus arose out of Chatfield's personal interests. Allowed to use warships to enforce British claims in Nicaragua and Honduras, Chatfield ordered the military actions that took place to defend *his* interests. Further encouraged by the superintendent of Belize, British expansion on the Mosquito Coast was inspired by Chatfield, who subsequently persuaded the Foreign Office of the desirability of the protectorate once the deed was done. The atypical gunboat diplomacy Britain employed on the Atlantic coast of Central America between 1839 and 1850 must be attributed to Chatfield rather than British policy. On one of the few occasions that the Foreign Office was better informed of Chatfield's antics, namely his attempt to seize the island of Tigre in the Gulf of Fonseca in 1849, he was severely censured. The poor communications which existed even between the Foreign Office and the Colonial Office in London are evident in that in 1852, the Colonial Office created the colony of the Bay Islands without letting the Foreign Office know. Similarly, when the Foreign Office surrendered the colony, seven years later, it did so without consulting the Colonial Office.

The US victory in the Mexican–American War (1846–48), and its consequent acquisition of California, paired with the discovery of gold in the new US state in 1848, seriously undermined British influence in Central America. With both the United States and Britain competing to control any railway, canal or road that was built to connect the Atlantic with the Pacific, the USA was in a position to halt British interventionism. Nevertheless, Britain was still sufficiently dominant to prevent the USA from doing so either for the next three decades. The 1850 Clayton–Bulwer Treaty prevented both the USA and Britain from claiming an exclusive sphere of influence in Central America, as it was agreed that

> neither...will ever obtain or maintain for itself any exclusive control over the said ship canal...that neither will erect or maintain any fortifications commanding the same...or occupy, or fortify, or assume, or exercise any domain over Nicaragua, Costa Rica, the Mosquito Coast, or any part of Central America.

The British withdrew from Greytown, conceded the Bay Islands to Honduras in 1859 and abandoned most of their claims to the Mosquito Coast in 1860, although it remained a British protectorate until 1906. All this said, the Belize settlement was formally transformed into the colony of British Honduras, as recognised by Carrera in the 1859 treaty. The recognition of British sovereignty in Belize was granted in return for a British promise to construct a road from the coast to Guatemala City. Once it became clear that the British were intending to terminate the road in Belize rather than in a Guatemalan port, the Guatemalans abrogated the treaty. Belize, like the Falkland Islands, remains a contested territory to this day.

French intervention in Latin America was far more heavy-handed. It was also less influential since it only affected Mexico. Most of the aims cherished by the republican revolutionaries who took to the streets of Paris in 1848 were postponed with the rise to power of Napoleon III in 1852. A modernising dictatorship came into existence, not too dissimilar from those that emerged in Latin America in the 1870s, and with it came a renewed attempt to extend the French Empire overseas. Against a backdrop of intervention in the Crimea, Italy, Indochina and Algeria, the possibility of increasing French influence in the Americas was perceived as a desirable aim. A dramatic growth in French industry was also important in highlighting French interests in Latin America. Between 1848 and 1860, French exports to Latin America (fine textiles and high-quality goods like wine) quadrupled in value.

Coinciding with the eruption of the US Civil War in April 1861, and in concert with a clique of conservative monarchist Mexican exiles, the idea of a Mexican adventure gathered momentum in the French imperial court. The Civil War represented an important distraction that would prevent the United States from being in a position to halt a European military expedition to Mexico. There was also a good excuse. On 17 July 1861, **Benito Juárez**'s radical liberal government decreed that all payments on the external debt would

Benito Juárez

### Benito Juárez (1806–72)

Born into a humble family with Zapotec origins, Juárez nonetheless studied law, becoming governor of the state of Oaxaca in 1847. As a radical liberal, he opposed Santa Anna and was imprisoned and then exiled to New Orleans in 1853. He returned to Mexico in 1855 to join the revolution that overthrew the dictator. He became minister of justice in the liberal government that ensued and was responsible for the notorious 23 November 1855 law, which significantly reduced the civil power of the Church by abolishing its privileges. During the 1858–61 Civil War of the Reform, he led the Liberal forces, serving as the 'legitimate' president while the Conservative army imposed their own president in Mexico City. Following the liberal victory (25 December 1860), Juárez's presidency was prolonged through elections in March 1861. The reformism of his government was remarkable and far-reaching. However, between 1863 and 1867, following the French capture of Mexico City and the imposition of Maximilian I's empire, he was forced to move around the country to avoid capture, while leading the resistance. Once Maximilian's government fell in 1867, Juárez was able to complete his term in office, being re-elected in 1871. He died in 1872 and has become one of the most highly revered politicians in Mexican history.

be suspended for a period of two years. Britain, France and Spain reacted by signing the Tripartite Convention of London in October, agreeing to occupy the main Atlantic ports of Mexico to enforce debt payment. It was not long before Britain and Spain realised that the French intended to use this as a pretext to enforce a change of regime in Mexico. Therefore, in spring 1862, while Britain and Spain withdrew their forces, France embarked on its costly and ultimately disastrous Mexican campaign. The fact that the occupation of Mexico was not going to be an easy task was made apparent by Porfirio Díaz's victory over the French, outside Puebla, on 5 May 1862. Nevertheless, Mexico City was taken in June 1863, and from June 1864 to June 1867 the Austrian Habsburg prince, Archduke Ferdinand Maximilian, was placed on the Mexican throne by Napoleon III. The Second Mexican Empire was a fiasco. Juárez persevered as the legitimate President of Mexico (albeit forced to do so on the move, fleeing from the imperial forces that were sent out to arrest him), leading the forces that waged an unremitting guerrilla war on Maximilian. Maximilian, on the other hand, alienated both his Conservative Mexican allies, by pursuing liberal policies, and the French military command, by attempting to create an autonomous Mexican Imperial Army. After three bloody years, and with the US Civil War having come to an end, the French abandoned Maximilian and withdrew their forces. Supported by a handful of Mexican Conservatives, Maximilian refused to leave Mexico, and was executed outside Querétaro on 19 June 1867. In executing an Austrian Habsburg by firing squad, despite the many pleas that were sent to Mexico to spare Maximilian's life, Juárez turned the execution into a powerful signal to the European powers that intervention in Mexico would not be forgiven.

Spain's sphere of influence continued to decline in the region. It became increasingly difficult to exert control over Cuba and Puerto Rico. Spain experienced its own watershed during these years. Following the 1868 revolution that brought an end to Queen Isabel II's reign and ushered in six chaotic years, during which the First Republic was inaugurated (1873–74), the restoration of the monarchy in 1875 led to the triumph of a Spanish variant of conservative liberalism. Faced with a major uprising in the eastern part of Cuba, which lasted for ten years (1868–78), the liberal *Cortes* of the *Sexenio Revolucionario* (1868–75) sought political as well as military solutions to the crisis. The 1870 Moret Law freed all children of slaves born after 1868 and all slaves over the age of sixty. Slavery was actually abolished in Puerto Rico in 1873, although it was not abolished in Cuba until 1886. Among the concessions Spain made to its Caribbean colonies, Puerto Ricans were allowed to elect delegates to the Spanish *Cortes* in 1869. A year after the Ten Year War came to an end in 1878, Cubans were permitted to do the same. Where Spain did not give way was over liberalising the Cuban economy. The Cuban sugar industry expanded, coming to represent three-quarters of the island's export income. By 1860, after the United States and Canada, Cuba had the third-highest quantity of railway track in the Americas (682 kilometres). And yet the taxes Madrid imposed on Cuba made the export of sugar to Spain an expensive affair, forced the Cubans to import almost exclusively Spanish products and represented a major drawback in Cuban–US trade relations. By 1886, Cuba was selling 94 per cent of its sugar to the United States under circumstances that favoured neither US interests nor those of the Cuban elites. When the United States hijacked the Cuban War of Independence (1895–98) in 1898, it had strong economic reasons for doing so.

Apart from Spain's faltering control of Cuba and Puerto Rico, and its brief takeover of the Dominican Republic (1861–65), its only significant contribution to the emergent neocolonial order came in 1865. This was Spain's attempt to reassert its long gone authority in South America, seizing Peru's guano-rich Chincha Islands, having dispatched a 'scientific' expedition to the region in 1863. The intervention was a notable failure. In what was the only time in the nineteenth century that Ecuador, Peru, Bolivia and Chile put aside their historic differences, they consolidated a formal defensive alliance against the Spanish occupation forces. The Spanish naval squadron was repulsed, and although it bombarded the ports of Valparaíso and Callao in retaliation, the resistance that was summoned by the Peruvian forces succeeded in forcing the surrender and withdrawal of the Spaniards in May 1866.

Although the US intervention in Mexico and Central America cannot be overlooked, the disruption that resulted from the Civil War (1861–65) delayed its hegemonic position in the continent. It was only after the planters of the South were defeated in 1865 that the balance of power was decisively transferred to the industrialists and financiers of the North. Once they gained control of the country's economic development, the rise of the US empire proved unstoppable. Mirroring events in Britain, the dramatic period of industrialisation that ensued resulted in a situation whereby the United States needed to export its surplus manufactured goods. Following in Britain's steps, the United States found an outlet for its exports in Latin America, importing raw materials in exchange. By the 1870s, the rise in exports was such that the previously unfavourable balance of US trade was corrected and remained so until 1930.

Nevertheless, it would not be until the outbreak of the First World War in 1914 that the United States would overtake Britain as the dominant power in neocolonial Latin America. This, of course, excludes Mexico from the equation, since it was pressurised into selling the territory of La Mesilla in 1853, including Tucson (Arizona). It also excludes Central America and the Caribbean, since US intervention was particularly forceful in the region at the turn of the century.

## Order and progress

For the triumphant liberal governments of the day, after two decades of severe conflict, the political systems that were forged in the 1870s were described as representing 'order and progress'. The defeat of the conservatives and the emergence of a consensus among the elites paved the way for the imposition of a more stable political environment. The increase of British loans and investment enabled the economies of most Latin American countries to overcome their historic instability. The conservative liberal constitutions that were drafted proved longer lasting. For many, it appeared that the perceived chaos of the early national period had become a thing of the past.

Given that economic development needed political stability to flourish, the imposition of order became as sacred an objective for the 1870s Liberals as it had been for the 1850s Conservatives. In order to do this, the 1870s Liberals abandoned the idealism of their predecessors and embraced authoritarian (albeit constitutional) regimes. In Mexico, order was attained through a policy of conciliation towards dissident *caudillos*, a more sophisticated network of patronage and the use of repression. Porfirio Díaz's famous slogan *pan o palo* (bread or the stick) encapsulated his administration's philosophy, whereby everybody could gain from the government's patronage (promotions, jobs, concessions) if they supported it, or suffer a beating, arrest or death if they opposed it. The army was well paid and professionalised, to the extent that its high-ranking officers were deterred from starting or joining a revolt. A paramilitary mounted police, called the *rurales,* was created to bring an end to banditry. The regime which emerged claimed that, given that it represented the scientific improvement of the nation, its energy would be focused on administering the path towards modernity without the distractions of party politics. In Central America a very similar trend was followed. Justo Rufino Barrios (Guatemala), Santiago González (El Salvador) and Tomás Guardia (Costa Rica) led the so-called republican dictatorships of their respective countries along parallel lines. The professionalisation of the army was achieved through the institutionalisation of national military schools such as the Escuela Politécnica of Guatemala. Civil guards, like the *rurales*, were also formed in the region.

With the imposition of order, progress became a continental obsession. Positivism became the leading philosophy of the day. This was a world view proposed by Auguste Comte (1798–1857) that rejected metaphysics and approached politics recognising that only positive facts mattered. It glorified science, empiricism and material progress, in direct confrontation with the retrograde superstitions associated with spiritual or theological discourse. The role of the Church and traditional views of society needed to be replaced by a progressive, modern and, consequently, positivist state. In Venezuela, under the rule of Antonio Guzmán Blanco, the 'Civiliser', numerous railways, roads and bridges were built. An aqueduct was constructed to supply Caracas with water. Free and obligatory primary education for all children was decreed, and schools were erected throughout the country. In Chile, between 1861 and 1881, numerous irrigation canals were constructed, including the 120-kilometre Canal de las Mercedes. By 1882 there were nearly 1,931 kilometres of railway track in Chile. The telegraph line also received attention, and following the feat of the Chilean brothers Juan and Mateo Clark, who succeeded in linking Santiago to Buenos Aires, the laying of the Brazilian submarine cable in 1874 meant that Chile became connected with Europe. Education was also supported to the extent that by 1875, 17 per cent of the school-age population was receiving some form of primary education. Moreover, by an 1877 decree, women were awarded the right to enter higher education for the first time.

It was as an integral part of the Liberals' faith in progress that **Sarmiento**'s 1840s defence of 'civilisation' became the pretext for what, in the 1870s, amounted to the annihilation of the Indian tribes of the Southern Cone countries, in particular Chile and Argentina. While in Mexico and Guatemala the Liberal defence of 'civilisation' involved ending the *repúblicas de indios* and converting the Indians into Mexican or Guatemalan citizens, in Argentina the War of the Desert (1879–83) led to the ruthless extermination of the Indians of the pampas. In Chile, the 'Araucanian question' was resolved at the same time, along similar lines.

## The rise of the oligarchy

It was during these years that Latin America experienced the rise of the oligarchy. The term oligarchy is used here in its American (both

---

### Domingo Faustino Sarmiento (1811–88)

Born in remote San Juan, Sarmiento was mainly self-taught. He fought for the unitarians during the 1820s and was consequently forced into exile once Rosas became dictator in 1835. He was unable to return to Argentina until 1852. He established himself in Chile (1835–45), where he directed a teacher-training institution, and was subsequently sent to Europe and the United States by the Chilean authorities to research the educational systems there. In 1845 Sarmiento published *Facundo: civilización y barbarie*, in which he employed the biography of the *gaucho caudillo* Juan Facundo Quiroga to illustrate how Rosas' dictatorship represented the interests of the barbaric chieftains of the outback. Its main thesis, namely that the main conflict in Argentina, and by default in Latin America, was between civilisation and barbarism (between European–urban civilisation and rural–indigenous barbarism) became extremely influential. Following his return to Argentina, after the fall of Rosas, he went on to serve as ambassador in the United States (1864–68), being elected president of Argentina in 1868. His presidency (1868–74) was characterised by its vigour and by the progressive policies it implemented. Trade expanded, transportation improved, European immigration was promoted and education spread to encompass a large proportion of the population. He died in 1888 after spending the rest of his life as a director of schools in Buenos Aires.

Spanish and Anglo-American) sense, rather than its strict British sense of government or State governed by a small group of people. It refers to the elites who expanded and developed their political and economic control of their respective countries. Nevertheless, the original meaning of the term, stemming from the Greek *oligarkhia*, is not entirely absent in its application to the political system these elites came to sponsor. For although most post-1850s constitutions expanded the suffrage to include a much wider percentage of males than that permitted in the post-1830s charters, electoral fraud, paired with other methods of 'persuasion' (intimidation at the polling stations, purchase of votes, etc.), converted the majority of Latin American governments into the private enterprises of an extremely reduced group of privileged individuals.

The rise of the oligarchy was directly related to the triumph of liberalism and the emergence of the export economies that the shift in the global market brought with it. The demand for primary products on the part of industrialised Europe and the United States, paired with the auction of Church, communal and public lands instigated by the Liberals, led to the expansion of the *hacienda*. As a result, the landowning class increased its economic power and political sphere of influence, as their vast properties became even larger. Immense cattle ranches in Argentina expanded into the 'conquered' desert; coffee and banana plantations spread throughout Central America. The emergent oligarchy came to control land and water throughout their respective countries, usurping village resources. More significantly, they came to control the labour force as well.

The evident victims of the oligarchy's rise to prominence were the majority of people who lived in the countryside. Indians and peasants lost control of their communal lands and their small landholdings and were forced to work in the expanding *haciendas* to make a living. A rural proletariat came into being, but one which was, in certain cases, not that different from the suffering slave population in Brazil and Cuba. Debt peonage became a common feature of *hacienda* labour. The peons were advanced credit, and were forced to work until the debt was repaid. Instead of being paid a wage, the peons were given vouchers they could use in a company store, where, due to the overpriced merchandise and irregular bookkeeping, they soon ran up further debts that forced them to remain on the estate until they had repaid them. In some cases, the peons' children were expected to work for the *hacienda* to repay their parents' debts.

By the late nineteenth century, the rise of the oligarchy had led to a situation whereby a limited number of families were living in extreme opulence, at the expense of an impoverished rural majority. They expanded their *haciendas* and bought spectacular houses in the main cities of their countries. As positivist developmentalism led to the paving of streets in the main urban centres, the adoption of gas street lighting and the construction of lavish theatres and opera houses, the elites transformed their city homes into French-style mansions. The ladies ensured that they were wearing the latest fashions from Paris, adding a profusion of Latin American jewellery to their imported dresses. The gentlemen drank French rather than Chilean or Argentinean wine, and went on grand tours to Europe. For the majority, this was a foreign world with which they either had no contact or could not aspire to join. Notwithstanding this, an important yet often omitted fact about Latin America at the time is that, while in Ireland, parts of Britain, Spain and Italy people were being forced to emigrate because they were literally dying of hunger, in Latin America, however impoverished the population, food was never lacking.

## The empire of Pedro II (1841–1889)

In Brazil, the conflicts that characterised the 1850s and 1860s in former Spanish America were avoided by Pedro II's early liberal authoritarian developmentalism. During the first ten years of his rule (1840–50), he ensured that order was restored, bringing an end to the Rio Grande do Sul federalist revolt (1835–45) and quelling any other uprisings with unwavering resolve. Order and progress became as much a Brazilian objective as a Spanish American one. Progress was supported through the encouragement of foreign trade (which increased by 450 per cent during his reign), the building of railways (over 2,000 kilometres of track by 1878) and telegraph lines (over 7,000 kilometres), a policy that welcomed European immigration, and the 'conquest' and development of large parts of inland Brazil, in particular around São Paulo. Like the rest of Latin America, Brazil entered the neocolonial order by developing a thriving (yet dependent) export economy, almost exclusively based on its sale of coffee, rubber, sugar and tobacco.

The conservative liberalism of the regime preceded and mirrored that which surfaced in most Latin American countries post-1870. Benefiting from the consensus arrived at by the elites in 1840, Pedro II was able to forge a constitutional government whereby the Liberal and Conservative parties took it in turns to rule the country under the emperor's 'moderating powers'. He allowed freedom of speech and the press, and went as far as awarding the Assembly (parliament) freedom of action, as long as the final approval or rejection of its proposals was his. He pursued a distinctly liberal agenda in the way that he clashed with Church and army in the 1870s, defending a positivist agenda and refusing to increase military expenditure. He also promoted the establishment of elections and, in theory, appeared to defend the eventual creation of a truly democratic and representative political system. He appointed and removed prime ministers in order to make rotation in office possible, becoming an impartial arbiter who refused to side consistently with any of the main political factions that emerged post-1850. As a result, although Brazil was a constitutional monarchy with regular elections and a facade of democratic practices, in reality it was the emperor who ruled. Albeit in the name of maintaining the equilibrium of conflicting party interests, the emperor dissolved the Assembly on eleven different occasions, and ensured through patronage that the government supported his liberal and developmentalist ideals. The success of Pedro II's rule was such that his reputation as an able leader was admired throughout the world. The Venezuelan president, Juan Pablo Rojas, described Brazil as 'the only republic which existed in America', and the Argentinean, Bartolomé Mitre, went as far as claiming that Brazil was the 'crowned democracy of America'.

However, the issue of slavery remained the most controversial aspect of the empire, and one that would, in the long run, lead to the eventual demise of the monarchy. In 1850 there were 2.5 million slaves in Brazil; a third of the population. With the Brazilian economy depending heavily on coffee, which accounted for 41 per cent of exports in 1846–50, the need for slave labour remained as important as ever. Abolitionism was as difficult to accept in Brazil as it was in the south of the United States, where the picking of cotton, like coffee, was labour-intensive. In order to persuade the elites to free their slaves, the government would have to find the means of compensating them financially. Even then, it would be unlikely that they would easily accept such a proposal when it was obvious that providing wages for a labour force of a similar size, working similar hours, would significantly eat into the profits they were accustomed to reaping. Evidently, the intensification of British naval activities off the shores of Brazil and Africa was not only the result of a philanthropic commitment to ensuring a worldwide end to slavery. As long as Brazil and Cuba continued to use slave labour, the British plantations in the West Indies would never be able to compete.

In Brazil, a change in attitude over the slavery issue was going to be difficult when the wealth of much of the elite was strongly linked to its existence. Nevertheless, Brazil was forced to contemplate the possibility that slavery would eventually be abolished. The zeal with which British warships intercepted slave-trading frigates after 1848 resulted in a dramatic fall in Brazil's ability to import slaves. While Brazil was still importing around 60,000 slaves in 1848, this figure was reduced to 22,856 in 1850, coming to an abrupt end in 1853. However, although the slave trade was consequently terminated, slavery itself survived for another thirty-five years.

Unable to bring any more slaves from Africa, the issue arose of how to replenish the workforce. By the 1870s, increasing numbers of peasants and Portuguese and Italian immigrants started to form an alternative labour force. It became obvious that free wage labour did not represent such a dramatic loss of profit after all. Given that the planters had no choice in the matter, forced as they were to replace the dwindling slave population, an abolitionist movement developed in the main urban centres of Brazil which brought discredit to the monarchy. Pedro II responded by passing the law of *ventre livre* in 1871, by which all children born of slaves were free. But it was not enough. Slavery came to represent the extent to which the empire was illiberal and anti-quated, however much it had stressed the need for progress and claimed to champion democracy and modernisation. The emergent middle classes of the cities came to view slavery as evidence of the reactionary tenets of the regime, and by the early 1870s republicanism began to gather prestige among a younger generation of liberals. They started to campaign for wider suffrage, for federalism and for an end to the emperor's moderating power.

Following a decade of recession, increasing tensions between Church and State, and the rise of discontent in the armed forces, who felt badly treated and underfunded in the wake of the War of the Triple Alliance (1864–70), the abolition of slavery, on 13 May 1888, marked the beginning of the end of the empire. Coinciding with one of Pedro II's trips to Europe, where he was convalescing in Milan, afflicted by diabetes, his daughter, Princess Isabella, abolished slavery without offering compensation to the slave owners. The consequent loss of support of the slave-owning elite, paired with the conflagration of issues that characterised 1880s Brazil, resulted in the revolt of 15 November 1889. With the support of São Paulo's oligarchy, the republican movement and a significant number of affronted high-ranking officers, in what was an uneasy alliance, a bloodless revolt deposed the emperor and banished him and his family into exile, inaugurating the First Republic (1889–1930).

## Major Latin American wars (1864–1883)

Between 1850 and 1880 there were only two major Latin American wars: the War of the Triple Alliance (also referred to as the Paraguayan War, 1864–70) and the War of the Pacific (1879–83). In both cases, the economic context of the early neocolonial period played a significant part in pushing the conflicting parties onto the path of war. Control of the upper Paraná river in Paraguay and the nitrate-rich Atacama desert in Bolivia became key concerns, in a context in which international trade had become a major part of the countries' fast-developing economies.

The War of the Triple Alliance erupted for a number of convoluted reasons. It is clear that both Brazil and Argentina shared territorial ambitions over the upper Paraná basin, but the aggressive policies pursued by the Paraguayan dictator, Francisco Solano López, cannot be overlooked. In as far as the motivation of the Brazilian, Argentinean and Paraguayan governments can be summarised: Brazil wanted to extend its boundaries; Argentina wanted to control navigation along the Paraná river; and Paraguay wanted free access to the River Plate in order to fully develop the landlocked nation's trade with the outside world.

The conflict broke out in September 1864, when the Brazilian army entered Uruguay to support Venancio Flores' *colorado* insurgents in their revolt against the *blanco* government. Paraguay's Solano López declared war on Brazil in solidarity with the Uruguayan *blancos*, and brought Argentina into the war by crossing Argentine territory after permission to do so had been denied, in order to attack Rio Grande do Sul. With the *blancos* ousted from power in Uruguay, the *colorado* government in Montevideo joined Argentina and Brazil in a Triple Alliance, with the ostensible objective of punishing and overthrowing Solano López. Behind the scenes, Brazil and Argentina signed a secret treaty in which they agreed to divide between themselves over half of Paraguay's territory once the war was over.

The war that ensued proved to be far longer lasting and sanguinary than either Brazil or Argentina had expected. From May 1865 to January 1869, the Paraguayans put up an extraordinary show of resistance against the invading army. The invaders' advance up the River Paraguay was slow and costly. By the time Asunción fell to the allies, over 100,000 of their troops had died. For the Paraguayans, the loss of human life caused by the war was even more devastating. It is estimated that the male population of Paraguay was reduced by nine-tenths. Some estimates claim that half the country's population perished in the conflict. The end result was the fall and execution (without judicial process) of Solano López in March 1870, and almost 40 per cent of Paraguay's territory falling into Brazilian and Argentine hands.

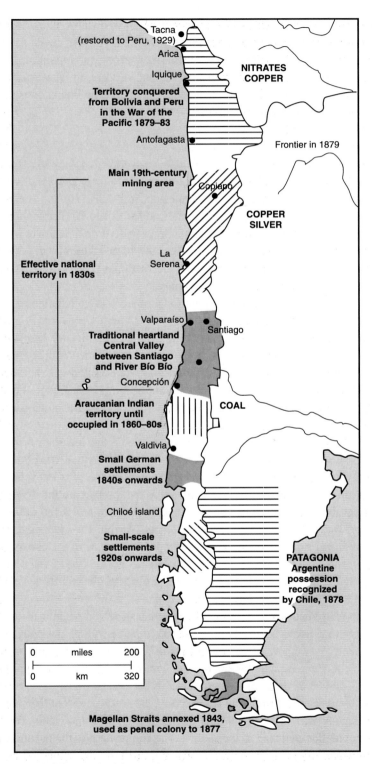

Map of Chilean territorial expansion

The War of the Pacific (1879–83) was equally important in the way that its outcome changed the territorial make-up of South America. Problems arose initially from the generous concessions the Bolivian government granted the Chilean–British Compañía de Salitres y Ferrocarril de Antofagasta, to allow it to extract nitrate in the Bolivian section of the Atacama desert. By 1878, as a consequence of these concessions, most of the inhabitants on the littoral were Chilean, forming almost a state within a state. When the Bolivian government raised the tax it imposed on the Chileans to extract the nitrate, contravening the original agreement, tensions flared. The company refused to pay and the Bolivian government threatened to confiscate it if it did not do so. In order to prevent the Bolivians from taking such action, the Chilean government declared war on Bolivia, occupying the port of Antofagasta in February 1879. Peru found itself dragged into the conflict since it had signed a secret treaty with Bolivia in 1873, pledging to defend its ally in the case of war with a third party.

The war was initially characterised by naval warfare, the main battles being those of Iquique (May 1879) and Cape Angamos (October 1879). After nine months of maritime conflict, Chile gained control of the sea and was subsequently able to send large armies to the northern deserts by sea. Following three major campaigns in Peru and Bolivia, the last of which entailed the Chilean capture of Lima following the battles of Chorrillos and Miraflores (January 1881), Chilean victory was essentially confirmed. Nonetheless, Peruvian guerrilla forces kept the war going for another two years, until the Treaty of Ancón was signed in October 1883. Peru lost Tarapacá, Arica and Tacna (until 1929) to Chile, and Bolivia lost the Atacama, becoming a landlocked nation and remaining so to this day. Chile increased its national territory by one-third. Chile's 1870s crisis (caused by the collapse of the copper and silver mining industries) was overcome with the possession of the nitrate fields of Peru and Bolivia.

Anybody visiting Latin America in the 1880s, after thirty years' absence, would have realised that the continent had changed dramatically in that time. Railways were being laid everywhere, the streets in the main cities were paved and progress was the word on everybody's lips. They would have been impressed by the sense of order that had come to prevail in the region, at least in comparison to the situation in 1850. They would have been struck by the fact that revolutions were no longer as frequent or as common, and that the governments of the day, albeit authoritarian, defended liberal values and modernisation. They would have noticed the existence of numerous European and US enterprises, and would probably have been astonished to find that they could send or receive a telegram from Paris even when they were in remote Santiago de Chile. If they had belonged to the middle or upper classes they would have celebrated the opportunity to see Italian opera companies perform in Rio or Buenos Aires, and would have been dazzled by the extent to which the elites had extended their wealth and properties. A visit to an *hacienda* or an *estancia* would have amply confirmed to them that their prosperous relatives or friends had more than surpassed their wildest dreams of power and opulence. They may have noticed the squalor in which the majority lived and worked, but they would have been assured that things could only improve. The governments were promoting education, and as

> **casino**
> Social club; gentlemen's club in the nineteenth century.

long as the economy was thriving, the less privileged members of society would find work and, with time, improve their situation. The fact that increasing numbers of Italian, Spanish and Portuguese immigrants were arriving in the main ports was evidence enough of how desirable it had become to live in the Americas. The foreign press, available in any luxury hotel, cafe or **casino**, would have further convinced them that they were extremely fortunate to have men such as Porfirio Díaz, Justo Rufino Barrios, Antonio Guzmán Blanco or Pedro II running their countries, defending order and progress with plenty of positivist administration and no divisive politics. Of course, had they looked closer they would have seen that the disparities which were emerging between their few privileged acquaintances and the oppressed majority would be difficult to sustain forever. Had they stopped to consider the dangers of total dependence on their export economies, they might also have realised that major upheavals lay ahead. The next thirty to forty years would see the consolidation of the neocolonial order, but they would also see the emergence of violent social revolutions, the development of anarchist and Marxist movements, and the collapse of the export economies.

## Exhibit 3.1: Excerpt from Juan Bautista Alberdi, *Bases y puntos de partida para la organización política de la República Argentina* (Buenos Aires: Imp. Argentina, 1852)

Es preciso traer las capitales a las costas, o bien llevar el litoral al interior del continente. El ferrocarril y el telégrafo eléctrico, que son la suspensión del espacio, obran este portento mejor que todos los potentados de la tierra. El ferrocarril innova, reforma y cambia las cosas más difíciles, sin decretos ni asonadas.

Él hará la unidad de la República Argentina mejor que todos los congresos. Los congresos podrán declararla una e indivisible; sin el camino de fierro que acerque sus extremos remotos, quedará siempre divisible y dividida contra todos los decretos legislativos.

Sin el ferrocarril no tendréis unidad política en países donde la distancia hace imposible la acción del poder central. ¿Queréis que el gobierno, que los legisladores, que los tribunales de la capital litoral, legislen y juzguen los asuntos de las provincias de San Juan y Mendoza, por ejemplo? Traed el litoral hasta esos parajes por el ferrocarril, o viceversa; colocad esos extremos a tres días de distancia, por lo menos. Pero tener la metrópoli o capital a veinte días es poco menos que tenerla en España, como cuando regía el sistema antiguo, que destruimos por ese absurdo especialmente. Así, pues, la unidad política debe empezar por la unidad territorial, y sólo el ferrocarril puede hacer de dos parajes separados por quinientas leguas un paraje único.

Tampoco podréis llevar hasta el interior de nuestros países la acción de la Europa por medio de sus inmigraciones, que hoy regeneran nuestras costas, sino por vehículos tan poderosos como los ferrocarriles. Ellos son y serán a la vida local de nuestros territorios interiores lo que las grandes arterias a los extremos inferiores del cuerpo: manantiales de vida…

Para tener ferrocarriles, abundan medios en estos países. Negociad empréstitos en el extranjero, empeñad vuestras rentas y bienes nacionales para empresas que los harán prosperar y multiplicarse.

Sería pueril esperar a que las rentas ordinarias alcancen para gastos semejantes; invertid ese orden, empezad por los gastos, y tendréis rentas. Si hubiésemos esperado a tener rentas capaces de costear los gastos de la guerra de la independencia contra España, hasta hoy fuéramos colonos... Lo que hicimos para salir de la esclavitud, debemos hacer para salir del retraso, que es igual a la servidumbre: la gloria no debe tener más títulos que la civilización.

Pero no obtendréis préstamos si no tenéis crédito nacional, es decir, un crédito fundado en las seguridades y responsabilidades unidas de todos los pueblos del Estado. Con créditos de cabildos o provincias, no haréis caminos de fierro, ni nada grande. Uníos en cuerpo de nación, consolid la responsabilidad de vuestras rentas y caudales presentes y futuros, y tendréis quien os preste millones para atender a vuestras necesidades locales y generales; porque si no tenéis plata hoy, tenéis los medios de ser opulentos mañana. Dispersos y reñidos, no esperéis sino pobreza y menosprecio.

## Exhibit 3.2: Excerpt from Domingo Faustino Sarmiento's speech to a group of Argentineans, in Paris, on 4 July 1868, on accepting his election as president

Nuestra situación no es, sin embargo, desesperada ni irremediable. Si la población nos falta para llenar tan vasto territorio, el mundo no nos pide más que seguridad y leyes protectoras para darnos en pocos años su población superflua por millones de hombres; si las distancias son enormes, el vapor las acorta. Pero, todos estos recursos deben ser distribuidos y utilizados por leyes previsorias y equitativas para evitar que mientras los elementos de civilización se acumulen en las costas, lo restante del país sea entregado a la barbarie, y que salgan luego del bien aparente nuevas calamidades y desórdenes.

Las tierras públicas, sometidas a un régimen equitativo de distribución, fijarán la población que carece hoy de hogar, lo darán a los millares de emigrantes que vienen en busca de una patria para sus familiares, y pondrán coto al vagar de las hordas del desierto, suprimiendo el desierto mismo, su teatro y su elemento. Algunas leyes orgánicas de la educación bastarán para asegurar a las generaciones futuras la prosperidad que debemos prepararles. Las naciones, como los individuos, son casi siempre víctimas de la imprevisión de sus predecesores, respecto a los males que las aquejan.

Esparcir la civilización sobre aquella parte de la República que no goza aún de sus ventajas, proveer eficazmente a la defensa de las fronteras, dar seguridad a la propiedad y a la vida son condiciones tan esenciales como el cumplimiento mismo de las prescripciones de la Constitución, porque todas concurren al mismo fin. Una mayoría dotada con la libertad de ser ignorante y miserable, no constituye un privilegio envidiable para la minoría educada de una nación que se enorgullece llamándose republicana y democrática...

La obra solidaria del progreso humano viene también a ayudarnos en nuestro camino... La abolición del tormento, la desaparición de la esclavitud, la libertad de conciencia, la 'declaración de derechos' que hemos inscrito en la Constitución, no son una conquista nuestra, sino un legado que debemos conservar incólume. Un millón de hombres muertos en los campos de batalla de la gran República ha sellado para nosotros y para todas las repúblicas federales este gran principio: De hoy más no hay nulificadores ni separatistas, sino traidores y criminales.

Podemos a lo menos por este lado descansar tranquilos... Una mayoría me ha traído al poder...y tengo por lo tanto derecho para pedirle...que se mantenga unida... Debo también pedirle que atraiga a esta obra a todos los que pueden figurar decorosamente en sus filas por sus propósitos patrióticos y sus ideas liberales.

*continued*

Protegido por el auxilio de la Providencia, en la que confío, con la activa cooperación de mis conciudadanos, dirigidos por vuestras prudentes leyes, honorables senadores y diputados, ilustrado por el saber de mis consejeros, teniendo por guía la Constitución, y como auxiliar la fuerza que ella pone en mis manos, alcanzaré a realizar algunas de las esperanzas que he bosquejado, entregando al que me suceda en este puesto íntegra la República, prósperas las rentas, un número mayor de hombres felices y educados, la ley respetada, y acaso, aunque no lo espero, bendecido el gobierno.

*Source:* Victoria Galvani (ed.), *Domingo Faustino Sarmiento* (Madrid: Ediciones de Cultura Hispánica, 1990), pp. 117–21.

## Topics for discussion in class

■ Provide a summary, in your own words, of the key points made by Alberdi in Exhibit 3.1, regarding the impact the railway will have in Argentina.

■ How does Alberdi believe Argentina can finance such a major and costly revolution in transport technology?

■ What evidence is there in Exhibit 3.1 that Alberdi was already, in 1852, representing the ideals of the triumphant Liberals of the 1870s?

■ Which points, raised in Exhibit 3.2, strike you as being characteristic of mid-century Latin American liberalism?

■ Which points, raised in Exhibit 3.2, indicate that the government Sarmiento will represent will favour certain authoritarian measures?

## Topics for essays and presentations

Making use of the recommended texts (see Further reading, p. 161) and/or others that may be available to you in your local library, write an essay/give a seminar presentation on **one** of the following topics.

1 Analyse the liberal–conservative divide in a Latin American country of your choice (1850–67).

2 Assess the impact of the liberals' reforms in mid-century Latin America, with reference to *at least two* countries.

3 Provide a comparative analysis of the reigns of Emperor Maximilian I and Emperor Pedro II.

## CHAPTER 4

## World context

**B**etween 1880 and 1913, European imperialism resulted in the partition of Africa. The rivalries that arose from European expansionism came to a head when the First World War broke out in 1914. The bloodshed and destruction the First World War entailed (1914–18) brought about the end of the age of European predominance and initiated a modern era of global politics in which the United States became a world power. This was also a period of intense political upheaval. In the industrialised world, the emergence of an exploited urban proletariat led to the formation of anarchist parties and unions, which strove to improve the conditions of the working classes. Strikes became a common means to force governments and employers to listen to the workers' demands. These were regularly crushed by the police or the army, resulting in numerous bloody clashes. However, the revolution so many Marxists predicted would unfold in industrialised Europe actually erupted in an agrarian society, changing the history of the modern world. The 1917 Russian Revolution initiated the age of modern revolutions; it

# The development and fall of the neocolonial order (1880–1930)

Between 1880 and 1930, the neocolonial order became fully established. Following the triumph of liberalism throughout the region, notions such as 'order and progress' became the pillars of oligarchical governments that supported an agenda based on authoritarian developmentalism. The *haciendas* expanded and the dependency on Latin America's export economies deepened. Although the decline of British trade, following the outbreak of the First World War, initiated a period of crisis in the 1920s, the neocolonial order was maintained with the ascendancy of the United States. US interventionism became rampant in Mexico, the Caribbean and Central America after 1898. The pressures placed on the peasantry and the emergent working classes by the export economies also gave rise to significant social tensions. The first labour movements of Latin America came into existence, leading to a period of strikes and brutal repression, and, in the case of Mexico, a major social signalled to the world that Marxists could forge a socialist society and it inspired revolutionaries throughout the globe to pursue parallel paths to power. Alongside the proliferation of labour movements, middle-class women took to the streets in an attempt to give women equal rights to men. In the wake of the First World War, nationalism grew into a powerful creed in most countries, in particular in all those regions that had suffered the brunt of European, US and Japanese colonialism.

revolution (1910–20). Although the rise of US imperialism, paired with the post-war crisis, inspired the creation of multiple nationalist movements in the region, the neocolonial order only collapsed once the world market came tumbling down in the wake of the 1929 Wall Street Crash.

## The triumph of the liberal State

The trends set in the 1870s gathered momentum during the following three decades. The early triumph of conservative liberalism in Mexico, Guatemala, El Salvador, Honduras, Costa Rica, Venezuela, Colombia, Chile, Argentina, Uruguay, Haiti and Brazil succeeded in spreading to Nicaragua, Ecuador, Peru, Bolivia, Paraguay and the Dominican Republic by the turn of the century. Prior to the outbreak of the First World War, British hegemony in the region as the leading partner in the emergent neocolonial order was fully established. The Latin American oligarchies that had begun to control the political and economic destinies of their respective countries in the 1870s further tightened their dominant role in society, as their *haciendas* expanded and the dependency on their export economies deepened. Railways continued to be laid down at a breathtaking pace. In Argentina, the rail network grew from 1,313 kilometres in 1880 to 34,000 kilometres in 1914. In Ecuador, the Quito–Guayaquil railway, built against all odds and in highly controversial circumstances between 1895 and 1908, became a symbol of the republican will of the liberal (and authoritarian) president, General Eloy Alfaro (1895–1901, 1906–12). In Mexico, on the eve of the revolution, in 1910, there were 19,205 kilometres of railroad, where there had only been 472 kilometres in 1873.

In those countries where the triumph of liberalism came later (i.e. in the 1890s), the developmentalist authoritarianism that came into place mirrored that of those countries where the conservatives had been defeated in the 1860s to 1870s. In Nicaragua, the reformism of José Santos Zelaya (1893–1909) was typical of the period. In Ecuador, following the 1895 revolution, under the rule of Alfaro and his successor, General Leónidas Plaza (1901–06), the Church was assaulted at all levels. Its properties were confiscated; the press was freed from ecclesiastical censorship; education was secularised; ecclesiastical taxation was abolished; civil marriage became obligatory; divorce was legalised; laws were passed against political preaching from the pulpit; and Roman Catholicism ceased to be the religion of the State. By the time the 1906 Constitution was drafted, the Church was not mentioned in it once.

In Peru, following the disastrous War of the Pacific (1879–83), it was General Andrés Cáceres (1886–95) who started the process of a liberal reconstruction of the country by pushing the signing of the Grace Contract in 1890. In it, the entrepreneur Michael Grace, at the head of a corporation of bondholders, committed himself to cancelling the entire national debt and granting the government an annual payment of £80,000 for 33 years. This was agreed in exchange for the government granting his company owner-ship of the Peruvian railways for a period of 66 years, free navigation of Lake Titicaca, and the right to extract up to three million tons of guano. The economic stability gener-ated by the Grace Contract served as the perfect footing on which a new liberal, oligarchic and neocolonial order could develop. While Cáceres was overthrown in the 1895 revolution, having alienated his liberal (*civilista*) allies by ignoring their demands to have a civilian as his successor, his fall from power did not result in the demise of his positivist ideology. His antagonist, Nicolás de Piérola (1895–99), perhaps surprisingly (considering his ultra-Catholic tendencies), did not instigate a return to conservative, pro-clerical, protectionist politics, but instead pursued the conservative Liberal agenda Cáceres had initiated. Piérola inaugurated the 'Aristocratic Republic' (1895–1919), a period noted for its level of political stability and economic progress.

In Bolivia, the defeat in the War of the Pacific proved fundamental in bringing an end to the *caudillo*-led military regimes of the previous decades. Evidently, the trauma of losing its direct access to the sea would not be easily overcome. However, the loss of prestige suffered by the military as a result of the defeat ushered in a period of civilian-dominated governments that resulted in the establishment of a modern political party system. Although the Bolivian conservatives hung on to power from 1884 to 1899, their ideology, like that of Rafael Núñez (1882–94) and Miguel Antonio Caro's (1894–98) conservative governments in Colombia, espoused a positivist, developmentalist agenda that did not differ greatly from that of the liberal administrations elsewhere. Evidence of this would come with the comparatively peaceful transfer of power to the Liberal party in 1899. Likewise, it was between 1880 and 1930 that Bolivia witnessed the rampant expansion of the *hacienda*. While in 1880 the Indian population owned half the rural land in the country, by 1930 they owned less than a third. Characteristic of the common trends of oligarchic rule in Latin America, suffrage restrictions and require-ments meant that between 1880 and 1932, national politics were determined by just over 10 per cent of the population. The Indians, representing over three-quarters of the population, were not allowed to vote. Integrated into the neocolonial order, the growth of the export sector (silver production, 1880–99, and tin production, 1900–29) resulted in the increasing dependency of the Bolivian economy on international forces.

In Paraguay, following ten years of political intrigue and instability in the wake of the War of the Triple Alliance (1864–70), it was General Bernardino Caballero (1880–86) who initiated a period of stability that lasted for almost twenty-five years. He rose to power in the coup of September 1880, and inspired a familiar assault on State proper-ties that led to the rise of a formidable oligarchy and a highly dependent economy. By 1900, 79 individuals owned almost half of Paraguay's land. By 1930, with these trends further supported by the more overtly liberal governments that rose to power between 1904 and 1923, 19 proprietors, most of them foreign companies, owned more than half of Paraguay's territory.

In the Dominican Republic, the triumph of conservative liberalism came with rise to power of the black general Ulíses Heureaux (1882–84, 1887–99). Heureaux's authoritarian developmentalism motivated a dramatic rise in the country's export economy. Between 1888 and 1897, sugar exports doubled, cacao exports more than tripled and coffee exports almost quadrupled. The country's infrastructure was significantly improved; the education system was given prime attention; and the army was duly professionalised. The values of order and progress became as important in the Dominican Republic as elsewhere. However, sharing the fate of most countries in the Caribbean (stemming from their proximity to the United States), Heureaux's achievements were short-lived. His assassination in 1899, and the instability that ensued (1899–1907), led first to indirect US intervention (1907–16), and ultimately to direct US intervention, with the eight-year US occupation of the Republic (1916–24).

✳ The triumph of the liberal State resulted in the consolidation of oligarchic governments which favoured free market economics, the expansion of the *hacienda* and export-led economies, based above all on primary products, under the banner of order and progress. Between 1870 and 1930, most Latin American countries witnessed a wide range of developmentalist programmes, including the building of roads and railways, paired with attempts to professionalise the armed forces, promote education and curtail the power of the Church. In broad terms, a particularly small percentage of the population became spectacularly rich, while the conditions of the majority became significantly worse. The sale of public, communal, Indian and Church lands turned a minority into the owners of most of their respective countries' territory, forcing the majority into peonage. The economies of most Latin American countries became profoundly dependent on the needs and demands of Britain and the United States, in a neo-colonial order that would collapse dramatically in the wake of the 1929 Wall Street Crash.

However, in most Latin American countries, the authoritarian oligarchic and developmentalist governments were based on constitutional systems that involved transfers of power between elected presidents and even, in some cases, between different parties. Although repression was exercised, a combative press did exist, and parliamentary debates were generally animated and unrestrained. Moreover, as the new century unfolded, these governments became increasingly aware that the disparities of wealth which had come to characterise their societies needed to be addressed. Although in general they failed to tackle adequately what became known as the 'social question', the rise of more 'radical' presidents in the early twentieth century, such as José Batlle y Ordóñez (Uruguay, 1903–07, 1911–15), Hipólito Yrigoyen (Argentina, 1916–22, 1928–30), Arturo Alessandri (Chile, 1920–25) and, at least initially, General Juan Vicente Gómez (Venezuela, 1908–1935), is evidence that not all oligarchic governments were impervious to the rising discontent of the working and middle classes. From as early as the late 1880s, some oligarchic presidents, such as José Manuel Balmaceda (Chile, 1886–91), sensed that there was a need to balance their increasing dependency on Britain and the United States, seeking ways to control the boom of the export economies. Balmaceda endeavoured to encourage State ownership of the ʼlean railways and defended greater Chilean involvement in the nitrate sector, ·ɡ that it harmed the country's interests to allow a foreign monopoly of the ᵗo develop any further.

What few liberal politicians could have suspected in the 1870s, and what few could ignore by the 1900s, was that the expansion of the *haciendas* had resulted in the formation of a more homogeneous and aggrieved rural proletariat than there had ever been before. The accelerated development of mining industries (nitrates in Chile, tin in Bolivia) brought about the formation of a hardened miners' movement. The fast growth and development of the main cities and ports led to the emergence of an equally aggrieved urban working class. The radical political movements the working classes would espouse in the early twentieth century, with Mexico representing its most extreme manifestation, would have far-reaching consequences once the neocolonial order collapsed.

## The First Republic of Brazil (1889–1930)

The conflictive experience of the First Republic in Brazil, while sharing some similarities with the few other Latin American countries where civil conflict resurfaced during this period, nonetheless differed greatly from the rest. Whereas in most Latin American countries, bar the rise of social unrest, this was a period of noted, albeit repressive, political stability, in Brazil, the demise of the monarchy resulted in a period of major upheaval.

The escalation of violence that spread throughout Brazil during the First Republic can be attributed to two key factors:

- the 1891 Constitution; and
- the conflicting interests of the Brazilian oligarchies.

The 1891 Constitution created a federal system whereby the country's twenty provinces acquired far-reaching powers, including the right to raise their own armies, foreign loans and taxes. In order to counterbalance this devolution of power to the provinces, the national president was given a prominent role whereby he could nominate his ministers and forcefully intervene in the newly formed states, should such a need arise. The contradictory tenets of this constitutional compromise contributed significantly to the instability that ensued as the provinces went their own way and federal military intervention became frequent. The federal structure exacerbated intra-state and elite competitiveness, granting what are often described as the 'feudal fiefdoms' of the large landowners a dangerous degree of autonomy and power in the interior. One of the direct consequences of the Constitution was the emergence of powerful *coronéis*. Another was the rise in intra-state conflicts, as different regions (such as São Paulo and Minas Gerais) competed to dominate the federal government.

The conflicts of the opening years of the First Republic included the overthrow of President Deodoro da Fonseca, only days after the new Congress assembled, in November 1891; a major revolt in Rio Grande do Sul (1893–95); and the revolt of Canudos (1893–96), in Bahia, which was crushed in 1896, after three military expeditions had

> ### *coronéis*
> Portuguese term for strongmen, chieftains; Brazilian equivalent of *caudillos*.

failed to defeat António *Conselheiro* (the Counsellor) and his 30,000-strong insurgent army. The Canudos rebellion and the brutal repression used to end it would be powerfully recreated in Euclides da Cunha's novel, *Os sertões* (1902), and in Mario Vargas Llosa's *La guerra del fin del mundo* (1981). The national government survived the turmoil of these years because the oligarchies of the two wealthiest provinces, São Paulo and Minas Gerais, reached an agreement whereby the presidents, chosen from their own regional constituencies, would loosely alternate in power. This formula became known as the *política dos governadores* (politics of the governors). From 1894 to 1930, there were six São Paulo presidents and four from Minas Gerais, out of a total of thirteen. The oligarchies of the other states allowed their counterparts from São Paulo and Minas Gerais to assume power on the understanding that they were allowed to do pretty much as they pleased in their own provinces. However, the tensions of these years remained high. The São Paulo and Minas Gerais alliance, popularly known as *café com leite* (white coffee), after the coffee elites of the one and the cattle barons of the other, was never an easy one. In the presidential elections of 1910, their divisions almost led to violence when the Minas Gerais candidate, Hermes da Fonseca (Deodoro's nephew), marginally defeated São Paulo and Bahia's candidate, Rui Barbosa. Notwithstanding this, with only 3 per cent of the population eligible to vote, no official candidate for the presidency lost the elections before 1930.

Where Brazil followed a trend more familiar to other Latin American countries was in its oligarchies' pursuit of a common economic policy. Free market economics (occasionally controlled through State intervention), coupled with the development of the country's agriculture-based export economy, led to the dramatic expansion of coffee, sugar and cotton plantations, with the subsequent enrichment of a limited few at the expense of an exploited majority. By the 1920s, 461 individuals owned over 27 million hectares of land, contrasting with over 464,000 small or medium-sized farmers, whose combined ownership of land did not amount to more than 15.7 million hectares. The dependency on British and US economic interests deepened. Although the collapse of the Amazonian rubber boom between 1910 and 1914 served as a clear signal that **monoculture** paired with an overdependence on agricultural exports could prove seriously detrimental to Brazil, little was done to diversify the Republic's economy. Coffee became the main produce of Brazil, to the detriment of other sectors. Indicative of this is the fact that by the

### monoculture

Agricultural policy pursued in response to global market forces within a neocolonial order, whereby specific primary products were grown exclusively, to the detriment of others. Instead of encouraging diversity in Latin America's market potential, including the kind of industrialisation that might have allowed the region a degree of self-sufficiency, monoculture converted most countries into producers of one or two products. The manner in which bananas were cultivated in Honduras is an example of monoculture. This specialisation of export produce made recovery a near-impossible task once Europe and the USA stopped purchasing Latin American produce in the wake of the 1929 Wall Street crash.

1920s Brazil was importing four-fifths of its grain. The opposition of foreign interests and the plantation-owning oligarchy proved too strong for anything other than a light industry (food-processing plants and textile mills) to emerge. By 1929, with an external debt of $1,181 million, costing a third of the annual national budget in repayments, the collapse of the coffee market in the wake of the Wall Street Crash could not have been more devastating. The price of coffee fell from 22.5 to 8 cents a pound, and the neocolonial order came tumbling down with it.

## The rise of US interventionism

By the outbreak of the First World War, in which most Latin American countries remained neutral, US investment in Latin America had risen from $320 million in 1898 to $1.7 billion. It was during the First World War that US investment rose by 50 per cent, with the value of US exports to Latin America trebling between 1914 and 1929. By 1929, the United States was the main buyer of Latin America's minerals and tropical food-stuffs, with over 30 per cent of the region's exports going to the USA. The United States had clearly become the dominant power in the mature neocolonial period. This can be attributed to three factors. The first was the impact the First World War had on Britain. Britain's involvement in the war severely weakened its economic standing in the world. Its wartime debt, which had risen to $4.1 billion by 1918, meant that Britain would no longer be in a position to dominate the Latin American economies as their main source of trade and loans. British foreign investment fell dramatically, and its trade with countries like Brazil, whose main produce, coffee, was not perceived to be essential for the war effort, declined rapidly. The second cause was the emergence of new industries and technologies in which the United States had become the leading power. The rise of the automobile, along with the growing demand for oil, and the emergence of radio and cable communications, were all innovations that hit the world at a time when Britain was not in a position to compete. The United States broke the more traditional commercial hegemony of Britain, exporting cars, agricultural machinery and a whole new range of household electrical appliances. The third and perhaps the most obvious reason was that by the time the United States entered the First World War in 1917, it had become one of the world's leading industrial and financial powers.

US domination in Latin America developed in four different spheres of influence: trade, economic penetration, political pressure and military intervention. Trade relations between the USA and Latin America expanded at a great pace between 1880 and 1914, with the United States supplanting Britain as the dominant partner once the First World War erupted. This was, similarly, a relationship whereby the United States imported raw materials from Latin America, exporting surplus manufactured goods to its republics in exchange. In 1885, US trade with Latin America did not amount to more than 3.74 per cent of its exports. Notwithstanding this, the USA at that point already controlled 64.5 per cent of Guatemala's exports and imports, 41.6 per cent of Venezuela's, 39.4 per cent of Mexico's, 36.6 per cent of Colombia's and 26.8 per cent of Brazil's. By 1929 it accounted for over 30 per cent of the western hemisphere's exports, resulting in a situation whereby Latin America's fully developed export economies were highly dependent on US demand for its products. Of Cuba's exports, 80 per cent were going to the United States, and a similar percentage could be found in Central America as well as in the Caribbean republics. Sugar became the main product of Cuba, Puerto Rico and the Dominican Republic. Coffee and bananas became those of the Central American republics, Haiti and Colombia. In Brazil, coffee remained the main export, while in Uruguay and Argentina, wool, beef exports and wheat assumed an even greater role. In Chile, the nitrate mining industry was given pre-eminence, while in Bolivia, the tin industry reached an all-time high by 1929, with the export of 47,000 tons of tin. The extent to which the Latin American economies came to depend on the United States meant that their governments were forced to listen to US political demands and expectations. However, the dependency that was forged became even greater given that, while British hegemony was mercantile-based, US hegemony entailed direct ownership of the means of production.

US companies penetrated the markets of the majority of Latin American countries. The United Fruit Company penetrated the Central American market so effectively and became so powerful that some would argue that their high-flying executives made up the so-called Banana Republics' government in all but name. By 1930, taking the whole of Central America, including Panama, of the 103 million bananas that were exported, 63 per cent of them were owned by the United Fruit Company. Although its power may be deemed exaggerated, the series of conflicts that developed between Honduras and Guatemala after 1913 stemmed directly from the existing rivalry between the United Fruit Company and the Cuyamel Fruit Company. It is no coincidence that when the two companies merged in 1929, these conflicts came to an abrupt end. Those who defend the impact the United Fruit Company had in Central America note that it was both 'the largest and certainly the best employer of labour' in Central America, that it improved the region's communications networks, created thousands of jobs, motivated economic development, and taught the 'native population something of modern industrial methods and hygiene'. For those who condemn it, the 1928 strike and the subsequent massacre that ensued in the United Fruit Company's banana plantations in Colombia, vividly depicted in García Márquez's *Cien años de soledad* (1967), represent a bleaker interpretation of the exploitation the company's activities entailed.

With the discovery of oil in Argentina, Bolivia, Mexico, Peru and Venezuela, US penetration proved equally dramatic. In those countries where there was no oil, Standard Oil became the leading oil importer, controlling its distribution and taking the largest share in the sales of automobile fuels. In those where there was the possibility of extracting it, Standard Oil ensured that it was granted all the necessary concessions and rights to dominate the market. Standard Oil took over the nascent oil industries in all the oil-producing countries, with the notable exception of Venezuela. To General Juan Vicente Gómez's credit, his government pursued a line that maintained a tight balance between Standard Oil, the British-owned Royal Dutch Shell and Venezuelan ownership of the oil industry. This was to have a long-lasting effect on Venezuela's economic stability. It allowed the country to benefit from the boom of its oil industry. By 1926 oil was Venezuela's leading export, with production rising to 15 million tons by 1928, making Venezuela the second-largest producer of petroleum in the world, after the United States. It gave Gómez's government an atypical stability in the 1920s. Oil revenues led to the cancellation of the national debt in December 1930, and Gómez was able to survive the crisis of the world Depression. His government ended when he died a natural death on 17 December 1935. Elsewhere in Latin America, Standard Oil acquired such a prominent role that once nationalism started to develop as a powerful force in the wake of the First World War, it became a symbol of US imperialism and the obvious target of nationalist politicians. In the late 1920s, Hipólito Yrigoyen's second presidential campaign was based on a nationalist platform, whereby he claimed he would nationalise the oil industry in Argentina, directing all his vitriol against Standard Oil alone.

However, it was the extensive use of US military intervention that significantly changed the nature of the neocolonial order. President Theodore Roosevelt (1901–08) legitimated the use of force in 1905, with the defence of a policy which became known as the Roosevelt Corollary to the Monroe Doctrine. Consistent with his belief that 'A just war is in the long run far better for a man's soul than the most prosperous peace', Roosevelt's 1905 Corollary gave the United States the right to send its marines to any country in the western hemisphere where the political situation was deemed problematic in terms of US interests. As he noted himself, as long as the different Latin American governments acted with 'reasonable efficiency', maintaining order and paying their dues, then they 'need fear no interference from the United States'. However, 'chronic wrongdoing, or an impotence which results in a general loosening of the ties of civilised society' would force the United States, 'however reluctantly', to intervene as an 'international police power'.

Although US military intervention had already taken place in a number of Latin American countries prior to the formulation of the Roosevelt Corollary, after 1905 it became far more common and widespread. Between the Mexican–American War (1846–48) and 1905, US troops were dispatched to Cuba (1898–1902), Puerto Rico (1898) and Panama (Colombia, 1902 and 1903). Cuba was placed under a US military government from 1899 to 1902 and, albeit indirectly, from 1906 to 1909, with further intervention in 1921. The establishment of the naval base at Guantánamo, which still belongs to the USA, dates from 1903. Puerto Rico became a possession of the United States after the 1898 invasion, and has remained one ever since, although its inhabitants were not granted US citizenship until 1917 (voting to become 'an associated, free and sovereign' State in 1952). The Dominican Republic was occupied from 1916 to 1924, after nine years (1907–16) of not altogether successful Washington intervention in the politics of the Republic, which involved imposing and deposing presidents, depending on how well they served US interests. Haiti was occupied for a longer period, stretching from 1915 to 1934. In Mexico, US marines took Veracruz by force in 1914, and sent a punitive expedition into Chihuahua in 1916 to seek out Pancho Villa after the revolutionary had raided Columbus in the USA (becoming the first and only Latin American to have attacked mainland USA). The United States sent troops to Central America in 1906, and occupied Nicaragua from 1912 to 1933. In Panama (Colombia), in the wake of the civil War of a Thousand Days (1899–1901), Colombian refusal, in 1903, to ratify the Herrán–Hay Treaty, which granted the USA complete control of the planned fortified canal that would eventually link the Atlantic with the Pacific, led to US inter-vention. US marines assisted Dr Manuel Amador's secessionist Panamanian movement, brought about the independence of Panama, and went on to obtain permission for construction of the canal as well as control of a canal zone sixteen kilometres wide. Panama, like Cuba, became a pseudo US protectorate, and the canal was opened in 1914.

The rise of US imperialism was viewed with great unease by a wide range of Latin American intellectuals and politicians. From as early as 1837, the Mexican politician José María Tornel had noted that 'The dominant thought of the United States has been for fifty years, in other words, since its political infancy, to occupy a large part of the territory that was Spanish before.' By 1850, the Mexican conservative ideologue Lucas Alamán had become convinced that it was only a matter of time before the whole of Spanish America would be taken by the Colossus of the North. For obvious reasons, it was Mexican writers who first started to express their fears of US supremacy ('so far from God, so close to the United States'). By the mid 1890s, however, a new generation of Latin Americans started to voice their rejection of US values, as well as their imperial behaviour.

At a cultural level, there was a significant shift from what amounted to a movement preoccupied with defining its respective countries' identity to one that did so in response to US influence. The late nineteenth-century *costumbrista* movement, which attempted to describe the national and regional identities of its respective countries, became increasingly concerned with what it meant to be Haitian, Nicaraguan or Uruguayan vis-à-vis US values and identity. The event that contributed most signifi-cantly to the formation of a cultural and subsequently political repudiation of the United States was the outcome of the Cuban War of Independence (1895–98).

After the Ten Year War (1868–78), although the Spanish government had attempted to appease Cuban discontent by abolishing slavery (1886) and granting the island a certain degree of political autonomy, by 1895 the reality remained that the island's political and economic development was oppressively subjugated under Spanish domi-nation. Given that by 1894, Cuba was exporting around $8 million worth of sugar to Spain, contrasting with the $93 million worth it was exporting to the USA, the inflexi-bility of Spain placed Cuba commercially in a situation that invited US intervention. After two long years of conflict between Cuban revolutionaries (originally led by **José Martí**) and the Spanish army, on 15 April 1898 the United States entered the war, as President William McKinley put it, 'in the name of humanity, in the name of civilisation, and on behalf of endangered American interests'. Following the US entry into the war and the subsequent defeat of the Spanish forces in the summer of 1898, US marines occupied Cuba until 1902, when the Republic of Cuba was proclaimed. Cuba became a pseudo US protectorate under the Platt Amendment (lasting until 1934), which stipu-lated that 'Cuba consents that the United States may exercise the right to intervene for the preservation of Cuban independence, the maintenance of a government adequate for the protection of life, property, and individual liberty'. US involvement in Cuba sparked a trend whereby many Spanish Americans developed a re-discovered love for Spain and its cultural legacies. It signalled the emergence of the USA as an imperial power in the twentieth century. And it inspired a wave of anti-US publications.

Probably the most influential text of the period, regarding this emergent Latin American rejection of US influence, was the Uruguayan José Enrique Rodó's *Ariel* (1900). Rodó proposed that it was the duty of young Latin Americans to be idealistic. He stressed that they needed to seek a moral and political regeneration of their continent, upholding an aesthetic high ground. The most influential section of *Ariel* was chapter V, in which Rodó's venerable teacher, Próspero, warns his pupils of the degrading tenets of US materialism. The association he drafted between an ethereal-spiritual-aesthetic idealism, as represented by Ariel, with Latin America, and a gross-aggres-sive-selfish and empty materialism, as represented by Calibán, with the United States, was to be taken up by a wide range of Latin American writers. The modernist Nicaraguan poet, Rubén Darío, dedicated his *Cantos de vida y esperanza* (1905) to Rodó. It is in *Cantos* where poem VIII, *A Roosevelt*, is to be found. Echoing Rodó's continental dichotomy, Darío's poem juxtaposes a parallel vision of the United States (modern, imperial-istic, aggressive, vulgar) with one of a spiritual and ancient, indigenous Spanish America that will never be conquered fully because of the spiritual void the United States represents. In Haiti, the cultural movement J.C. Dorsainvil initiated with his articles in *Le Matin* (1907–09), defending the view that the Haitian people were essentially African in racial composition and cultural heritage, became one that was virulently anti-US by the 1920s. Writers such as Jacques Roumain, Carl Brouard and Emile Roumer rejected their forebears' Francophilia and openly condemned the US occupation of Haiti.

### José Martí (1853–95)

Born in Havana, Martí's early political activism led to his arrest by the Spanish authorities at the age of sixteen. Thereafter he was banished to Spain, and although he returned to Cuba (1878), he was forced into exile again. The last time he went back would be at the head of the Cuban independence movement in 1895. During his years in exile, Martí studied law in Zaragoza (Spain) and worked as a journalist and a teacher in France, Mexico, Guatemala and the USA. He was one of Latin America's leading modernist poets, and a writer of essays and pamphlets that demanded Cuban independence and challenged US supremacy. Based in New York (1891–95), he strove to unite the numerous yet divided Cuban factions into an all-inclusive independence movement that culminated in his *Cuba Libre* campaign. Unlike the revolutionaries of the Ten Year War, he appealed to Cubans of all races and classes. His ardent faith in democracy led him to seek a quick victory by inspiring a mass rebellion throughout the island. He feared, rather prophetically, that a long, drawn-out campaign would be counterproductive, since it would encourage the rise of military *caudillos*, destroy Cuban wealth and lead to US intervention. He died in an ambush in Dos Ríos, only a month after having reached Cuba to join the insurgency.

At a political level, it was the more radical presidents of the first decades of the twentieth century who expressed more openly their unease over the increasing power of the United States. José Batlle y Ordóñez, twice president of Uruguay (1903–07 and

1911–15), sought to promote a protectionist programme in 1912 that aimed to expand the Uruguayan manufacturing industry. He strove to limit the extent of foreign penetration in the economy and inspired the creation of a number of significant State-owned companies. By the end of his second presidency, sectors of the economy, such as telephones, railways and insurance, were State-owned. He had also succeeded in nationalising the capital of the Banco de la República. On the whole, however, Batlle y Ordóñez was more the exception than the norm. In more general terms, it was not until the 1920s that this rejection of the neocolonial order and US imperialism became widespread in Latin America at a political level.

## The impact of immigration

While the lives of most Latin Americans were affected by US imperialism, immigration was to become another major influence in the development of their societies. Population growth in most Latin American countries had already proven dramatic during the nineteenth century. The major cities had grown at an incredibly fast rate, even before the arrival of European, Chinese and Syrio-Lebanese immigrants at the end of the century. In those countries where immigration was not as significant, such as Mexico, Chile and Colombia, these patterns of growth continued unrestrained. Between 1877 and 1910, Mexico's population grew from nearly ten to over fifteen million. In Colombia, the population grew from just under three million in 1870 to just over seven million by 1928. It was in those countries where immigration was more systematically encouraged, however, namely Argentina, Uruguay and Brazil, that its impact was greatest.

The 1.8 million Argentineans recorded to have made up the country's population in 1869 became almost four million in a matter of twenty-five years, rising to eight million by 1914. Between 1870 and 1914, around six million immigrants from Spain and Italy arrived in Argentina. Foreign immigrants represented 12.1 per cent of the population in 1869, 25.4 per cent in 1895 and 29.9 per cent in 1914. In addition to immigration, between 1870 and 1914, Italian peasants came and went every year during the European winter to participate in the wheat harvests in Argentina, earning themselves the name of *golondrinas* (swallows). In Brazil, the wave of Italian, Spanish and Portuguese workers arriving between 1872 and 1930 amounted to around 2.2 million. São Paulo became known as an 'Italian city', after the foreign population rose to 54.6 per cent of the total in 1893. In Uruguay, by 1908, immigrants amounted to 17 per cent of the entire population. Even in those countries where the arrival of immigrants was more modest, their impact was nonetheless considerable in economic, social and cultural terms. The 1908 census of Lima showed that 10 per cent of the capital's population (16,649) was foreign-born, with Italians (3,944) making up about a quarter of the total.

In terms of immigration patterns, Argentina and Uruguay saw the arrival of mainly Italian (and French, in the case of Uruguay) immigrants. Scottish and Welsh farmers went to Patagonia, and large German colonies established themselves in the south of Chile. In Brazil, 31 per cent of all immigrants were Italian, 30 per cent were Portuguese,

13.8 per cent were Spanish, 4.5 per cent were Japanese and 4 per cent were German. Cuba witnessed the arrival of large numbers of Spaniards (mainly Galicians, Catalans and Asturians), even after the 1898 debacle. Chinese coolies had a major impact in Peru,

> ### *gamonales*
> Peruvian term for large estate owners. (See *hacendados, estancieros, latifundistas.*)

working as semi-free contractual labourers, imported initially as a measure to avoid draining off Indian labour from highlands *haciendas* when the guano boom erupted in the 1860s. It is estimated that over 100,000 Chinese workers settled in Peru between 1860 and 1880.

The impact of immigration, the growth of the native population and the dramatic expansion of the main urban centres had several significant consequences. In terms of cultural identity, there is no doubt that immigration drastically transformed countries like Argentina and Uruguay, giving them that 'European' distinctiveness that differentiates their population to this day from that of the rest of Latin America. In social terms, immigration within a context of accelerated urban development contributed to the establishment of an expanding middle class. Spanish shopkeepers, French tailors and Syrian merchants fuelled the demands of Latin America's developing bourgeoisie. Nevertheless, the middle classes in Latin America were far less influential than in the industrialised world. The Peruvian Marxist ideologue José Carlos Mariátegui was probably correct in arguing, in 1927, that in Peru, and by default in Latin America, with its predominantly agrarian society, the middle classes represented such a reduced percentage of the population that they hardly deserved a mention in a society characterised by the opulence of the few and the abject poverty of the majority. According to Mariátegui, they had either become *proletarizados*, like himself, joining the working classes, or had been absorbed into the ranks of the **gamonales**. In his view, the agrarian feudalism of Latin America had not been eradicated since independence, and remained too powerful to have been replaced by a bourgeois-led industrial capitalist system. It is perhaps no coincidence that those countries which witnessed a significant increase in their middle-class population during these years were the same ones to welcome a major wave of immigrants. Given that literacy is considered a middle-class trait, figures for newspaper circulation, *c.*1910–14, provide a reliable means for assessing the extent to which the middle classes had grown in Latin America at the time. Mexico, which was to undergo the major 1910 revolution and which was the country to attract the smallest number of immigrants, had the smallest middle class in Latin America, with only twelve newspapers being sold per thousand people. The countries to have the strongest middle classes were Argentina (eighty-seven copies per thousand people) and Uruguay (eighty copies).

It was in terms of politics that the impact of immigration was to prove particularly influential. Anarchist, Marxist and socialist ideas spread throughout Latin America, as the changing context of the working classes became particularly receptive to the radical ideas brought by Italian and Spanish immigrants. This was especially true in the main cities. In Buenos Aires, half of the population were immigrants by 1914. In the state of São Paulo alone, by 1920, 58 per cent of those employed in the transport sector were foreigners. Their influence cannot be underestimated. It was an Italian, Errico Malatesta, who, in exile in Argentina from 1885 to 1889, published numerous anarchist pamphlets and was responsible for drawing up the statutes of a union of bakery workers, among others, in Buenos Aires. By the early 1900s in Brazil, thirty-three different anarchist newspapers aimed at the urban working classes were being published *in Italian*. Latin American intellectuals, such as the Peruvian Manuel González Prada, were quick to pick up this European influence and make it their own. It was González Prada who defined and defended the anarchists' ideal of 'unlimited freedom and the highest possible well-being of the individual with the abolition of the State... The Anarchist rejects laws, religions, nationalities and recognises one power only: that of the individual.' The receptiveness of Latin America's working classes to anarchism, anarcho-syndicalism, socialism and communism was evidently the result of their conditions at the beginning of the twentieth century. Workers' and peasants' discontent, in a context where the disparity of wealth between the few and the majority had become untenable, would become known as the 'social question'.

## The 'social question'

The growth of the main cities, and the need for labour that was generated by the railways, the trading sector (dockyards) and emergent light industries (food-processing plants, tobacco factories and textile mills), led to the development of a large urban working class. Their living and working conditions soon became the cause of major discontent. In the 1914 census for Buenos Aires, it was estimated that the working classes made up two-thirds of the population. Forced to live in highly unhygienic households, whether it was the improvised slums that surfaced in the cities' outskirts or occupying the rooms of rundown **conventillos** or **casas de vecindad**, their exploitation by the oligarchy and foreign companies became increasingly severe. Their circumstances were characterised by low wages, no minimum wage, long hours, no day of rest, no insurance against accidents, no job security and no paid vacations. Evidence of the dire conditions the working classes lived in can be found in the figures for infant mortality. In Chile, between 1890 and 1915, 293 out of every 1,000 children died before reaching the age of five.

The period 1880–1930 was characterised by the working classes' organisation of trade unions and other proletarian movements, as they were influenced by radical immigrants, but also thrust into mobilisation by their living conditions. Between 1886 and 1926, numerous unions were founded, such as the FOCH (Chilean Workers' Federation) and the Central American Labour Council. As the anarchists evolved into a more restrained anarcho-syndicalist movement, which sacrificed its outright anticapitalist stance for a more pragmatic one that restricted itself to improving, through trade unions, the conditions of the working classes within a capitalist framework, socialist and

**conventillos (South America)/casas de vecindad (Mexico and Caribbean)**

Former colonial houses converted into tenement houses.

communist syndicates and political parties started to proliferate. The socialist UGT (General Workers' Union) surfaced in Argentina in 1907. The Chilean Luis Emilio Recabarren founded the *Partido Obrero Socialista* (Socialist

> ### soldaderas
> Mexican female revolutionary soldiers.

Workers' Party) in 1912. Communist parties emerged in Central America between 1920 and 1931, as they did elsewhere. By the end of the 1920s, the writings of José Carlos Mariátegui (see Exhibit 4.1) had become extremely influential throughout Latin America.

In tandem with the rise of working-class unions and political parties, the women's movement became a force in its own right. With increasing numbers of working-class women joining the industrial sector (textile and tobacco factories, and food-processing plants), as well as the service sector (domestic work), the demands for equal rights, including the right to vote, became an essential part of the social question. In Peru, a generation of middle-class female intellectuals sought to improve the condition of women in general, including working-class women, with the formation of a women's organisation, *Evolución Femenina*, in 1914. By 1919, María Jesús Alvarado and Zoila Aurora Cáceres had transformed their *Evolución Femenina* into the far more combative *Comité Femenino de la Lucha Pro-Abaratamiento de las Subsistencias,* calling on 'all women without distinguishing between classes' to fight against hunger and the rising prices of basic foods. Alvarado went on to become secretary of the International Women's Suffrage Organisation in 1924. In 1922, and typical of other parallel movements that surfaced throughout Latin America, the Brazilian activist Berta Lutz founded the FBPF (Brazilian Federation for the Advancement of Women) to protect 'female labour, which has been subject to inhuman exploitation'. By 1930 she was advocating female suffrage, civil equality, equal pay for equal work, paid maternity leave for working women, affirmative action in government employment, a minimum wage, the eight-hour day, paid vacations, and medical, disability and retirement insurance. Between 1900 and 1930, women became as active as men, participating in strikes, calling meetings and fighting in those countries where social unrest led to open revolts. Women were notoriously combative during the Mexican Revolution, with the **soldaderas** becoming one of the most enduring icons of the 1910–20 conflict.

The dramatic expansion of the *hacienda* in the countryside was equally important in creating a more homogeneous and aggrieved peasantry. Indians and peasants lost their communal lands and their smallholdings to the ever-expanding *latifundios*. They were forced to become peons in a system where they were often paid in vouchers or coupons, where there was no limit to the hours they were expected to work, and where the houses they were forced to live in were unhygienic and unsafe. While levels of literacy were already low in the main urban centres, in the countryside and among the peasant classes illiteracy was rampant. In Argentina, in 1914, compared to an illiterate 35.2 per cent of the population in Buenos Aires, 57.6 per cent could not read or write in the vast interior of the country. Although some may view Jorge Icaza's depiction of the horrendous conditions in which the Ecuadorian Indian peons had to live, in his

**Augusto César Sandino (1893-1934)**

More of a nationalist than a socialist, Sandino became the leader of one of Latin America's most tenacious anti-US resistance movements. Employing guerrilla warfare, and intensely popular in the countryside, Sandino succeeded in inflicting numerous defeats on the US troops that were dispatched to dislodge him. After seven years of conflict, US marines, stationed in Nicaragua since 1912, withdrew. In 1934, as peace negotiations were nearing an end between Sandino and President Juan Bautista Sacasa, he was assassinated by Anastasio Somoza's National Guard.

disturbing novel *Huasipungo* (1934), as somewhat exaggerated, most accounts of the period would appear to confirm his assessment. Peasant uprisings exploded in western El Salvador from as early as the 1880s, following the confiscation of communal lands. There were over 300 peasant uprisings in Peru between 1901 and 1930, the most famous of which was the 1915 Puno revolt. The Mexican Revolution, particularly between 1910 and 1917, was fought by dissatisfied peasants.

Both in the countryside and in the cities, the inevitable clash between working-class/peasant movements and the oligarchical, neocolonial establishment was to give a particularly bloody feel to these years. This was a period of strikes and repression. In 1905, the so-called *Semana Roja* (Red Week) in Santiago led to 60 dead and over 300 wounded. In June 1906, a strike in the textile factory of Río Blanco, in Veracruz, was suppressed with ruthless brutality and executions. The massive general strike of 1919 in Lima transformed the streets into a battleground. In January 1919, the *Semana Trágica* (Tragic Week) erupted in Buenos Aires, following a strike of metallurgical workers that began in December 1918. In Chile, strikes rose from 16 in 1916, involving 18,000 workers, to 105 in 1920, involving 50,000 workers. In Central America, the strikes that became common in the 1920s led to the emergence of radical politicians such as Agustín Farabundo Martí (El Salvador) and **Augusto Sandino** (Nicaragua).

Most oligarchical governments sought peaceful means to resolve the problems posed by the often-cited social question. From 1906 onwards, the more radical governments implemented measures that were intended to tackle the workers' main grievances. However, even the more progressive governments fell back on repression once the workers' demands and actions got out of hand. Nonetheless, reforms were carried through, aimed to respond to a situation that was becoming explosive. In Chile, a law meant to improve and protect workers' housing was passed in 1906. Obligatory Sunday rest was imposed in 1907, and laws that granted the workers insurance against industrial accidents were approved in 1917. In Uruguay, under Batlle y Ordóñez, the eight-hour working day for all urban workers was legislated in 1915.

Although the rise in worker and peasant mobilisation was significant enough to force certain changes in the law, it would be wrong to overemphasise the impact their political movements had in the cities and the countryside. Even as the crisis of the 1920s set in, and regardless of the example of the 1917 Russian Revolution, with the exception of Mexico, most Latin American oligarchies remained in control and the neocolonial order prevailed. There are numerous reasons for the failure of both the workers' movements in the cities and the Indian–peasant uprisings in the coun-tryside to transform their countries and overthrow the capitalist systems they opposed. In spite of a combative anarchist press or the exertions of a small number of active political agitators, the illiteracy and lack of education of the masses proved too big an obstacle for a purely ideological revolution to prosper. Distance, ethnic and regional differences, issues that had been so important in complicating the exer-cise of government in the nineteenth century, were to prove an equally difficult chal-lenge to overcome when it came to attempting to generate any large-scale revolutionary activity at the beginning of the twentieth century. Mariátegui lamented, in 1927, that the understandable lack of a national spirit among the majority of the oppressed Indians in the Andes, depicted in José María Arguedas' novel *Yawar fiesta* (1941), prevented them from joining forces to combat the injustices of Peru's feudal form of oligarchic neocolonial capitalism. As exemplified in Icaza's *Huasipungo* or Miguel Ángel Asturias' *Hombres de maíz* (1949), most peasant revolts only came about as a very last resort, when there was nothing left for the Indians to do but fight or be left homeless.

Divisions among the leaders of the more prominent unions and radical political parties did not help either. While the original anarchists rejected capitalism and the parliamentary political system altogether, they soon became divided, as the syndicalist branch of the movement sought to improve the workers' conditions within the very system they condemned. Socialists and communists turned against each other, with the former defending a gradualist approach that accepted the capitalist stage of develop-ment they were in, defended parliamentary representation and acknowledged the need to form pragmatic alliances with other progressive parties. The communists' intransi-gence lost them many of their initial supporters, with the notable exception of Chile, and in some cases they ended up being accused of representing an elitist, academic and antinationalist agenda. In the 1920s, most workers were still more interested in improving their circumstances than overthrowing capitalism. Nonetheless, while most urban strikes and peasant revolts did little to bring the oligarchic–neocolonial order to an end, the same cannot be said of the Mexican Revolution.

## The Mexican Revolution (1910–1920)

Although the Mexican Revolution must be understood as a long and bloody civil war in which agrarian discontent was at the heart of the intense violence that characterised these years, it would be wrong to assume that the Revolution erupted in Mexico because the exploitation of both workers and *campesinos* was more extreme there than elsewhere. What needs to be highlighted is that in Mexico, unlike in the rest of the region, where the expansion of the *hacienda*, the triumph of authoritarian developmen-talism and the emergence of a neocolonial order had all been experienced along similar lines, the oligarchic system collapsed. It was the acute divisions which surfaced among the Mexican oligarchy that unwittingly gave the aggrieved peasantry an opening for revolutionary activity in a way that was unparalleled in the rest of the continent. The key difference, on the eve of the 1910 revolution, was that, unlike the rest of Latin

America, Mexico had been governed by one man for over thirty years (1876–80, 1884–1911). Elsewhere, the oligarchic systems had allowed for a relatively regular transfer of power between alternating presidents and parties, even if these had represented shared interests. In Mexico, Porfirio Díaz's longevity in power became a problem in itself once it became evident that there was no clear provision as to who should succeed him after his death. The first signs of oligarchic discontent appeared between the ageing Díaz's fifth and sixth re-elections (1904–06). Anti-re-election clubs emerged in most cities, although they were divided over who they wanted to succeed the general. Díaz went on to exacerbate elite tensions when, having stated in an interview with a US journalist (the Creelman interview) in 1908 that he would be standing down in the 1910 elections, he announced, only three months later, that he would be going for further re-election. Faced with the prospect of Díaz's seventh term in office, a major Coahuila landowner, Francisco I. Madero, founded the Anti-Re-electionist Central Club in May 1909, published his highly influential *La sucesión presidencial en 1910*, and started to campaign openly against Díaz. The government's response was to ban his movement in June 1910 and to have Madero arrested. With Madero in gaol, Díaz ensured that he was re-elected. With no choice but to resort to violence, Madero escaped to the United States and called the Mexicans to arms, setting 20 November 1910 as the date on which the revolution was to begin. This it did, with major peasant uprisings throughout the country. Emiliano Zapata led the *campesinos* of Morelos. Pancho Villa led the revolt in the north. By May 1911, Díaz had been forced to resign and Madero was voted president.

Having mobilised the disaffected peasants of the countryside, expectations of major agrarian reforms ran high. Madero failed to comply with their demands and his situation became increasingly precarious. Zapata, in Morelos, and Pascual Orozco, in Chihuahua, rebelled, demanding the long-awaited redistribution of land that had not materialised following Díaz's overthrow. The Porfirian establishment attacked Madero for being weak, and a large sector of the middle classes lost faith in his democratic ideals, terrified by the prospect of social dissolution. In February 1913, after fifteen months in power, a military coup, supported by the reactionary General Victoriano Huerta, ended his short-lived government, ordering his arrest and execution. Thereafter, the situation degenerated into an appalling bloodbath.

The complexities of the revolution, with its numerous rival revolutionary armies, are difficult to summarise. There were four main armies in the field in 1913:

1  The *Huertistas* or the Federal Army.
2  The *Villistas,* led by Pancho Villa.
3  The *Zapatistas,* led by Emiliano Zapata.
4  The *Carrancistas*, also known as the Constitutionalists, led by Venustiano Carranza.

The *Huertistas* were a throwback to the *Porfiriato*, albeit without Díaz, who died in exile in Paris in 1915, at the age of eighty-five. The *Villistas* and the *Zapatistas* were all committed peasant revolutionaries, intent on redistributing the land among the people. However, Villa's loyalty to Madero led to the *Villistas* fighting against the *Orozquistas* in

Mexican revolutionaries

1912, and, by default, against the *Zapatistas*, for having revolted against Madero's government. After much bloodshed, the revolutionaries' differences were temporarily put on hold, under Carranza's leadership, in a concerted effort to take Mexico City and bring down Huerta in 1914. This they did, forcing Huerta into exile, after *Villistas* and *Zapatistas* converged in the capital in December 1914. At this point, Villa and Zapata could have dramatically changed the course of Mexican history. However, neither faction could agree on a lasting political situation, and neither Villa nor Zapata was interested in occupying the presidential palace, preferring to return to their home provinces. It was then that Carranza, a landlord like Madero, who was not known for his commitment to agrarian reform, seized the day and led his revolutionary movement against Villa and Zapata, entrusting the leadership of his main divisions to the revolution's best general, Álvaro Obregón. Obregón took Mexico City in January 1915. On 6–7 and 13 April 1915, in the two battles of Celaya, he routed the *Villistas* by employing First World War tactics with which Villa was unfamiliar. (He used trench warfare, setting up strategically placed machine guns, against Villa's old-fashioned cavalry charges.) With Obregón pursuing the retreating *Villistas* in the north, and other *Carrancista* divisions forcing the *Zapatistas* into Morelos, Carranza became president in 1917. Under Carranza (1915–20), the 1917 Constitution came into place while Villa and Zapata fought on, albeit at the head of dwindling armies. Zapata was assassinated in 1919. Villa was amnestied in 1920, and subsequently assassinated in 1923. The long-term defeat of the *Villistas* and the *Zapatistas* had the inevitable effect of curtailing significantly the impact their aims were meant to achieve. The landowning political class from Sonora that came to run the country, Carranza (1915–20), Obregón (1920–24) and Plutarco Elías Calles (1924–28), ensured that Zapata's ideals, as voiced in his 1911 Plan of Ayala (see Exhibit 4.2), and later in the Agrarian Law of 1915, were not fulfilled as intended. The expectation that a comprehensive agrarian reform would succeed the triumph of the revolution, in which the large private estates would be broken up and redistributed among the dispossessed peasant communities, was never followed through to its ultimate consequences.

It would be misleading to argue that after a decade of brutal civil war little had changed. Nevertheless, it remains the case that, for many, the years of post-revolutionary reconstruction represented a major betrayal of the beliefs that had inspired so many people to take up arms in the 1910s. The most enduring novels that have been written about the Mexican Revolution tend to focus, with great bitterness, on the opportunity that was lost to truly transform land ownership and class relations in Mexico. In Juan Rulfo's *Pedro Páramo* (1955), the *hacendado* survives the revolution by buying off the revolutionaries who attempt to occupy La Media Luna, and backs whichever band is the strongest as the conflict unfolds. In Mariano Azuela's *Los de abajo* (1915), there comes a stage where the protagonists appear to lose sight of what they are fighting for, as the bloodbath becomes a way of life. Carlos Fuentes' *La muerte de Artemio Cruz* (1962) reconstructs Cruz's loss of innocence and charts the protagonist's rise to wealth, fame and reactionary politics, in a tragic and critical interpretation of the corrupt and treacherous path many revolutionary leaders pursued once the revolution was over. Ironically, by the time Calles came to power, serving first as president (1924–28) and subsequently as *Jefe Máximo* (Big Boss), controlling the actions of his nominated successive presidents (1928–34), Mexican politics had returned to a path which mirrored that of most countries in the region. Nationalism had emerged, in the wake of the First World War, as a major political force in most Latin American republics, whether they had undergone a major social revolution like Mexico or not.

## The crisis of the 1920s and the emergence of nationalism

The emergence of nationalism was related to the crisis of the 1920s and to the forceful ascendancy of US interventionism in the region. Although many harboured the hope that once the First World War had come to an end, trade relations with Britain would be restored to the way they had been prior to 1914, Britain's standing in the world had changed beyond recognition. The extent to which countries like Argentina, Uruguay and Chile had come to depend on Britain drastically affected their economies after the Treaty of Versailles in 1919. However much their respective oligarchies and British entrepreneurs wanted to return to the 'golden age' of the 1880s–1900s, the economic context of post-war Britain made such a dream impossible. The British economy was no longer in a position to allow its banks and companies either to invest in Latin America or to purchase Latin American primary products to the extent they had done before. Although the rise of US economic penetration kept the neocolonial order going, this did not entail a straightforward transfer of trading partners from Britain to the United States. Those Latin American companies and *haciendas* that had become entirely dependent on British demand went into recession. The rise of US hegemony prevented the neocolonial order from collapsing for another ten years, but the first clear signs that monoculture and an excessive dependency on external market forces could be a risky and dangerous business had become too strong to ignore. The rise of nationalist political movements owed much to this daunting realisation.

However, there were other issues at stake. The rise of the middle classes in the cities had started to have an impact on the very fabric of the political class. The traditional landowners and oligarchs began to be replaced by less affluent politicians who, in many cases, felt closer ties to the aggrieved working classes. Social unrest was on the rise as well. In spite of the brutal repression that had been employed over the previous two decades, strikes were increasing. The example offered by the 1917 Russian Revolution represented both a threat and an inspiration to a political class which was perfectly aware of the similarities that existed between most Latin American countries and the Tsarist Russia that had been destroyed by the Bolshevik Revolution. It is no coincidence that the formation of most of Latin America's communist parties dates from the 1920s. Faced with the post-war crisis, most oligarchical governments opted to adapt to the demands of the period to survive. In other words, the different governments of the day, influenced both by their own ranks and by some dissatisfied high-ranking officers, started to advocate nationalist and protectionist policies. Their rhetoric evolved into one that openly condemned US interventionism. They condemned the power which foreign companies had come to exert on their soil. Arising from both the left and the right of the political spectrum, nationalism, coupled with populist promises aimed at controlling the working classes, became the dominant creed of the late 1920s. Alfredo Zayas (Cuba, 1921–25), Plutarco Elías Calles (Mexico, 1924–28), Hernando Siles (Bolivia, 1925–30), Carlos Ibáñez del Campo (Chile, 1927–31) and Hipólito Yrigoyen during his second term in office (Argentina, 1928–30) are the most obvious examples that come to mind. Although the tendencies of most Latin American countries in the 1920s anticipated the extremes that would become dominant in the 1930s, it would nevertheless take the 1929 Wall Street Crash for them to become profoundly rooted in the political life of the region.

Two European novels that synthesise the problems of Latin America during the mature neocolonial period, in the imaginary countries of Costaguana and Santa Fe de Tierra Firme are Joseph Conrad's *Nostromo* (1904) and Ramón del Valle-Inclán's *Tirano Banderas* (1926). The triumph of the liberal state, the emergence of authoritarian developmentalism, the rise of US interventionism, immigration, the 'social question' and the violence that featured so often during these years are all described, to a greater or lesser extent, by Conrad and Valle-Inclán. D.H. Lawrence, albeit somewhat idiosyncratically, subsequently captured the nationalist mood of 1920s Mexico in his novel *The Plumed Serpent* (1926). Yet what neither they nor their Latin American contemporaries could predict, in spite of the post-war crisis, was the extent to which Latin America would be transformed once the Great Depression kicked in. The neocolonial order collapsed, but what followed was not necessarily a period of emancipation.

## Exhibit 4.1: Excerpt from José Carlos Mariátegui, *7 ensayos de interpretación de la realidad peruana* (Lima: Biblioteca Amauta, 1928)

El grado de desarrollo alcanzado por la industrialización de la agricultura, bajo un régimen y una técnica capitalistas, en los valles de la costa, tiene su principal factor en el interesamiento del capital británico y norteamericano en la producción peruana de azúcar y algodón. De la extensión de estos cultivos no es un agente primario la aptitud industrial ni la capacidad capitalista de los terratenientes. Estos dedican sus tierras a la producción de algodón y caña financiados o habilitados por fuertes firmas exportadoras.

Las mejores tierras de los valles de la costa están sembradas de algodón y caña, no precisamente porque sean apropiadas sólo a estos cultivos, sino porque únicamente ellos importan, en la actualidad, a los comerciantes ingleses y yanquis. El crédito agrícola, subordinado absolutamente a los intereses de estas firmas,…no impulsa ningún otro cultivo. Los de frutos alimenticios, destinados al mercado interno, están generalmente en manos de pequeños propietarios y arrendatarios. Sólo en los valles de Lima, por la vecindad de mercados urbanos de importancia, existen fundos extensos dedicados por sus propietarios a la producción de frutos alimenticios. En las haciendas algodoneras o azucareras, no se cultiva estos frutos, en muchos casos, ni en la medida necesaria para el abastecimiento de la propia población rural.

El mismo pequeño propietario, o pequeño arrendatario, se encuentra empujado al cultivo del algodón por esta corriente que tan poco tiene en cuenta las necesidades particulares de la economía nacional. El desplazamiento de los tradicionales cultivos alimenticios por el del algodón en las campiñas de la costa donde subsiste la pequeña propiedad, ha constituido una de las causas más visibles del encarecimiento de las subsistencias en las poblaciones de la costa… La producción de algodón no está regida por ningún criterio de economía nacional. Se produce para el mercado mundial, sin un control que prevea en el interés de esta economía, las posibles bajas de los precios derivados de períodos de crisis industrial o de superproducción algodonera…

El suelo del país no produce aún todo lo que la población necesita para su subsistencia… Un interés urgente…de la economía peruana exige, desde hace mucho tiempo, que el país produzca el trigo necesario para el pan de su población. Si este objetivo hubiese sido alcanzado, el Perú no tendría ya que seguir pagando al extranjero doce o más millones de soles al año por el trigo que consumen las ciudades de la costa.

¿Por qué no se ha resuelto este problema de nuestra economía?… [L]a resistencia a una solución, se encuentra en la estructura misma de la economía peruana. La economía del Perú, es una economía colonial. Su movimiento, su desarrollo, están subordinados a los intereses…de los mercados de Londres y de Nueva York. Estos mercados miran en el Perú un depósito de materias primas y una plaza para sus manufacturas. La agricultura peruana obtiene, por eso, créditos y transportes sólo para los productos que puede ofrecer con ventaja en los grandes mercados. La finanza extranjera se interesa un día por el caucho, otro día por el algodón, otro día por el azúcar. El día en que Londres puede recibir un producto a mejor precio y en cantidad suficiente de la India o del Egipto, abandona instantáneamente a su propia suerte a sus proveedores del Perú. Nuestros latifundistas, nuestros terratenientes, cualesquiera que sean las ilusiones que se hagan de su independencia, no actúan en realidad sino como intermediarios o agentes del capitalismo extranjero.

## Exhibit 4.2: Excerpt from Emiliano Zapata, *Plan de Ayala* (Morelos, Mexico: 25 November 1911)

5  La Junta Revolucionaria del Estado de Morelos no admitirá transacciones ni componendas hasta no conseguir el derrocamiento de los elementos dictatoriales de Porfirio Díaz y de Francisco I. Madero, pues la Nación está cansada de hombres falsos y traidores que hacen promesas como libertadores y al llegar al poder, se olvidan de ellas y se constituyen en tiranos.

6  Como parte adicional del plan que invocamos, hacemos constar: que los terrenos, montes y aguas que hayan usurpado los hacendados, científicos o caciques a la sombra de la justicia venal, entrarán en posesión de esos bienes inmuebles desde luego, los pueblos o ciudadanos que tengan sus títulos, correspondientes a esas propiedades, de las cuales han sido despojados por mala fe de nuestros opresores, manteniendo a todo trance, con las armas en las manos, la mencionada posesión, y los usurpadores que se consideren con derecho a ellos lo deducirán ante los tribunales especiales que se establezcan al triunfo de la Revolución.

7  En virtud de que la inmensa mayoría de los pueblos y ciudadanos mexicanos no son más dueños que del terreno que pisan sin poder mejorar en nada su condición social ni poder dedicarse a la industria o a la agricultura, por estar monopolizadas en unas cuantas manos, las tierras, montes y aguas; por esta causa, se expropiarán, previa indemnización, de la tercera parte de esos monopolios, a los poderosos propietarios de ellos, a fin de que los pueblos y ciudadanos de México, obtengan ejidos, colonias, fundos legales para pueblos o campos de sembradura o de labor y se mejore en todo y para todo la falta de prosperidad y bienestar de todos los mexicanos.

8  Los hacendados, científicos o caciques que se opongan directa o indirectamente al presente Plan, se nacionalizarán sus bienes y las dos terceras partes que a ellos correspondan, se destinarán para indemnizaciones de guerra, pensiones de viudas y huérfanos de las víctimas que sucumban en las luchas del presente Plan.

*Source:* Jesús Silva Herzog, *Breve historia de la Revolución mexicana*, Vol. 1 (Mexico City: Fondo de Cultura Económica, 1973), pp. 286–93.

# Topics for discussion in class

■ Provide a summary, in your own words, of the key points Mariátegui makes in Exhibit 4.1, regarding the impact of the neocolonial order in Peru.

■ Why does Mariátegui blame Peru's export economy for the misuse of the country's agricultural resources?

■ What points, raised in Exhibit 4.1, can be seen to be under attack in Exhibit 4.2?

■ In Exhibit 4.2, what does Zapata mean by 'ejidos, colonias, fundos legales'?

■ Provide a summary, in your own words, of article 6 of the Plan de Ayala.

■ In article 7, Zapata states that only a third of the large haciendas will be confiscated and redistributed among the peasants. Does article 8 confirm that his intentions were to confiscate and redistribute all of the large estates?

# Topics for essays and presentations

Making use of the recommended texts (see Further reading, p. 161) and/or others that may be available to you in your local library, write an essay/give a seminar presentation on **one** of the following topics.

1  Explain how the export economy model became hegemonic in late nineteenth-century Latin America, with reference to *at least two* case studies.

2  Analyse US interventionism in **one** of the following countries: Cuba, Haiti, the Dominican Republic, Panama, Nicaragua (1898–1934).

3  Account for the long duration of the Mexican Revolution (1910–20).

4  Discuss the emergence of the women's movement in **two** of the following countries *c.*1910–*c.*1930: Argentina, Brazil, Chile, Peru, Venezuela, Uruguay.

## CHAPTER 5

World context

The years between the 1929 Wall Street Crash and the end of the Second World War (1939–45) were ones of great upheaval throughout the world. Most countries' economies were devastated by the Great Depression that succeeded the crash. Extremist ideologies such as communism and fascism became particularly influential as nationalist leaders rose to power, benefiting from the popular discontent provoked by the world recession. The rise of Adolf Hitler in Germany, Benito Mussolini in Italy and Joseph Stalin in the Soviet Union, along with the Spanish Civil War (1936–39), were all events that characterised the polarities and violence of this period. It would take six years of global warfare for many of the issues that had plunged the world into such extremes to be resolved. Thereafter, the age of European imperialism drew to a close with the emergence of forceful independence movements in Africa and Asia. Nevertheless, aided by the US Marshall Plan, the reconstruction of post-war Europe and Japan enabled those countries that had been

# Reaction and revolution (1930–1970)

The 1929 Wall Street Crash signalled the end of the neocolonial order. The subsequent boom and bust cycles caused by the Second World War (1939–45) confirmed to the Latin American political elite that the time had come to abandon the export-led economic model. While the Depression ushered in a period of populist–nationalist authoritarianism, most governments responded to the severe economic crises by encouraging import-substituting industrialisation (ISI) and import-substituting agriculture (ISA). By the 1950s, most Latin American countries had become inward-looking, and it was only in the 1960s that moves were made to open up their economies once more. Nonetheless, interventionist states had been formed with large bureaucracies, and authoritarianism remained a common feature as the Cold War inspired the United States to prevent the spread of communism by backing right-wing dictatorships and the Soviet Union to support the Cuban Revolution.

## The 1929 Wall Street Crash and its consequences

It is difficult to overstate the importance of the stock market crash on Wall Street, in New York, in October 1929. In Latin America it brought a dramatic end to the neocolonial order and, paired destroyed by the conflict to recover. By 1970, nations such as Britain, Germany and Japan had booming economies once more and remained among the richest in the world. However, two world powers had emerged from the Second World War: the United States and the Soviet Union. In the wake of the division of Germany and the Chinese Revolution (1945–49), the Cold War gathered momentum, with the outbreak of the Korean War (1950–53). The world was divided into capitalist and communist blocs. With the United States striving to contain the spread of communism, and the USSR attempting to promote it, the following four decades (1950–90) were characterised by numerous contained conflicts in the so-called Third World, in which the two superpowers clashed with each other while avoiding direct confrontation.

with the subsequent effect the Second World War would have on world trade, would lead to a major change in the management of the different countries' economies in the region. The crash led to a catastrophic reduction in consumer demand. The main importers of the neocolonial order found themselves unable or unwilling to continue building stocks of primary products. Between 1928 and 1932, the unit value of Latin American exports fell by more than 50 per cent. Although the prices of imports also fell, most Latin American countries were no longer in a position to pay for them, having lost their main source of income.

Badly hit by the Depression, many British and US banks requested the immediate repayment of the loans they had extended to Latin America. Unable to respond to this demand, most republics (with the exceptions of Argentina and Haiti) found themselves defaulting on the payment of their external debt, finding it impossible to raise further credit abroad. Most Latin American currencies were devalued. The dependency on export economies, monoculture and agriculture had proved fatal faced with the Great Depression. Chile suffered an 83 per cent fall in purchasing power of exports. Export prices went on falling until 1934, and it was only after five years of acute recession that a new cycle began. Nonetheless, the shock of the crash significantly altered the relationship between Latin America's economies and the world market.

In response to the crisis, most Latin American governments had no option but to pursue economic policies that fostered import-substituting industrialisation (ISI) and, in the case of Central America and the Caribbean, import-substituting agriculture (ISA). It became imperative to find the means to replace over forty years of dependency with a self-sufficient national economy. The reliance on the import of manufactured goods from Britain and the United States needed to be curtailed through the development of national industries. The problems that stemmed from monoculture had to be balanced with an active encouragement of agricultural diversification that would enable the different republics to provide their population with basic food commodities. ISI became the means to combat in Mexico and South America an over-dependency on industrial imports, and to correct a situation whereby monoculture had led certain countries to import primary products (wheat, for example) that had been neglected through the expansion of export-orientated *hacienda* production.

Free market economics was replaced by a tendency to favour protectionist policies. In most Latin American countries there was a significant rise in tariffs on imports, aimed at safeguarding the development of their nations' emergent industries. The pursuit of protectionist policies came hand in hand with indirect State intervention, leading to the formation of an increasingly powerful State. This led to the development of a large State bureaucracy, but it also led to the creation of State agencies aimed at promoting the formation of new manufacturing activities, such as the CORFO (the Chilean *Corporación de Fomento de la Producción*), set up in 1939. There was also an increase in direct State intervention. The most obvious example was the 1938 nationalisation of the oil industry in Mexico. Highly controversial at the time, Mexican public ownership of what had been mainly US oil refineries based in Mexico represented a bold step in what was perceived to be a bid to achieve full economic independence on the part of a Latin American country.

Representative of the kind of industrial activity that was pursued in Mexico and South America in the 1930s, in the hope of fostering both ISI and ISA, was the construction industry, in particular the transport system. While by the 1930s the railway boom was over, the development of the road system was just starting. Characteristic of 1930s economic policies, the roads that were built were generally financed by the State. This was a popular and nationalistic move, as only local raw materials were used and much-needed employment was generated. In the long run, these were highly successful and noteworthy ventures. The network of roads permitted isolated regions to market their agricultural surplus and to contribute to the required growth of domestic use agriculture (DUA).

Although the 1930s witnessed a major shift in Latin America's economies away from the export sector and towards ISI and/or ISA, their slow recovery, only emerging in the late 1930s, was still based on the traditional export sector. However, the export economies of the 1930s were different from those of the neocolonial order. Monoculture had been replaced by diversification. In Brazil, cotton was grown alongside its traditional export products. In Costa Rica, cacao was grown on the abandoned banana plantations. Moreover, a new trade partner surfaced in the mid 1930s, contributing to this recovery of the export sector: Nazi Germany. By 1938, 10.3 per cent of all Latin American exports were being shipped to Germany. Germany was also supplying 17.1 per cent of all Latin American imports. The emergence of a new market for coffee allowed the export economies of Brazil, Colombia, Guatemala and Costa Rica to experience a notable recovery in the late 1930s. The 1930s were therefore characterised by a mixed approach to the economy that promoted ISI and/or ISA, while seeking a means to rebuild the export sector.

However, by the 1950s, Latin America was fully committed to ISI, and most governments in the region were particularly outspoken in their condemnation of export-oriented economic principles. As a direct result of the Second World War (1939–45), from the late 1940s to the mid 1950s, a drastic rejection of the old, export-led growth model developed, with the consolidation of the new, inward-looking ISI model of economic growth. This was because the end of the Second World War represented the final blow to the export sector. The Second World War served to demonstrate that economic growth could not continue to depend on an unstable and unpredictable world market. After September 1939, Britain blockaded Germany, preventing trade with the latter from prospering any longer. After the summer of 1940, with Germany and Italy in control of continental Europe, and the British fleet patrolling the Atlantic, Latin America lost its access to the entire European market, with the exception of the British Isles. The loss of the European market enforced the need to foster ISI. Nevertheless, the export economy received a second boom once the United States were drawn into the war in December 1941.

Following the boom-and-bust cycle of 1938–40 came the even more dramatic boom-and-bust cycle of 1941–45. The moment the United States entered the war, significant pressure was placed on Latin America to sever diplomatic and commercial relations with the Axis powers. With the exception of the Southern Cone countries (Argentina, Paraguay and Uruguay), Latin America gave in to US pressure and opted to openly support the Allied forces. Mexico and most Central American and Caribbean states declared war on the Axis powers in 1941, following the US entry into the conflict. Brazil did so in 1942, Bolivia in 1943, Colombia in 1944 and Argentina in 1945. Those countries that supported the Allies quickly benefited from reciprocal preferential treatment. The export sector boomed again, as the United States favoured their economies, generating a high demand for a number of strategic materials. The US-based Export–Import Bank made credit available once more to the Allied Latin American countries, assisting them with numerous projects, including the building of roads, the most famous of which was the Pan-American Highway. Between 1941 and 1945, practically every country in the region experienced export growth with the United States. Brazil's foreign reserves increased by 635 per cent between 1940 and 1945, Colombia's by 540 per cent, Mexico's by 400 per cent, Chile's by 214 per cent, Argentina's by 156 per cent and Peru's by 55 per cent. The main problem with this last export-based boom, apart from the fact that it created a new dependency on the United States, was that it was based on the abnormal context of the war. Once the war came to an end, the demand for the specific strategic products on which the boom had been founded declined dramatically. A fourth export-related crash ensued. Nonetheless, the moves that had been made in the 1930s towards generating ISI and ISA, albeit modest, were sufficient to protect their economies when access to the world market was cut off in 1939–41. The same could be said about the post-Second World War crisis, except that by the time the United Nations Economic Commission for Latin America (ECLA) came into existence in 1948, it was clear to most Latin Americans that it was time to abandon the export sector. While the choices made by the authorities in the 1930s marked an important stepping stone on the way to the intellectual revolution associated with the United Nations ECLA, the explicit development of the import-substitution model came after the Second World War. Inspired by the Argentinean Raúl Prebisch, ECLA stressed the need for the deliberate government promotion of industrialisation as the only means of achieving true economic independence.

The result of ECLA's recommendations and the general pessimism caused by Latin America's recent financial experiences was an extreme reaction against primary exports and an overemphasis on ISI. The 1950–73 post-war reconstruction resulted in a period of unprecedented prosperity and expansion in Europe, the USA and Japan. Aided by the US Marshall Plan, which injected millions of dollars into aiding the reconstruction of those countries that had been badly affected by the war, the developed market economies (DMEs) boomed, with a return to liberal economic principles. The same could not be said for Latin America, where exports fell due to the stress on ISI; and with no equivalent to the Marshall Plan being directed at Latin America, the hoped-for prosperity proved elusive. It was the increasing awareness of the problems that became equated with the extreme ISI model of the 1950s which led to an eventual relaxation of the anti-export bias during the 1960s. However, a large interventionist State, often riddled with corruption, had been formed in most countries, with a vast bureaucracy with links to private businesses. Although the subsequent liberalisation period of 1960–73 proved dynamic, with Latin America's exports of manufactured goods expanding at a yearly rate of 11 per cent (manufactured goods came to account for 21 per cent of total exports in 1973), the 1973–74 oil crisis represented another blow to the region's sustained development.

## Land of dictators

The crisis that succeeded the Wall Street Crash, coming as it did at a time when nationalism had become a powerful force and the unresolved 'social question' was becoming particularly explosive, contributed significantly to the polarisation of politics which characterised the 1930s. With the exceptions of Juan Vicente Gómez's government in Venezuela and that of the embryonic Mexican *Partido Revolucionario Institucional* (founded as *Partido Nacional Revolucionario* in 1928, becoming the PRI in 1946), most 1920s governments collapsed in the early 1930s, overthrown, in their majority, by military *coups d'état.* Representative of the so-called age of extremes, most Latin American countries were ruled either by authoritarian parties or military dictators. While fascism and Nazism surfaced with extraordinary vigour in continental Europe, in Latin America a parallel stress on a populist and authoritarian brand of nationalism became hegemonic.

Although it is tempting to generalise, the authoritarian regimes that surfaced in most Latin American countries were by no means the same. In the same way that European fascism acquired different characteristics in Hitler's Germany, Mussolini's Italy and Franco's Spain, in Latin America the populist nationalistic dictators and governments that came to the fore provided, in each case, their own distinctive brand of authoritarianism. For the sake of simplification, the 1930s–1950s witnessed the emergence of four different kinds of regimes, all of which were markedly different from each other. There were military governments with fascist tendencies, such as those led by Rafael Leonidas Trujillo Molina (Dominican Republic, 1930–61), Maximiliano Hernández Martínez (El Salvador, 1931–44), Jorge Ubico (Guatemala 1931–44) and Juan Perón (Argentina, 1945–55). There were civilian-led governments with fascist tendencies, such as those of Arturo Alessandri (Chile, 1932–36), who renounced his past radicalism during his second term in office, and José María Velasco Ibarra (five times president of Ecuador, 1934–35, 1944–47, 1952–56,

1960–61, 1968–72). There were reformist socialistic authoritarian governments, such as those led by Getulio Vargas (Brazil, 1930–45, 1950–54) (which also displayed fascist tendencies at times!), Lázaro Cárdenas (Mexico, 1934–40), David Toro (Bolivia, 1936–37) and Juan José Arévalo (Guatemala, 1945–50). And there were troubled democracies which exceptionally avoided the onslaught of authoritarian politics, despite numerous problems, such as Colombia (1930–53), Haiti (1934–56) and Costa Rica (1919 to the present).

In those republics where the authoritarian governments failed to consolidate their hold on their respective countries, these were years of great instability, with numerous *coups d'état* and frequent changes of government. In Ecuador, there were fourteen different presidents between 1931 and 1940. In Peru, between 1930 and 1956, there were four different military dictatorships, two major coups (1930 and 1948) and one democratic government (José Luis Bustamante, 1945–48). The founder and leader of the APRA (American Popular Revolutionary Alliance), Víctor Raúl Haya de la Torre, spent most of these years either in prison or in exile, depending on the greater or lesser degree of openness of the successive military regimes, and violence paired with repression was the order of the day.

Attempts to bring back democratic practices also characterised this period during the brief spells between the fall of one dictator and the rise of another. In Venezuela, a popular revolt in 1945 brought Rómulo Betancourt to the presidential seat, inaugurating what could be viewed as a characteristic brief transition to democracy. The novelist Rómulo Gallegos, author of *Doña Bárbara* (1926), a particularly original and vivid recreation of *hacienda* life and conflict set in the Llanos, went on to win the 1947 elections at the head of *Acción Democrática,* only to be overthrown ten months later by another military coup.

Echoing the importance of constitutionalism during the early national period, democratic values were equally recognised, albeit in rhetorical terms, even by some of the most authoritarian regimes of the 1930s and 1950s. Getulio Vargas claimed that in Brazil his *Estado Novo* (New State) was 'a new kind of democracy'. In many cases, the imposition of dictatorships did not entail an end to elections either. The facade of democracy was maintained, while elections were carefully managed so that the dictator or the governing party was guaranteed a secure victory. In Mexico, the PNR (subsequently PRI) won every presidential election (held every six years, as stipulated in the 1917 Constitution, with the re-election of the president becoming illegal) from 1928 to 2000.

Moreover, there were numerous cases of governments that were authoritarian in their dealings with the communist opposition, but who were, nonetheless, prepared to uphold free elections for those parties not deemed to be extremist. Gabriel González Videla's 'democratic' government (Chile, 1946–52), was particularly heavy-handed in the way it dealt with the communists, as evidenced in several of the poems Pablo Neruda directed at him in his *Canto general* (1950). Having come to power on the back of a strategically important alliance with the left, González Videla outlawed the Communist Party in his so-called 1948 *Ley maldita* (Accursed Law), set up a concentration camp for left-wing militants and pursued a more conservative agenda.

Nevertheless, when the 1952 elections took place, he did not prevent a reconstructed democratic General Ibáñez del Campo from being voted to the presidency. Similarly, General Eleazar López Contreras (Venezuela,

> ### descamisados
> Literally, 'the shirtless ones'; refers to the Peronist popular classes.

1935–41) exiled forty-seven critics in 1937 on charges of communism, while ensuring that General Isaías Medina Angarita could win the 1941 elections.

The most obvious example of the ambiguities and paradoxes to be found when grappling with the nature of Latin American authoritarianism (*c.*1930–*c.*1960) revolves around the increasing participation of women in politics during these years. Against a backdrop of relative forms of dictatorship, and notwithstanding a generally fraudulent electoral process, women gained the right to vote at the same time as suffrage restrictions (literacy, property, etc.) were gradually abandoned. Female suffrage occurred between 1932 and 1955, a period in which most Latin American republics were ruled by authoritarian governments. Representative of the complexity of Latin American politics at the time is the role played by Eva Duarte (Evita) during Juan Perón's dictatorship.

Perón was a high-ranking officer who had spent several years in Europe during the 1930s. Influenced by some of the key teachings of Italian fascism, when he joined the 1943 military coup that overthrew the Concordancia government of Ramón Castillo, he became, as head of the Ministry of Labour and Welfare he created, an outspoken defender of the urban proletariat. This was a common feature of populist authoritarianism as it broke away from the oligarchic traditions of the 1900s–1920s, actively seeking to secure the support of the growing industrial working classes, through co-option and patronage. His progressive social policies included establishing the National Institute of Social Security, the implementation of a collective bargaining policy, the promotion of a dramatic rise in workers' wages, the investment of a significant sum of money to build inexpensive housing, and the provision for compulsory, annual, paid holidays. Typical of 1930s–1940s populism, Perón encouraged the formation of unions, while ensuring that these were controlled by a reconstituted General Confederation of Labour (CGT), dominated by his own supporters. He co-opted the majority of unions, establishing a particularly resilient network of patronage that granted the workers numerous rights in exchange for their outright support. Those who did not support him were beaten up or imprisoned. Perón's endeavours as Minister of Labour transformed him into the hero of the working classes. While serving as vice president, he was imprisoned in the 1945 coup led by a group of dissatisfied generals. The *descamisados*, encouraged by Eva Duarte, a twenty-six-year-old radio performer and friend of the colonel, took to the streets of Buenos Aires, demanding his release. Once freed, Perón married Evita and became president, gaining 54 per cent of the vote in the 1946 elections.

Perón's government (1946–55) went on to consolidate the populist 'worker-friendly' agenda he had pursued as Minister of Labour. It also became remarkably repressive. The anti-*peronista* press was censored, closed down or taken over. A private army of thugs, the National Liberating Alliance, was used to intimidate all political opposition. The federal police force became a much-feared institution, with imprisonment, torture,

Eva Perón

purges and exile becoming commonplace. And yet, at the same time, with Evita by his side, women were included in the suffrage in 1947. The Peronist Feminist Party was formed, the number of women admitted to universities more than doubled and a wide range of women's centres were established in the poorer neighbourhoods, providing medical, social and legal services. Her philanthropic Social Aid Foundation distributed medicine, clothes and food to needy people throughout Argentina, and by the time the 1951 elections took place, seven women senators and twenty-four women deputies were elected, the largest female representation in any government in the whole of the Americas.

Notwithstanding these achievements, Evita's feminism has since been the source of much controversy. In part, this has arisen from her support of Perón. However, most importantly, the controversy has revolved around the very nature of her feminist outlook. Evita was the leading proponent of a Latin American brand of feminism known as *Marianismo*. Emerging from the Latin American cult of the Virgin Mary (*Marianismo* originates from María), this was a belief which took as its main premise that mother- hood resulted in women being superior to men, both morally and physically. The experience of motherhood entailed qualities such as caring and self-sacrifice that were unique to women. A *Marianista* agenda was one that viewed the woman's role as mother as all-important. The inferior men were allowed by the women to carry out all the secondary tasks, such as earn the bread, serve in the army or pursue a career in politics. The women controlled them within the domestic realm, governing the home in a femi- nine, motherly and caring way, extending their influence in society through more informal fora, such as charitable organisations. Men were viewed as children who needed to be humoured and reprimanded. Using the home front as the starting point of all progress, it was women's duty to guide their men, to motivate them to work hard and succeed in their jobs, while they nurtured the new generation and spread their female moral high ground in the nursery, the school and at charity events. Subsequent generations of feminists would condemn *Marianismo* as a disguised form of *machismo* for the way in which it paradoxically limited women's role in society.

Nevertheless, Evita's untimely death in 1952, at the age of thirty-three, resulted in a process of deification that gave her a mythical importance no other woman has succeeded in achieving in Latin America to this day. Her story, from rags to riches, coupled with her beauty, charisma and the extraordinary impact she had on women's lives in Argentina, not only inspired successive generations of Latin Americans, but became acknowledged throughout the world.

Many aspects of Perón's rule were shared by the numerous authoritarian regimes that surfaced in the 1930s–1950s. More often than not they were developmentalist, and through the formation of a powerful state they encouraged ISI and/or ISA. In Honduras, Tiburcio Carías Andino, during the sixteen years he was in power (1932–48), actively promoted road building, the modernisation of agriculture, stockbreeding and the construction of schools. They were praetorian in their outlook, granting the armed forces a privileged status in society, while employing systematic repression as the most effective means of guaranteeing their permanence in power. The emergence of State-inspired paramilitary groups was also a generalised phenomenon. Examples of paramilitary activity extend from Alessandri's Republican Militia in Chile (1932–36) to the armed bands depicted in Graham Greene's novelistic account of the persecution priests were subjected to in Mexico during Calles' *Maximato* in *The Power and the Glory* (1940).

Their longevity depended on how successful they were in pleasing oligarchical and popular interests at the same time. The common means by which the oligarchy's support was obtained was through combining private business interests with a State-run system. Needless to say, corruption was rife, as one State or another granted influential businessmen preferential treatment in State-inspired ventures such as the construction industry. The common means of appeasing the working classes was through populist politics that co-opted them through patronage, stifling opposition and plurality with State-run unions. In Brazil, under **Getulio Vargas**, the working day was fixed at eight hours, an impressive social security system was established, a minimum wage came into force and the working class lost its freedom of expression, as all trade unions became official agencies run by the Ministry of Labour. In those cases where this balancing act between pleasing business interests and pursuing a populist agenda floundered, the outcome was generally an oligarchic-backed coup. In Bolivia, Colonel David Toro's commitment to 'socialisation' (1936–37), with its corresponding land reform and assault on the interests of the great landowners, led to his inevitable overthrow by army officer Germán Busch (1937–39).

Most of these authoritarian regimes avoided ideological terms, such as fascism or socialism, and claimed to represent a nationalist platform that was solely interested in the good of the mother country. Antipolitics became an essential ingredient in most

of 17 million hectares of land, with the andholdings (*ejidos*), the 1938 nationalisa-  t support towards the Spanish Republican 9). However, pragmatism prevailed when it  ondemnation of the Axis powers, Cárdenas g the Allied boycott. Rodolfo Usigli's play *El* l politicians as liars and performers, inter- of the double standards of 1930s populism. tality in most of Latin America. Individual :d or forced into exile. The Spanish novelist, ate which the Basque refugee, Jesús de o's dictatorship in *Galíndez* (1990). In the re often fed to the sharks. Organised oppo- was forcefully repressed. Under General a (1940–42), the horrific 'Catavi massacre' :ico, ostensibly the least tyrannical of Latin er 1968, 325 students (according to official  the square of Tlatelolco (Mexico City), for  the eve of the Olympics. For disturbing :arlos Monsivais, *Días de guardar* (1970), 0), Carlos Fuentes, *Los años con Laura Díaz* (1991). It is not surprising that so much of  hereafter was concerned with the themes of : two novels that deal with the subject of  *ñor presidente* (1946) and Gabriel García :ssential reading.

the perpetuation of authoritarian regimes degree, Soviet interventionism. One of the : was the emergence of two world powers, h of which became notoriously wary of the SA dedicated to containing the spread of  China prepared to support it, the Cold War he Korean War (1950–53). Fear that an esca- nic or nuclear war that would destroy the at avoided direct confrontation. It became  flicts in which the United States and the de, without ever actually officially fighting

In Latin America, fear of the spread of communism resulted in a US policy that actively supported military right-wing dictatorships. The first casualty of the Cold War was the Guatemalan government of Jacobo Arbenz (1950–54). His marked communist

*Getulio Vargas (1883–1954)*

### Alfredo Stroessner (1912–2006)

Born in Encarnación, Stroessner was educated at the Military College in Asunción. He acquired a heroic status for his actions during the Chaco War (1932–35), becoming chief of the armed forces in 1951. In 1954 he led the coup that overthrew Federico Chávez's government and established one of the longest-lasting dictatorships in twentieth-century Latin America (1954–89). Stroessner used the army and the Colorado Party to cement his personalist rule. Repression and censorship were used consistently to crush all opposition. Numerous notorious dictators and Nazi war criminals found refuge in Stroessner's Paraguay. His rabid anticommunism also earned him the support of the United States throughout his years in office within the context of the Cold War. Deposed in 1989 by his second-in-command, Stroessner went into exile in Brazil, where he died in 2006.

(some would prefer nationalist) tendencies, exemplified by the Agrarian Law of July 1952, which entailed the nationalisation and redistribution of foreign-owned properties, including the plantations of the United Fruit Company, alarmed Washington. In July 1954, the USA backed the overthrow of Arbenz by a military junta, replacing him with Colonel Carlos Castillo Armas as a US puppet president. Similarly, the USA supported the long-lasting dictatorship of General **Alfredo Stroessner** (Paraguay, 1954–89). And in September 1957, the USA assisted the rise and perpetuation in power of the dictator François Duvalier in Haiti (1957–71). Following 'Papa Doc' Duvalier's death, the USA went on to support his son, Jean-Claude Duvalier (1971–86). By 1965, as outlined in President Lyndon B. Johnson's 'Johnson Doctrine', the United States openly awarded itself the right to intervene to suppress any 'communist' activity in Latin America. The US Central Intelligence Agency (CIA) went on to orchestrate a number of *coups d'état*, including the September 1973 military overthrow of Salvador Allende's government which placed General Augusto Pinochet at the head of the Chilean state (1973–90). President Franklin D. Roosevelt's well-meaning 1945 'Good Neighbour Policy', which espoused the view that no American state should interfere in the affairs of another, did not prosper once the Cold War got under way. The one event in twentieth-century Latin American history that was to throw US paranoia about communism into a state of hysteria was the 1956–59 Cuban Revolution.

## The Cuban Revolution (1956–1959)

In Cuba, the Wall Street Crash resulted in a violent change of government. The dictator Gerardo Machado (1925–33), unable to control the high levels of popular discontent and unrest the Depression (paired with his brutality) had generated in the island, fled Cuba in August 1933, as Havana mobs looted his homes. The provisional, 'made in Washington' government that was formed under Carlos Manuel de Céspedes was then overthrown, only twenty-one days later, by Sergeant Fulgencio Batista. Batista became strongman-cum-dictator from 1934 to 1959, allowing an eight-year 'democratic' interlude to take place from 1944 to 1952.

military dictatorships, since they argued that they were above the dirty world of parliamentary politics, which they equated with civilian-led oligarchical system of the 1920s. In some instances, where individual dictators succeeded in hanging on to power for a longer period of time, personality became a regular feature, developed through the building of monuments, the naming of squares and streets, and the organisation of public holidays and parades. Leonidas Trujillo Molina, dictator of the Dominican Republic from 1930 until his assassination in 1961 (Mario Vargas Llosa's novel *La Fiesta del Chivo* (2000) provides a controversial account of his murder), renamed Santo Domingo after himself, calling it Ciudad Trujillo. In his own decrees (see Exhibit 5.1), he went on to refer to the period of his government as 'the Trujillo era'. In Nicaragua, under the Somoza dynasty (Anastasio Somoza 1936–56), Luis Somoza (1956–63) and Anastasio Somoza Jr (1966–79)), the extent to which the Somoza name was celebrated in monuments, streets and stadiums is beautifully captured in Ernesto Cardenal's poem *Hora desveliza la estatua de Somoza en el Estadio Somoza* (1951). Almost inevitably, these dictators ended up being presented as the living personification of their respective countries, and any criticism of them was viewed not only as subversive, but also as unpatriotic.

The nationalist rhetoric of their regimes hid a less patriotic and more pragmatic agenda, which sought to avoid confrontation with the United States. In spite of Perón's nationalistic, anti-imperialist discourse, the US-owned Standard Oil was allowed to renew its activities in Argentina in 1953, and key foreign-owned industries, such as sugar refining and meat packing, were not nationalised. In Mexico, Lázaro Cárdenas' achievements (1934–40) included an agrarian

Cuba's post-Wall Street Crash experience was entirely different from that of other Latin American countries. The move towards ISI and ISA that surfaced throughout the region (1930s–1950s) was absent in the island. Although the Depression had a disastrous effect on the Cuban economy, Cuba's recovery was achieved through the very same export sector that had suffered so intensely as a result of the 1929 debacle. By the 1950s, Cuba was once more buying 75 per cent of its imports from the United States, with over 65 per cent of its sugar exports going to the USA in return. Both monoculture and dependency were as great in the 1950s as they had been during the neocolonial period. The great economic contrasts that existed between the few and the many towards the end of the neocolonial period had grown even greater in Cuba. More Cadillacs were apparently sold in Havana in 1954 than in any other city in the world, and yet most of them belonged to not more than one hundred families. Unemployment was high, illiteracy was generalised and health care remained a privilege for those who could afford it.

It was a year after Batista's second coup of March 1952, and on the 100th anniversary of José Martí's birth, that Fidel Castro, a twenty-six-year-old Cuban lawyer, attempted to overthrow the dictator by storming the Moncada barracks in Santiago de Cuba on 26 July 1953. Castro's assault failed. He was taken prisoner, put on trial, sentenced and eventually pardoned under an amnesty. At the time, Castro was an ardent defender of democracy who called for the re-establishment of the 1940 Constitution. However, Castro's world view started to change in 1955, when he went to Mexico to prepare for a new revolution. In Mexico, he met the charismatic and inspiring freelance Argentinean revolutionary, Dr Ernesto Guevara, whose political awakening is captured in Walter Salles' film *The Motorcycle Diaries* (2004). Guevara's constant use of the very Argentinean 'Che' before and after every other word led his Cuban acquaintances to call him 'Che' Guevara, and he eventually became known quite simply as *El Che*. With Che Guevara by his side, Castro launched his second attempt to topple Batista, sailing back to Cuba in the autumn of 1956. Employing guerrilla warfare, Castro, his brother Raúl, Guevara and an ever-increasing army, took control of the Sierra Maestra mountains in the eastern part of the island, and over a period of three years expanded their circle of influence until, on 1 January 1959, the Batista regime collapsed.

Once in power, supported by the majority of Cubans, Castro initiated his lengthy period as dictator (1959 to the present), by implementing a dramatic transformation of the economic and social structures on the island. As expressed in *The First Declaration of Havana* (see Exhibit 5.2), Castro condemned the exploitation of underdeveloped countries by 'imperialist capital', and his regime was, in its origins, determined to eradicate the levels of poverty, inequality and social injustice that characterised the island in 1959. During the first eighteen months of Castro's regime, foreign-owned estates and industries were nationalised. The large sugar plantations were turned into co-operatives and State-owned farms, with a stress on collectivising the means of production. The emphasis that was placed on both education and health was awe-inspiring. Before 1959, 40 per cent of children aged six to sixteen did not receive any form of education. By 1961, the year in which Castro publicly proclaimed his allegiance to Marxism-Leninism, this proportion had been reduced to 20 per cent. Moreover, the 1961 literacy campaign reduced illiteracy from 23 per cent to 3.9 per cent. By 1965, the percentage of children attending school was well above the Latin American average, by over 50 per cent. Hospitals were built at a breathtaking pace, vaccination campaigns significantly reduced high levels of mortality, and a major effort went into training doctors and nurses in order to replace all those upper middle-class Cubans who had fled to Miami. As expressed in Nicolás Guillén's enduring poem *Tengo* (1964), most Cubans came to feel in the 1960s that, thanks to the Revolution, they had, *'vamos a ver'* (let's see), what they deserved to have.

Needless to say, few of Castro's achievements would have been as dramatic or as long lasting had it not been for the support his regime received from the Soviet Union. Despite Che Guevara's attempts, as Minister of Industry, to diversify the Cuban economy, pursuing an aggressive strategy of ISI, it became evident that Cuba could not end its dependency on the sugar industry. Although Che Guevara became notoriously critical of the Soviet Union, arguing that Cuba should consolidate its independence, following China's model, for Castro and his governing elite a more pragmatic approach towards the economy was all-important. Unable to break away from the bonds of a monoculture economy, Cuba ended up depending heavily on the Soviet Union. The Soviet Union went on to become the island's main buyer of sugar, and Cuba's financial debt to the USSR steadily mounted to billions of dollars.

Following the US-backed overthrow of Arbenz in Guatemala, it seemed appropriate to employ a parallel strategy in Cuba. In April 1961, with the support of the CIA, an invasion of Cuba was attempted by an army of anti-Castro Cuban exiles. This invasion was easily repelled by Castro's militias in the Bay of Pigs. Nonetheless, the prospect of further US-backed attempts to overthrow the regime remained a major cause for concern. In order to guarantee Cuba's independence, Castro actively sought military assistance from the Soviet Union. The Soviet Union satisfied Castro's requests by dispatching arms, including nuclear missiles, to the island. It was in October 1962, when it was brought to President John F. Kennedy's attention that Soviet missiles were being unloaded in Cuba, that what is known as the Cuban missile crisis broke out. Kennedy threatened Nikita Khrushchev with total nuclear war if the Soviet Union did not withdraw the missiles immediately. For two weeks, time stood still while Khrushchev pondered on what action to take, with most Cubans urging the Soviet Union to call Kennedy's bluff. Khrushchev gave in, agreeing to withdraw the missiles as long as the United States agreed, in return, not to invade Cuba again. Peace was maintained, and although the United States imposed a trade embargo in 1962, which remains in effect to this day, no further attempts were made to invade the island. Although the Cuban–Soviet love affair went through a patch of estrangement in the wake of Khrushchev's perceived weakness vis-à-vis the United States, their relationship was rekindled, lasting until the collapse of the Soviet Union in 1991.

During the following two decades, while Castro's revolutionary government was consolidated on the island, and the Cuban health system became the envy of Latin America, Che Guevara led the way in defending the need to export the revolution abroad. He was personally involved in revolutionary activity in the Congo, in Africa, in the mid 1960s; and thereafter, claiming that 'the Andes would become the Sierra

Maestra of Latin America', led a revolutionary expedition to Bolivia in 1967. Che Guevara hoped that the use of guerrilla warfare in Bolivia would generate the same kind of revolutionary support he and Castro had received in Cuba, leading to the eventual fall of capitalism in South America. The Bolivian adventure, however, was a disaster. The revolution did not spread and Che Guevara was tracked down and executed. Freddy Alborta Trigo's photograph of Che's corpse, taken in order to prove to the world that the Bolivian armed forces had indeed killed him, ironically gave the revolutionary a Christ-like image that was to acquire an iconic status only comparable to that of Evita. It is evident that Che's premature death enabled him to become the most idolised revolutionary of the twentieth century.

While Castro persevered in supporting the export of the revolution, sending 20,000 Cuban troops to Angola (Africa) in 1975 to support the Angolan war of independence, by the 1980s he had become more concerned with Cuban affairs. The revolution, with all its extraordinary achievements in the fields of health, education and social equality, and its adamant defence of socialism only a few kilometres from the interventionist Colossus of the North, created, nonetheless, an undemocratic and personalist dictatorship. Praised and idealised in works such as Julio Cortázar's short story 'Reunión' (1966), praised yet criticised in films such as Tomás Gutiérrez Alea's masterpiece *Memorias del subdesarrollo* (1968), and virulently condemned in the songs of Miami-based exiles such as the pop star Gloria Estefan (particularly popular in the 1980s–1990s), the revolution led to the emergence of two Cubas, one on the island, the other in exile. Representative of the repression that characterised Castro's regime was the treatment homosexuals received following the triumph of the revolution. Labour camps were created, to quote Guevara, for 'people who have committed crimes against revolutionary morals'. The horrendous persecution the gay community suffered under Castro would surface in films such as Tomás Gutiérrez Alea's *Fresa y chocolate* (1993) and Julian Schnabel's *Before Night Falls* (2000). Although it would be misleading to equate homophobia with Cuban communism (Manuel Puig's *El beso de la mujer araña* (1976) provides an interesting parallel text, set in Argentina in the mid 1970s), the existence of repression under Castro cannot be overlooked.

## Struggling democracies

Albeit not always long lasting, a number of relatively democratic systems did surface during these years. This can be seen to have been the case in Colombia between 1930 and 1950, and subsequently since 1958. In 1930, the first peaceful transfer of power in the history of Colombia, from Conservative to Liberal rule, took place with the election of Enrique Olaya Herrera (1930–34) to the presidency. The Liberals continued to hang on to power through the electoral process, albeit with some difficulty, until 1946. In 1946, however, following a period of much discontent, corruption and upheaval, including a failed *coup d'état*, the conservative Mariano Ospina Pérez (1946–50) was elected president. The fragile nature of Colombia's democracy was then seriously tested, given that Ospina Pérez's conservative restoration had resulted from the divisions which had surfaced within the liberal camp between the supporters of Gabriel

Turbay and Jorge Eliécer Gaitán, rather than from support of his political agenda. With Gaitán succeeding in uniting the Liberal Party behind him, the already saturated atmosphere of acute antagonism between Liberals and Conservatives became particularly intense. Ospina Pérez's response, decreeing a state of siege in 1947, did not help matters, and when Jorge Eliécer Gaitán was assassinated on 9 April 1948, Bogotá was plunged into an orgy of violence. The *Bogotazo* riot provoked in Bogotá by the news of the assassination was probably the worst in the twentieth-century history of Latin America. It led to major disturbances elsewhere. The situation degenerated in the countryside into an almost permanent state of conflict, labelled '*la violencia*'. With Colombia torn apart by civil war, the repression that ensued under Laureano Gómez (1950–53) effectively ended twenty years of democratic life. The Liberal–Conservative coalition that subsequently overthrew Gómez by force gave way to the bloody dictatorship of General Gustavo Rojas Pinilla (1953–57). Although the path towards democracy was eventually restored under Alberto Lleras Camargo in 1958, a more openly competitive electoral process was not put in place until 1974. Ever since 1958, however, large parts of Colombia have remained dominated by rural guerrilla activity, a situation that would only worsen with the emergence of powerful drug barons in the 1980s.

Bolivia underwent a period of democratic change following the 1952 revolution. Víctor Paz Estenssoro (1952–56, 1960–64), founder and leader of the MNR (National Revolutionary Movement), together with his vice president, Hernán Siles Zuazo (1956–60), consolidated a democratic civilian government with socialist tendencies, which introduced universal suffrage, nationalised the mines and succeeded in implementing a dramatic agrarian reform, involving the break-up of the large *haciendas*, redistributing the land among the peasants. These reforms were all undertaken with the support of the United States, as Paz Estenssoro deliberately combined his 'revolutionary' liberal zeal with a pro-US and anticommunist agenda. However, notwithstanding the twelve years of MNR government, democracy in Bolivia was put on hold once more following the 1964 coup of General René Barrientos (1964–69).

Uruguay experienced a thirty-year spell of democratic practices from 1942 to 1972, standing out for having replaced the president with an original nine-member executive in 1951, an experiment which lasted until 1967. Uruguay was nonetheless different from most Latin American countries because of the democratic foundations José Batlle y Ordóñez had laid during his two terms in office (1903–07 and 1911–15). Under Batlle y Ordóñez, great advances were made in reducing the country's economic dependency within the neocolonial order. Thanks to Batlle y Ordóñez, Uruguay was the first Latin American country to have a welfare state, and by 1929 many Uruguayans enjoyed a good standard of living. It was because of this exceptional past that Uruguay avoided much of the turmoil that surfaced elsewhere following the Wall Street Crash. Nonetheless, authoritarianism did make itself felt under Gabriel Terra (1931–38), and then under his brother-in-law, General Alfredo Baldomir (1938–42), although Baldomir orchestrated a return to the republic's democratic traditions in 1942. Nevertheless, although this period of democracy survived for thirty years, as in Colombia they were not necessarily peaceful years. Inspired by the Cuban Revolution, the 1960s witnessed the emergence of numerous guerrilla movements in Latin America. It was in Uruguay that what was probably Latin America's most famous urban guerrilla organisation came into existence: the Movement of National Liberation, otherwise known as the *Tupamaros*. The *Tupamaros*, who included working-class activists from the poorer districts of Montevideo, as well as middle-class students, professionals and bureaucrats, destabilised society by robbing banks, setting off bombs, seizing business properties and kidnapping influential individuals, including the British ambassador, Geoffrey Jackson, in 1971. Mirroring their activities across the River Plate, in Argentina a parallel guerrilla movement, known as the *Montoneros,* emerged in the late 1960s, and they went as far as kidnapping and executing the former president and dictator General Pedro Aramburu (1955–58), in 1970. In both countries, the escalation of violence was ultimately countered with a return to military rule in the 1970s.

In contrast, Venezuela has experienced the second-longest spell of democracy, after Costa Rica, in twentieth-century Latin America, stretching from 1959 until the present. Nevertheless, like most democracies in the region, Venezuela's has not always been free from trouble. The rioting that hit Caracas on 27 and 28 February 1989, and the brutality with which Carlos Andrés Pérez's government (1988–93) dealt with it, killing over 400 people according to unofficial estimates, provide a less flattering view of Venezuela's democracy. In February 1992, Venezuela came very close to returning to military rule, when Lieutenant Colonel Hugo Chávez Frías launched a *coup d'état* that failed. However, for the purpose of this chapter, there is no doubt that Venezuela's democratic record, benefiting from its thriving oil industry, was among the most promising and stable in the region, even though, as was noted by Rafael Caldera (president in 1969–74 and 1994–99), it was a democracy that failed to provide the majority of Venezuelans with food or 'put a stop to the terrible round of corruption that...eroded the institutional legality of the country'.

Costa Rica remains the country to have enjoyed the longest-lasting democracy in Latin America. Following the Wall Street Crash, when every other Central American country succumbed to the rise of brutal and authoritarian regimes, Costa Rica's democratic institutions survived the 1932 revolution, and went on to become firmly consolidated following José Figueres' election to the presidency in 1953. The situation in Costa Rica came close to degenerating into authoritarian politics when, in 1948, a revolutionary group attempted to topple the elected president, Otilio Ulate. Figueres led the civilian uprising that quelled the revolt and ensured that Ulate remained in place until his term in office was over. Once elected, Figueres went on to govern Costa Rica twice (1953–58 and 1970–74), with an avid commitment to uphold, as he put it, 'the American conceptions of the stability of representative government, the fundamental freedoms, and the respect for human dignity'. As a pragmatic socialist, Figueres succeeded where Arbenz did not in Guatemala, by avoiding confrontational politics. He convinced the United Fruit Company to allow the Costa Rican government a 30 per cent share of its profits, and likewise guaranteed US support (like Paz Estenssoro in Bolivia) through his public condemnation of all dictatorships, including communist ones. Figueres also recaptured the ideals of the 1848 Constitution, abolishing the Costa Rican army. He relied on an Inter-American Treaty of Reciprocal Assistance, backed by the United States and the Organisation of American States (OAS), on the two occasions that

Anastasio Somoza's Nicaragua attempted to invade the country, in 1949 and 1955. Ever since, Costa Rica's democratic practices have become deeply rooted in the country, representing one of the most striking exceptions in a region which, overall, has been characterised by the authoritarianism of its regimes.

## Latin American wars (1932–1969)

From 1930 to 1970, only three major wars broke out in Latin America: the Chaco War (1932–35), the Ecuador–Peru conflict (1941) and the Football (also known as Soccer) War (1969). Of these three wars, only the first one was markedly devastating. The origins of the Chaco War remain, to this day, a matter of controversy. There are three broad interpretations of why the conflict erupted. Bolivian and Paraguayan expansionism in the disputed territory of the Chaco account for the first two. The third blames the British Royal Dutch Shell and the US Standard Oil companies. According to the latter, the prospect of extracting oil in the Chaco led Shell in Paraguay and Standard Oil in Bolivia to pressurise the respective countries, from which they had received numerous privileges, to extend their frontiers in the area in order to expand their own companies' spheres of influence.

The war, which lasted until the 1935 truce, resulted, as confirmed in the 1938 peace treaty, in a Paraguayan victory. Paraguay gained 20,000 square miles. However, the loss of life the war entailed was horrific. Between 60,000 and 70,000 Bolivians died. An estimated 40,000 Paraguayans were killed. There is no doubt that, initially, the odds were stacked in Bolivia's favour to achieve a quick victory. Their troops greatly outnumbered the Paraguayans, their army had been drilled by the German General Hans Kundt, and they had succeeded in importing a large quantity of military equipment left over from the First World War. However, for the Bolivian army of Indians, accustomed to the bleak altitudes of the Andes, the heavy jungles and desert plains of the Chaco proved a powerful obstacle to victory. Decimated by malaria, the Bolivians were eventually defeated by Colonel José Félix Estigarribía's *'corralito'* tactics, which entailed sending small battalions behind the Bolivian forces, cutting off their line of supplies (including water) and communications.

In Bolivia, the defeat ushered in a period of marked instability. From a Paraguayan perspective, the victory gave the military caste the kind of prestige that would enable the veterans of the Chaco War to become the leading figures in the country's political scene. Six of the presidents who held office thereafter, including Stroessner (1954–89), were 'war heroes' from the Chaco War. The suffering and loss caused by the war was to leave, nevertheless, an enduring sense of grief and injustice. This is exemplified in Augusto Roa Bastos' *Hijo de hombre* (1960). In what is one of the greatest novels of the twentieth century, Roa Bastos traces the lives of a group of oppressed and persecuted characters (*c.*1870–*c.*1935), with the climactic chapters taking place during the Chaco War.

The Ecuador–Peru conflict (1941) shared two features with the Chaco War: first, the war was motivated in part by the prospect of drilling for oil in a sparsely inhabited jungle area that would otherwise have attracted scant attention from the two countries' governments; and second, the territory in question had been under dispute since independence, with both countries interpreting colonial demarcations to their advantage. Under Manuel Prado's military government (Peru, 1939–45), against a backdrop of reiterated claims and counterclaims over control of Ecuador's *Oriente* (Amazon) territory, Peruvian troops launched an invasion into the Ecuadorian coastal region of El Oro, in July 1941. Fighting continued until October, although the conflict was not brought to an end until Carlos Arroyo del Río's government (Ecuador, 1940–44) was pressurised into signing the Protocol of Rio de Janeiro in January 1942. In this peace treaty, Ecuador accepted the new frontier which gave Peru around 70,000 square miles of the disputed territory. At the time, with both countries supporting the United States in the Second World War, Washington diplomats exerted significant pressure on the Ecuadorian and Peruvian governments to bring the conflict to a speedy end. Nevertheless, the territory Peru conquered in 1941 has remained disputed ever since. In 1959, President Velasco Ibarra denounced the Rio Protocol and revived Ecuador's claim on the upper Amazon. War would break out once more between Ecuador and Peru in 1995.

The 1969 Football War only lasted five days (14–18 July). Nevertheless, over 4,000 men were killed and at least 100,000 Salvadoreans were left homeless. In this case, migration-related tensions were at the heart of the violence. For several decades, in particular the 1950s and 1960s, overcrowding in El Salvador had resulted in thousands of Salvadoreans moving to neighbouring Honduras. This situation was exacerbated by Colonel Julio Rivera (1961–67) and Colonel Fidel Sánchez Hernández's (1967–72) governments' pursuit of ISI policies, coupled with a major reduction of the labour force employed by the fruit companies in El Salvador. Unemployed and landless, many Salvadorean *campesinos* moved across the border to make a living in underpopulated Honduras. By 1968, there were an estimated 300,000 illegal Salvadorean immigrants in Honduras, and tensions were running high.

There were also economic reasons behind the growing hostility between the two countries. The Central American Common Market (CACM), formed in February 1960, had led to major disparities between the two countries' economies. Industrialisation had succeeded in turning El Salvador's manufacturing sector into the second most important in the region after Guatemala. El Salvador contributed 24 per cent of Central American manufactured goods, compared to Honduras' 7.7 per cent in 1968. Moreover, between 1960 and 1968, Salvadorean exports to Honduras increased by 500 per cent, while Honduran exports to El Salvador only doubled. The resentment Colonel Oswaldo López Arellano's government (Honduras, 1963–70) felt towards neighbouring El Salvador was great. It resented the debt it had incurred with El Salvador, rising to $5 million in 1969, as well as the disparity of wealth between the two countries and the perceived informal invasion of Honduran land by the Salvadorean immigrants.

Against this backdrop of increasing tensions between the two nations, López Arellano's Agrarian Law of July 1968 was formulated. López Arellano decreed that over 80,000 Salvadorean settlers were to be expelled from Honduras at the end of April 1969, and forced to 'return' their lands to the Honduran State for redistribution. When the two countries' soccer teams met in June 1969 to qualify for the 1970 World Cup in Mexico, Honduran troops were forcefully implementing the expulsion law. The three matches El Salvador and Honduras played (0–1, 3–0, 3–2), between 8 and 27 June, led to major clashes between the fans. It was against the backdrop of football violence that, pressurised into adopting a belligerent position by the military and most political parties, as well as stung into action following accusations of cowardice in the press, Sánchez Hernández's government responded to the crisis by invading the Honduran frontier on 14 July.

The war ended promptly, following OAS and US condemnation of the attack. However, while there is no doubt that in El Salvador the conflict was popular and that the nationalistic fervour it generated diverted the population's attention from a number of key domestic problems, its outcomes were far from positive. Both countries lost each other's markets. For El Salvador, this represented a loss of $23 million worth of trade. The return of over 100,000 Salvadoreans from Honduras seriously exacerbated the social crisis in the countryside. The number of landless and unemployed peasants rose to spectacular figures (41 per cent of the population in 1975), leading to major agrarian discontent, the emergence of guerrilla activity and government repression in the 1970s.

## Population

The problems of population pressure that provoked, in part, the 1969 Football War were representative of more general trends that characterised Latin America's development (*c*.1930–*c*.1970). One of the most striking features of Latin America since 1930 has been the dramatic growth of the population and the impact this has had on the region's societies. From 1930 to 1990, in a time span of only sixty years, the population of Latin America quadrupled, from round 110 million to 450 million. Population growth was higher in Latin America than anywhere else in the world, except Africa (that went from 155 to 642 million). The problems this growth generated were further exacerbated by a significant decline in mortality rates, and a generalised pattern of migration away from the countryside to the cities.

While birth rates increased, so did life expectancy. The creation of welfare states, paired with the advances that were made in the science of medicine, significantly reduced, post-1930, the impact of illnesses such as tuberculosis. The decline of infectious disease-related deaths amounted to a 21 per cent decline in mortality rates between 1950 and 1973. While in 1930 the average life expectancy in Latin America at birth was around 35 years, by 1970 this had extended to around 60. Infant mortality rates also fell, by 30–50 per cent between 1950 and 1980. Evidently, although great advances were made during these years, and although it remains true that, at the time of writing, mortality in Latin America is low compared to other developing regions, major health problems remain an issue. On average, taking infant mortality as an example, in most of Latin America around sixty-one babies under the age of one die out of every thousand. This remains six times the level of infant mortality in developed countries. It is also evident that the section of the population that has benefited the least from the introduction of new health technology has been the low-income groups, who continue to have little or no access to health services.

Population growth and a decline in mortality rates increasingly put pressure on the State-led systems that were consolidated post-1930. Unemployment figures rose in most Latin American countries as a consequence of there being four times more people looking for work in the 1990s than there had been in the 1930s. The different welfare states, underfunded in most cases, were further taxed, forced as they were to cater for an increasing under-age *and* ageing population. The need to offer schooling to a fast-growing population, along with the need to offer care for the elderly, became an expensive area to support in countries that were in dire straits from the outset. This situation was not aided by the stress on ISI policies that became hegemonic in the 1950s. The shift from agriculture to manufacturing industrial activities that were not labour-intensive reduced work opportunities precisely at a time when the need to create jobs had become essential. The desperate need to find work initiated a process of migration away from the countryside that continues to this day. While the export-led economies of the neocolonial period (1870–1930) had resulted in Latin America remaining a predominantly rural-based region (only 17 per cent of the population lived in cities in 1930), by the 1980s, two-thirds of the population lived in urban localities.

The problems caused by the urban concentration generated by this migration were, and are, both grave and many. In some countries, such as Mexico, Peru and Brazil, certain cities came to command a disproportionate share of their nations' urban population and amenities. By the year 2000, almost 25 per cent of Mexico's entire population (100 million) was living in Mexico City (24 million). It was in the 1950s that this demographic shift started to take its toll on Latin American societies, as the average rate of urban growth rose by 64 per cent. Unemployment rocketed, urban poverty became endemic, and the stress on urban services became acute. Crime and political unrest became common features in most Latin American cities. The emergence of poverty belts around the main urban centres, with slum housing and shanty towns mushrooming in the outskirts of the main cities in the 1950s and 1960s, went on to expand relentlessly to the present day.

Population growth was to become one of the greatest challenges for Latin America's political class. Between 1930 and 1970, populist authoritarianism was perceived as the most viable political creed for those who succeeded in controlling their countries' destinies. Faced with a fast-growing population, in a context of repeated economic crises, governments were forced to appease the impoverished masses with measures that, at least on paper, paid lip service to defending their needs and interests. An inability to control popular discontent meant that repression and dictatorship became common features in Latin America's political landscape. In those countries where democracy made important gains, its position was soon weakened by the near impossible task of balancing the republics' accounts while finding the means to improve the conditions of an impoverished majority whose numbers had grown by 400 per cent. Revolutionary organisations on the one hand, and restless high-ranking officers on the other, made the most of the inevitable discontent population growth generated, by attempting, sometimes successfully, to overthrow the few democratic governments that were actually formed. By the end of the 1960s, there was, nonetheless, the hope that all this might change. The opening up of most Latin American economies, after three decades of ISI and ISA, appeared to offer the prospect of a more prosperous future. Unfortunately, the 1973 oil crisis would stall such hopes and a new wave of authoritarian regimes would spread throughout the region.

In Isabel Allende's family saga *La casa de los espíritus* (1982), seventy years of Chilean history (*c*.1900–73) are depicted through the eyes of four generations of women and of the patriarch, Esteban Trueba. While the exceptionality of Chile must be noted, for the way in which dictatorship, as such, was avoided (*pace* Ibáñez del Campo's first government (1927–31)), the key issues that affected Latin America during these years, as discussed in this and the previous chapter, are nonetheless present. The expansion of the *hacienda* and the impact the export economy had on society are experienced through Esteban Trueba's control of Las Tres Marías. The authoritarianism of the political system is explored through the ways in which the elections were often rigged. The great achievements of the women's movement are traced from Nívea's activities as a suffragette at the turn of the century, to Alba's involvement in politics at the end. *Marianismo* can be seen to emerge in terms of Trueba's relationship with Clara. The increasing poverty of the masses and the impact of population growth both surface as the novel progresses, and Blanca falls in love with the songwriter Pedro Tercero García. The acute discontent of the popular classes which led to the electoral victory of Salvador Allende (1970–73) (the first and only Marxist to have come to power via democratic means), and the difficulties he had in implementing his programme, opposed by the oligarchy, the military and the CIA, are illustrated with great pathos. The novel ends, as does this chapter, with the advent of a new form of dictatorship that would spread through much of South America in the 1970s. Pinochet's CIA-backed coup of 11 September 1973 brings *La casa de los espíritus* to a close with Alba's horrific torture, Trueba's death and Blanca and Pedro Tercero's exile. Tyranny would now cease to be quasi-fascist or populist. Authoritarianism had become neoliberal.

## Exhibit 5.1: Excerpt from Rafael Trujillo's *Mensaje al pueblo dominicano, el 16 de agosto de 1931, con motivo del 68 aniversario de la restauración y ii del gobierno* (16 August 1931)

Al cumplirse en este aniversario de la Restauración Nacional, el primer aniversario de mi exaltación a la Presidencia de la República…, deseo aprovechar estas horas, en que el sentido nacional es propicio al recuerdo de los deberes patrióticos, para dirigirme al pueblo en mensaje de fraternal solicitud… Mi ideal de gobierno es sencillo como es sencilla toda mi vida… Mi ideal político descansa sobre bases de concordia y de amplia libertad democrática. No tengo prejuicio contra hombre alguno ni contra grupo político alguno. Veo en cada hombre un colaborador y sólo cuando esa colaboración me es negada…admito que debo prescindir de ella. He descartado, sí, la cooperación estipulada a base de un tanto por ciento, porque ésto, además de producir la anarquía en el Gobierno, está en pugna con mi ética de gobernante… [C]reo haber sentado en el Gobierno el principio de igualdad que es la esencia de la democracia. Llegado al Gobierno para servir a mi pueblo…, no creo que nadie pueda considerarse privilegiado… [S]i he sido ayer la cabeza de la mayoría, soy ahora el representante de la nación

entera… Si hasta hoy la mano del Poder ha sido fuerte para prevenir y contener a hombres injustamente desavenidos con el régimen que actualmente impera, el llamamiento que ahora les dirijo es el
anuncio de que ante ellos se abre un período de indulgencia… Nuestras condiciones económicas
siguen siendo difíciles…en este momento en que una crisis profunda afecta a todas las naciones del
mundo. El Gobierno pugna en este momento por eliminar las causas primarias del malestar interno.
Estamos abrumados por el pago violento de nuestra deuda exterior… Hasta ahora estamos cumpliendo
fielmente nuestro compromiso y espero que podremos cumplirlo siempre; pero, necesitamos vivir…
Tengo un ideal de paz y de trabajo como norma de gobierno. La paz está asegurada, y el trabajo, que
ha decrecido notablemente en el mundo entero, ha podido mantenerse entre nosotros… El Gobierno
lucha por crear mejores condiciones… En este glorioso día para la Patria me descubro reverente ante
las tumbas de nuestros próceres y ratifico ante el pueblo la formal e irrevocable promesa de luchar por
su mejoramiento…

*Source:* Rafael L. Trujillo, *Discursos, mensajes y proclamas*, Vol. 1 (Santiago: Editorial El
Diario, 1946), pp. 111–14.

## Exhibit 5.2: Excerpt from Fidel Castro's *Primera declaración de La Habana* (speech delivered on 6 September 1960)

[L]a Asamblea General Nacional del Pueblo de Cuba condena el latifundio, fuente de miseria para el
campesino y sistema de producción agrícola retrógrado e inhumano; condena los salarios de hambre y
la explotación inicua del trabajo humano por bastardos y privilegiados intereses; condena el analfa-
betismo, la ausencia de maestros, de escuelas, de médicos y de hospitales; la falta de protección a la
vejez que impera en los países de América; condena la discriminación del negro y del indio; condena la
desigualdad y la explotación de la mujer; condena las oligarquías militares y políticas que mantienen a
nuestros pueblos en la miseria, impiden su desarrollo democrático y el pleno ejercicio de su soberanía;
condena las concesiones de los recursos naturales de nuestros países a los monopolios extranjeros
como política entreguista y traidora al interés de los pueblos; condena a los gobiernos que desoyen el
sentimiento de sus pueblos para acatar los mandatos de Washington; condena el engaño sistemático a
los pueblos por órganos de divulgación que responden al interés de las oligarquías y a la política del
imperialismo opresor; condena el monopolio de las noticias por agencias yanquis, instrumentos de los
trusts norteamericanos y agentes de Washington; condena las leyes represivas que impiden a los
obreros, a los campesinos, a los estudiantes y los intelectuales, a las grandes mayorías de cada país,
organizarse y luchar por sus reivindicaciones sociales y patrióticas; condena a los monopolios y
empresas imperialistas que saquean continuamente nuestras riquezas, explotan a nuestros obreros y
campesinos, desangran y mantienen en retraso nuestras economías, y someten la política de América
Latina a sus designios e intereses.

La Asamblea General Nacional del Pueblo de Cuba condena, en fin, la explotación del hombre por el
hombre, y la explotación de los países subdesarrollados por el capital financiero imperialista.

*Source:* Fidel Castro, Osvaldo Dorticós and Raúl Roa, *Así se derrotó al imperialismo. Vol.
1. Preparando la defensa* (Mexico City: Siglo Veintiuno Editores, 1978), pp. 210–11.

## Topics for discussion in class

■ Which lines in Exhibit 5.1 strike you as being populist?

■ Which lines in Exhibit 5.1 illustrate Trujillo's personalist approach to politics?

■ In Exhibit 5.1, although Trujillo stresses his faith in democracy, what indication is there, in his speech, that he actually supports an authoritarian regime?

■ Does Exhibit 5.2 strike you as being obviously Marxist?

■ How fair is it to say that Exhibit 5.2 is first and foremost a condemnation of US imperialism?

■ What are the main differences between Exhibits 5.1 and 5.2? Are there any similarities?

## Topics for essays and presentations

Making use of the recommended texts (see Further reading, p. 161) and/or others that may be available to you in your local library, write an essay/give a seminar presentation on **one** of the following topics.

1 Provide a comparative analysis of the 1952 Bolivian Revolution and the 1956–59 Cuban Revolution.

2 Using *one* of the following governments as a starting point, provide a typology of the populist authoritarian regimes that came to power in much of Latin America in the wake of the 1929 Wall Street Crash: Rafael Leonidas Trujillo Molina (Dominican Republic, 1930–61), Getulio Vargas (Brazil, 1931–45) or Juan Perón (Argentina, 1946–55).

3 Analyse US foreign policy towards Latin America during the Cold War.

4 Account for the longevity of *one* of the following authoritarian regimes: Alfredo Stroessner (Paraguay, 1954–89), François Duvalier (Haiti, 1957–71) or Fidel Castro (Cuba, 1959–).

## CHAPTER 6

World context

The Cold War continued to engulf the world until the collapse of the Communist bloc in 1989–91. The United States was involved in a major conflict in Vietnam (1964–73), while the Soviet Union became embroiled in a war in Afghanistan (1979–89). However, following the reunification of Germany and the disintegration of the Soviet Union, the dynamics of the world political scene changed dramatically. The United States became the uncontested world power at the turn of the century. Neoliberalism also became hegemonic, as most countries' economies were integrated in the world market in a fast-track process that became known as globalisation. Most political parties in established democracies abandoned their traditional ideological discourses and embraced parallel moderate social democratic agendas within a triumphant capitalist context. War remained, nonetheless, a key feature. Britain was involved in the Malvinas/Falklands War (1982), and fought with the United States and other allied countries against Iraq (1990), Serbia (1999),

# Dictatorship and democracy since 1970

The late 1960s and early 1970s saw a return to authoritarian rule in most Latin American countries. Unlike previous dictatorships, however, these were characterised not only by their extreme use of repression, but also by their endorsement of neoliberal economic strategies. However, while neoliberalism, within a context of globalisation, went on to survive the military regimes, becoming hegemonic in the region, the end of the twentieth century was also characterised by multiple processes of democratisation. The twenty-first century thus began with both hopeful and worrying prospects for the future. On the one hand, the neoliberal model appeared to have consolidated democratic governments in most Latin American countries. On the other hand, the neoliberal model had broadened the wealth disparities in the region, generating rampant unemployment and increasing social tensions, while forging a new economic dependency that did not bode well for the future. As the United States became increasingly concerned with the Middle East and issues of national security, in the wake of the attack on the Twin Towers on 11 September 2001, Latin America witnessed a significant shift to the 'left'.

Afghanistan (2001) and
Iraq (2003). Conflicts in
the Middle East and Asia
also continued to erupt
throughout these years.
Moreover, although the
last Western European
dictatorships in Portugal
and Spain gave way to
democracy in the 1970s,
and apartheid was ended
in South Africa in the late
1980s, authoritarian rule
remained a common
feature in China and
many African and Middle
Eastern states. In Japan
and east Asia, a
spectacular, export-
orientated process of
industrialisation
transformed their
economies into the
fastest growing in the
world, benefiting from a
major technological
revolution that changed
people's lives worldwide,
with the advent of
television, CDs, personal
computers, mobile
phones and the Internet.
By the beginning of the
twenty-first century, China
and Cuba remained the
last bastions of
communism, albeit
integrated into the world
market following parallel
stages of economic
liberalisation. After 11
September 2001, the rise
in terrorist attacks, and
the violent response they
elicited from the United
States and its allies,
became a global concern.

## The last dictators

For many Latin American countries that appeared to be on the path towards consolidating democratic systems in the late 1950s, the mid 1960s and 1970s marked a devastating and depressing return to authoritarian rule. This was also the case in countries like Chile and Uruguay, which had experienced a longer spell of representative government and which also had stronger economies. The reasons for the collapse of democracy in the region continue to generate controversy. One school of thought accounts for the return of authoritarianism by arguing that the absence of a consolidated constitutional structure led to a situation wherein most Latin American democracies were unable to withstand the economic crises of the 1970s. Democratic values and institutions had not had the time to put down deep roots in society and were too weak to resist the unrest of the late 1960s and 1970s. Faced with a major crisis, a return to authoritarian rule was, if not inevitable, certainly understandable, given the political traditions of most Latin American countries. Another school emphasises issues of domestic socio-economic inequality and class structure. In a region where, according to the World Bank, the levels of inequality are, on average, the most extreme in the world, the need for basic commodities, including food, was always going to be more pressing for the majority than the ideal of democracy *per se*. Latin American democracy could not be stable or long lasting when the majority of people were living in abject poverty. These disparities were conducive to the politics of violence, especially in the wake of the 1973 oil shock, when oil prices quadrupled, plunging the world at large and, in particular, the less developed countries into deep recession. Last but not least, another school of thought continues to blame the United States for the return of military regimes, in a Cold War context wherein US administrations preferred to support authoritarian rulers rather than run the risk of allowing communism (or even socialism) to spread in their 'backyard'. There is evidently some truth in all these interpretations, and depending on the country in question, some are more accurate than others. What is undeniable is that for many Latin Americans, the brutal crushing of their democratic hopes in the 1960s–1980s would scar them for life.

In Brazil, a coup in March 1964 led to the establishment of a military regime that lasted until 1985. In Bolivia, also in 1964, a coup orchestrated by General René Barrientos led to the overthrow of Víctor Paz Estenssoro's second term in office (1960–64), resulting in eighteen years of almost uninterrupted military rule, with General Hugo Banzer's dictatorship (1971–78) emerging as the most long lasting of the different military regimes that surfaced prior to the return to democracy in 1982. In the Dominican Republic, following the crises that characterised the post-Trujillo period (1961–66), which included a coup in 1963 and US military intervention, a civilian-led authoritarian government was imposed under Joaquín Balaguer (1966–78). In Panama, a coup in 1968 placed General Omar Torrijos Herrera in power. Succeeded by General Rubén Darío Paredes (1981–83) and General Manuel Noriega (1983–89), the military remained in power until a US invasion toppled the latter in December 1989. In Peru, General Juan Velasco Alvarado imposed a military, albeit reformist, government (1968–75), which, under General Francisco Morales Bermúdez (1975–80) eventually paved the way to a return of electoral democracy in 1980. In Uruguay, a military junta took over the government from 1973 to 1984. In Chile, a military coup on 11 September 1973 overthrew **Salvador Allende**'s government and placed General

### Salvador Allende Gossens (1908–73)

Born into an upper middle-class family in Valparaíso, Salvador Allende became a Marxist as a student. He founded the Chilean Socialist Party in 1933 and, after serving as a deputy, minister of health and a senator, he was the favoured, albeit unsuccessful, presidential candidate of the left, in the 1952, 1958 and 1964 elections. In 1970, at the head of *Unidad Popular* (Popular Unity), a coalition of left-wing parties, he narrowly won the elections, with 36 per cent of the vote. In power, he sought to implement a major land reform (breaking up large estates and redistributing them among the labourers), nationalise major businesses and industries (copper, coal and steel) and invest in the provision of public services (health and education). The opposition to his measures was strong, especially on the part of US corporations. The CIA funded Allende's opponents to the tune of over $10 million, and assisted General Augusto Pinochet in the coup of 11 September 1973. During the coup, Allende refused to escape into exile and remained in the presidential palace, which was bombed by the military. Once the palace was taken, Allende's dead body was found. The Pinochet regime claimed he had committed suicide. Others believe he was assassinated.

Augusto Pinochet at the head of the nation for almost seventeen years, until March 1990. In Argentina, Generals Jorge Rafael Videla, Roberto Viola and Leopoldo Galtieri imposed a particularly violent dictatorship (1976–83). In Honduras and El Salvador, the military took over the government in 1978–82 and 1979–83 respectively, after brief spells of democratic rule.

In those countries where dictatorships were already in place, most of them survived the 1970s and only started to crumble in the 1980s. In Ecuador and Nicaragua, military rule ended ahead of other Latin American countries in 1979. In Ecuador, civil rule was restored after almost three decades of alternating military governments. In Nicaragua, the Somoza dynasty was finally overthrown during the 1979 *Sandinista* revolution. In Guatemala, military rule ended in 1985 after three decades of authoritarian government. In Paraguay, Alfredo Stroessner hung on to power for thirty-four years, until he was deposed in a palace coup in 1989. In Haiti, although Baby Doc Duvalier was forced into exile in 1986, military-dominated governments retained control of the nation until the 1990 election of Jean-Bertrand Aristide to the presidency. Unlike most other Latin American countries at the end of the twentieth century, the 1987–90 transition to democracy did not consolidate a representative government, given that a coup in September 1991 plunged the country once more into authoritarian rule. US sanctions and, eventually, military intervention were subsequently required to return Aristide to the presidency (1994–96). Aristide, however, would subsequently be the cause of more controversy and instability, and would eventually go into exile in 2004, following a three-month popular rebellion against his government. In Cuba, Fidel Castro continues in power at the time of writing (although his brother Raúl has taken over the day-to-day running of the government), having become the longest-lasting dictator of twentieth-century Latin America (1959–).

Colombia, Costa Rica and Mexico were the only three countries to retain civilian-led governments during this period. However, the violence that has characterised contemporary Colombian history (over 35,000 dead since 1987), and the control the PRI exerted over the Mexican government until the 2000 elections, means that talk of democracy or civilian rule needs to be qualified in the case of these two countries. The Mexican elections of 2006, moreover, were tainted with accusations of fraud. Following Felipe Calderón's marginal victory (by 240,000 votes), the defeated candidate Andrés Manuel López Obrador vowed to set up an alternative government that would oppose the administration of the president-elect. As a result, the legitimacy of Mexico's democratic institutions remains questioned and contested.

The case of Venezuela also makes any quick appraisal of the strength of democracy in the region difficult. Some believe that the riots of 27 February 1989, the attempted military coups of 4 February and 27 November 1992, and the impeachment and removal of President Carlos Andrés Pérez (May 1993) demonstrated that Venezuela's democracy from 1959 until 1998 was corrupt, unrepresentative and incapable of addressing the great wealth disparities that afflicted the population. Others argue that the end of the two-party system represented by Hugo Chávez's presidential victory (1998) and re-election (in 2000 and 2006), on an antiparty platform, paired with his determination to enact sweeping revolutionary measures by decree, amounts to a return to old-style Marxist authoritarian practices.

With some notable exceptions, such as General Velasco Alvarado's government (Peru, 1968–75), the dictatorships which became established between the mid 1960s and the mid to late 1980s were characterised by their systematic use of repression and their increasing dependence on neoliberal economic policies. These were two decades characterised by horrendous human rights abuses. Political assassinations both at home and abroad, widespread use of torture, and the disappearances and kidnappings of literally thousands of civilians became the order of the day. The massive exodus of Latin American refugees to the United States, Canada and Europe was highly characteristic of this period. In Chile, close to 3,000 people were killed by Pinochet's regime. Following the end of the dictatorship, the National Commission of Truth and Reconciliation docu-

> ### *desaparecidos*
> Literally translated as 'disappeared' or 'missing', it refers to the people who, for political reasons, were kidnapped and/or killed by the military under the Latin American dictatorships after the mid 1960s, and whose whereabouts – whether dead or alive and imprisoned – were never disclosed.

mented 2,279 cases of human rights victims killed by the regime, 957 of whom were 'disappeared' (i.e. kidnapped, killed, often quartered, and buried in locations that have not yet been found). The way in which the regime rounded up left-wing sympathisers in football stadiums prior to interrogating them and executing them would become one of the haunting images of Pinochet's terror. The manner in which the great songwriter Víctor Jara was killed, first having his tongue cut out and then his hands cut off (as a punishment for having sung left-wing songs and played the guitar) serves as a perfect example of the brutality that characterised the dictatorship. Numerous poems, songs, novels, plays and films, generally written by Chilean exiles, subsequently captured much of the horror of the regime's early years. Constantin Costa-Gavras' film *Missing* (1981) and Isabel Allende's novel *De amor y de sombra* (1984) provide a powerful indictment of the military's repression, from both a US and a Chilean perspective.

In Argentina, what became known as *la guerra sucia* (the Dirty War) amounted to a parallel use of institutional violence, State terrorism and repression. Between 1976 and 1977, according to Argentina's National Commission on Disappeared People, between 8,000 and 20,000 people were 'disappeared'. Secret detention centres and concentration camps, such as El Olimpo and El Banco, with torture chambers called 'operating theatres', were set up. The use of torture with electric prods was common practice, as were physical and psychological abuse, including rape. In many cases, the babies of 'disappeared' women were clandestinely put up for adoption. To comprehend the horror of these years, all one has to do is read the testimonies of the surviving victims contained in the report *Nunca más* (1984). It was the Argentinean novelist, Ernesto Sábato, author of key existentialist novels such as *El túnel* (1948) and *Sobre héroes y tumbas* (1961), who, as head of the commission that was set up in 1984 to investigate the fate of the ***desaparecidos***, introduced the report. Resistance to the regime, in the wake of such extensive and systematic repression, finally came down to an extremely courageous women's movement. Risking their lives, towards the end of the regime, the mothers of the 'disappeared' started to march around Buenos Aires' main square, the Plaza de Mayo, with posters of their missing relatives, acquiring the name of the *Madres de la Plaza de Mayo* (Mothers of the Plaza de Mayo). Although it is hard to accept, many Argentineans were either oblivious to the atrocities committed by the military *junta* or simply refused to believe that they were happening. As captured in

Rigoberta Menchú

Luis Puenzo's disturbing film, *La historia oficial* (1986), it was only once the dictatorship had collapsed in the wake of the *Malvinas*/Falklands War (1982) that the full extent of the horror became known.

Similar repressive strategies were employed in all other Latin American military regimes. Aided by the CIA, with most Latin American high-ranking officers having been instructed in the US-run military School of the Americas (Panama), policies such as Operation Condor united the military's efforts from a wide range of Latin American countries to track down and exterminate left-wing activists and sympathisers. Set up by the CIA as part of its policy to curb the spread of communism in the Americas, in 1974–75, and lasting into the early 1980s, Operation Condor brought together the intelligence services of the military in Chile, Argentina, Uruguay, Bolivia, Paraguay, Brazil and Ecuador. They combined their resources to establish a database of 'wanted leftists', and worked together to assassinate so-called 'top-level terrorists' in exile. The assassination of the former Chilean foreign minister, Orlando Letelier, in Washington, DC, in 1976, is but one example of how Operation Condor worked abroad. The dictatorships of the 1970s–1980s went two steps beyond any previous authoritarian regime. Advances in technology made repression far more sophisticated, effective and horrifying. What had previously been a regional affair had become an example of supranational state violence.

Needless to say, military repression was equally severe in those countries that were not formally integrated into Operation Condor. As was to be documented in Rigoberta Menchú's testimony, compiled by Elizabeth Burgos, *Me llamo Rigoberta Menchú y así me nació la conciencia* (1983), the abuses of the military in Guatemala, in particular towards the indigenous communities, were equally shocking. Rigoberta Menchú's extraordinary courage, and her passionate struggle for justice for the Indian peasant communities in

Guatemala, would eventually receive due international recognition when she was awarded the Nobel Peace Prize in 1992. Determined to end the injustices and exploitation to which her people were subjected, having experienced the brutal deaths of her father, her mother and one of her brothers at the hands of the military (another died of hunger and another died intoxicated by DDT), Menchú forced herself to learn Spanish to challenge the authorities through community action and, where possible, peaceful means. Her support for violence was almost always restricted to the idea of self-defence. Her dignity, humanity and inspiring ability to find hope in such dreadful circumstances make her one of the most remarkable Latin American women of the twentieth century.

Needless to say, the return of authoritarian governments coincided with a dramatic rise in guerrilla activity. The success of the Cuban Revolution (1956–59) served as an inspiring example to many radicals who could not see how they could liberate their countries from capitalist oppression, given the lack of education and ideological cohesion of the masses. It established the theory of the *foco*, an insurrectionary centre from where the revolution could spread. As was explained by Che Guevara:

> *foquismo*
>
> It is generally accepted that for a revolution to be successful, the following preconditions are necessary:
>
> 1 Widespread dissatisfaction with the political, economic and social situation (this must affect a variety of social classes).
> 2 Widespread politicisation of the people.
> 3 A generalised sense that the government is illegitimate.
> 4 There is a viable and preferable alternative on offer.
>
> *Foquismo*, based on the success of the Cuban Revolution (1956–59), argued that not all of these preconditions were necessary for a revolution to triumph. It stressed that a *foco* (insurrectionary centre), made up of a handful of committed revolutionaries, based in the jungle or in the mountains, employing guerrilla warfare, could generate all four preconditions if these were not yet fully established. The *foquista* model was to be the main strategy employed by the majority of guerrilla movements in Latin America.

We consider that the Cuban revolution has made three fundamental contributions to revolutionary strategy in Latin America: 1) The popular forces can win a war against the army; 2) It is not always necessary to wait until all the conditions for revolution are fulfilled – the insurrectionary centre can create them; 3) In underdeveloped America the terrain of armed struggle must basically be the countryside.

Evidently, in some republics it was the emergence of left-wing guerrilla armies in the late 1960s that led to a hardening of the military. Although many would dispute this, some would argue that the military in Argentina and Uruguay were provoked into taking over their countries' governments, given their perceived weakness vis-à-vis the threat posed by the revolutionaries (or terrorists). In other countries, such as Brazil, Guatemala and Nicaragua, it could certainly be said that it was precisely the imposition of repressive regimes that gave many little alternative but to join the armed struggle to seek social

### liberation theology

Originating from within the Roman Catholic Church, this is a religious and political philosophy which dates from the late 1950s, when a number of Latin American priests started to show concern over the problems relating to development in the region. It became fully established between 1968 and 1972, acquiring a particularly confrontational dimension once authoritarian rule became widespread again (1972–84). Thereafter, liberation theology has been exported outside Latin America and has become a global creed. It stresses a commitment on the part of the Church to defend the poor and the oppressed, and advocates the need for political action to bring an end to right-wing authoritarian regimes, social injustice and inequality.

justice. According to Rigoberta Menchú, in the case of Guatemala, people were radicalised by poverty, malnutrition, exploitation, discrimination and oppression. Talking about herself, she noted that 'they've killed the people dearest to me, and here I include my neighbours from my village among my loved ones. Therefore, my commitment to our struggle knows no boundaries nor limits'. Of the numerous guerrilla armies that were formed during these years, the following deserve a mention: FSLN (National *Sandinista* Liberation Front (Nicaragua)), URNG (National Revolutionary Guerrilla Unity (Guatemala)), FMLN (Farabundo Martí National Liberation Front (El Salvador)), FARC (Armed Revolutionary Forces of Colombia (Colombia)), *Sendero Luminoso* (Shining Path (Peru)), the *Tupamaros* (Uruguay) and the *Montoneros* (Argentina).

The radicalisation of politics, at the time, proved dramatically divisive at all levels of society, even within the Catholic Church. Rigoberta Menchú, among others, found herself siding with what became known as the 'Church of the people' or the 'Church for the poor'. As the repression of the military regimes increased and the poverty of the majority became more acute, what has been defined as **liberation theology** became a powerful creed among many priests, who found they could not ignore the plight of their parishioners. The Brazilian educationalist Paulo Freire, following the 1964 coup in Brazil, stressed through his belief in *conscientização* that it was the Church's duty to raise the political consciousness of the oppressed classes in order to prepare them for their eventual political liberation. As stated by the Salvadorean Archbishop, Oscar Romero, God was 'a God of justice and love who acts on the side of the poor and oppressed'. More so than anywhere else around the globe, liberation theology became one of the most enduring ideologies of a significant section of the Latin American Catholic Church. As a result, it was sections of the Church which, on many occasions, in Central America, Chile and Brazil, denounced the human rights abuses of their respective regimes and assisted those who were persecuted. Notwithstanding the emergence of liberation theology, many more traditional members of the Church, eventually backed by Pope John Paul II, denounced their 'Marxist' fellow theologians and attempted to have them excommunicated. In El Salvador, in 1977, right-wing leaflets abounded which stated 'Be a patriot! Kill a priest!' The assassination by right-wing death squads of notorious liberation theologians, such as Archbishop Romero, who was killed on 24 March 1980, became a common trait of the period.

The economic circumstances of the late 1960s and 1970s were evidently one of the major sources of unrest in the region. The shift from ISI policies to more open economies resulted in a rise of private enterprises at the expense of the public sector. The initial dismantling of the large bureaucratic states that had come into being (c.1930–c.1970), which would gather momentum in the 1980s and 1990s with the triumph of neoliberalism, led to significant cuts in public services. The resulting rise in unemployment, paired with cuts in what had never been an entirely successful welfare state, became all the more explosive in the wake of the 1973 oil crisis. As jobs became scarce at the same time as state subsidies started to be cut in the food, health, education and transport sectors, most Latin American currencies collapsed, hit by the oil shocks of 1973 and 1979. Between 1973 and 1981, Latin America's deficit rose from $10 billion to $40 billion. Inflation rocketed and most currencies were forced into devaluation on repeated occasions (at times by well over 40 per cent against the dollar). The debts most Latin American countries incurred to cope with the crisis became particularly acute in the 1980s. This is what has generally been labelled the 'debt crisis'; one which, according to dependency theorists, initiated a reprise of those very economic dynamics that had characterised the neocolonial period. It was in this highly volatile context, against a backdrop of increasing wealth disparity between the few and the many (as only a minority appeared to benefit from privatisation policies) and increasing military repression, that aggravated landless peasants and certain disaffected middle-class intellectuals resorted to taking up arms. Mario Vargas Llosa showed no sympathy towards such 'armchair Marxists', and was to ridicule well-meaning yet ultimately misguided middle-class intellectuals who supported the revolutionaries, in his compelling novel *Historia de Mayta* (1984). In contrast, for intellectuals such as the French Marxist Régis Debray, who was actually arrested in Bolivia in 1967 and sentenced to thirty years' imprisonment, charged with supporting Che Guevara's guerrilla activities: 'Under an autocratic regime, only a minority organisation of professional revolutionaries, theoretically conscious and practically trained in all the skills of their profession, can prepare a successful outcome for the revolutionary struggle of the masses.'

For the moderate majority, the extremes of these years made any form of political action difficult. On the one hand, a belief in democracy that necessarily entailed a critical view of the regimes' authoritarianism could lead an individual to suffer torture and imprisonment for subversive tendencies and alleged communist sympathies. On the other hand, a belief in bringing about a transition from within the regimes, with a pragmatic predisposition to overlook the military's atrocities and reject the revolutionaries' demands, could lead an individual to be killed or kidnapped by the guerrillas. Francisco J. Lombardi's film *La boca del lobo* (1988) highlighted only too well the quandary many Peruvians found themselves in, victimised by both the Maoist insurgent *Sendero Luminoso* and the repressive armed forces. Those who had the means to escape did so, forming entire communities of exiles abroad. It is estimated that over a million Chileans left Chile soon after the 1973 coup.

Moreover, the spiral of violence that exploded in many Latin American countries during this period, with savage crimes being committed by the military regimes and, to a lesser extent, the guerrilla armies, would make pacification and reconciliation with the return of democracy to the region particularly difficult aims to achieve. In Guatemala, when the 29 December 1996 peace treaty brought an end to the country's thirty-six-year conflict, people had to come to terms with a recent past in which more than 200,000 people had been either killed or 'disappeared', and in which thousands of others had suffered appalling physical injuries. The issue of whether the dictators or high-ranking officers who were responsible for the atrocities of these years could be forgiven became one of the most divisive issues of the late twentieth and early twenty-first centuries. For many, in order to consolidate the so-called third wave of democracy (c.1974–), it was preferable to forget the past and leave the military alone. Adopting a pragmatic stance, it made sense to avoid provoking the military into intervening in politics again by burying the memory of the terror. For others, in particular those whose friends and relatives were killed or 'disappeared', it was unacceptable that the murderers of so many people should go free and unpunished. In their view, so long as the authorities avoided placing the 'butchers' on trial, the idea that democracy had been consolidated would not be believed by anybody. Only Uruguay would succeed in overcoming this dilemma by holding a referendum in April 1989, in which a close majority of 52 per cent voted in favour of 'forgiving and forgetting'.

It was those moderate majorities who won through in the end, as most of the authoritarian regimes in Latin America crumbled by the late 1980s, allowing processes of democratisation to unfold. With the notable exception of Colombia, where guerrilla activity is ongoing, and without forgetting the emergence of a new and different kind of armed rebellion in Chiapas, Mexico, in the form of the EZLN (*Zapatista* Army of National Liberation, 1994–), most insurgencies were defeated. The armed revolts in Paraguay, Argentina and the Dominican Republic (1959), Venezuela and Colombia (1961), Guatemala and Ecuador (1962), Peru (1963), Bolivia (1967), Brazil (1964–70), Uruguay (1968–72) and Argentina (1969–76) failed to overthrow the regimes they opposed. This was hardly surprising given their lack of resources, inadequate preparation and the contrasting power of the armed forces, who benefited from US backing and US counterinsurgency tactics. One major exception was the *Sandinistas*, who entered Managua on 19 July 1979, overthrowing Anastasio Somoza Debayle (Tacho II) (1967–79).

## The *Sandinista* revolution (Nicaragua, 1979)

The *Sandinista* Front of National Liberation (FSLN) was founded by students in 1961, and, inspired by the Cuban *foquista* model of revolution, started a guerrilla campaign in the mountains. Although they attracted growing numbers of recruits as the years went by, they were repeatedly defeated by the armed forces. It was the 1972 earthquake that razed the centre of Managua to the ground which marked a change in the way the majority started to view the revolutionaries' cause. The way in which the Somozas and their cronies unashamedly pocketed large amounts of the funds collected by the international community to help Nicaragua recover from the devastation of the earthquake turned the apathetic middle classes against the regime. As public indignation grew and the *Sandinistas*' support broadened significantly, Anastasio Somoza Debayle's response became one of extending the brutality of the regime's repression to all sectors of society. The previous policy of killing, gaoling and torturing peasants and *Sandinistas* was extended to include members of the elites and middle classes. In January 1978, Somoza went one step too far when he had the outspoken and much-admired upper-class journalist Pedro Joaquín Chamorro assassinated.

In the wake of the Chamorro affair, the people responded with general strikes and major demonstrations. Somoza's dreaded National Guard dealt with these with unrestrained brutality. When, in August 1978, a *Sandinista* commando succeeded in seizing the National Palace, it was clear that the Somoza dictatorship was in its final throes. Somoza was forced to meet the *Sandinistas'* demands to have fifty-nine of their comrades released from prison, to pay out a significant ransom and to allow the commando in the National Palace a safe escape to Panama. The capture of the National Palace had two important consequences. It gave the *Sandinistas* the kind of widespread respect and popularity they had not previously succeeded in mustering, and it provoked Somoza into launching a retaliatory genocidal operation, which ultimately inspired all the opposed factions to unite in the final push that was to culminate in the overthrow of the regime. Somoza's air force bombed cities, and its National Guard launched a full-scale search for *Sandinista* sympathisers, killing over 5,000 people. Popular uprisings spread throughout the country in response. The violence of these years (1978–79) would result in a death toll of around 50,000 (i.e. 2 per cent of Nicaragua's population).

The United States, hoping to prevent the success of a socialist revolution in Central America, was working hard to find a peaceful solution, based on the idea of '*Somocismo* without Somoza' (i.e. remove the dictator, retain the system). However, Somoza refused to go quietly. In the meantime, while Somoza alienated his main supporters in the United States and the Organisation of American States, the *Sandinistas* succeeded in gaining key financial support from social democratic parties in Europe (such as the PSOE in Spain), and the governments of Costa Rica, Venezuela, Panama and Cuba. Well stocked with weapons, the *Sandinistas* led the final offensive in the summer of 1979. By 5 July they had surrounded the capital. On 17 July, Somoza accepted defeat and went into exile. On 19 July, the FSLN marched into Managua and formed a revolutionary government that included two priests (one of whom was the poet Ernesto Cardenal) and two bankers, as well as renowned Marxists such as Tomás Borge and Jaime Wheelock Román.

As can be gathered from the composition of the original revolutionary five-member junta, the *Sandinistas* did not intend to impose a Cuban-style communist regime in Nicaragua. While there is no doubt that their ideological origins were influenced by Marxist thought, once they came to power they sought to implement a socialist electoral democracy within a capitalist framework. Their socialism became evident in their promotion of social services, nationalisation of many companies, including the banking system, and expropriation of Somoza and his cronies' holdings. However, they also sought western loans and technology, and allowed the Nicaraguan private sector to retain 60 per cent of the country's gross national product. The early achievements of the *Sandinistas* were remarkable, especially when one considers that they inherited a

### contras

Name given to the Nicaraguan *contrarrevolucionarios* (counter-revolutionaries) who, backed by the Ronald Reagan administration, fought against the Sandinista government (*c.*1981–*c.*1987).

country with a national debt of $1.6 billion, whose material damages in the wake of the 1978–79 conflict amounted to a further $1.3 billion. Between 1979 and 1981, 1,327 state co-operatives and 1,200 independent co-operatives were formed. Illiteracy was reduced from 50 to 12 per cent. Around 4,000 new classrooms were built and the number of primary teachers tripled. Numerous clinics were constructed and an ambitious housing programme was implemented. In the 1984 elections, scrutinised by a large number of foreign observers, the *Sandinistas'* success was duly recognised, as evidenced by the fact that they secured 67 per cent of the vote. The exhilaration of the early years of the revolution was to be poignantly expressed in Gioconda Belli's poems, which consistently celebrate womanhood, love and the struggle for justice.

However, as was to happen with other socialist Latin American governments, such as that of APRA's Alan García's first term in office in Peru (1985–90), the pressures of international commerce and, above all, Ronald Reagan's US government (1980–88), seriously undermined the *Sandinistas'* achievements. On top of the natural disasters that had devastating consequences in Nicaragua, in particular the floods and drought of 1982 and hurricane Joan (1988), *Sandinista* Nicaragua was faced with a US trade embargo (1985–90) and a US-funded 'secret war'. Starting in 1981 and using neighbouring Honduras as the US base of operations, the Reagan administration went on to organise and finance a so-called low-intensity war against the *Sandinistas*. *Somocistas*, Vietnam veterans, CIA-paid mercenaries and Honduran troops were trained by US and Argentinean officers and sent into Nicaragua to destabilise its government. These counter-revolutionary forces became known as the **contras**, and went on raiding Nicaragua's villages until 1987, in spite of the fact that, in 1986, the World Court ordered the United States to end its military and paramilitary actions against Nicaragua. The war only ended after the Costa Rican president, Oscar Arias, succeeded in bringing peace to the region by conjuring up a set of agreements which the presidents of Guatemala, El Salvador, Honduras, Costa Rica and Nicaragua signed, barring each country from supporting insurgent forces in the other countries (for which he was awarded the Nobel Peace Prize), and after the Iran–*contra* scandal hit the headlines. The Iran–*contra* scandal erupted at the end of 1986, when it was discovered that the Reagan administration had illegally used a percentage of the proceeds of an arms sale to Iran (carried out in exchange for the release of some US hostages in Lebanon) to finance the *contras* in Nicaragua.

The US-backed war against the *Sandinistas* (1981–87) resulted in a death toll of over 60,000 and over 28,000 wounded. It also prevented the Nicaraguan economy from ever recovering, since, as time progressed, more and more funds needed to be channelled into the war effort. The impact of the *contra* war was devastating, as depicted in Ken Loach's moving film *Carla's Song* (1996), and it can be blamed, ultimately, for the failure of the *Sandinista* Revolution. After years of war, with a disastrous economy in which food shortages had become widespread and hyperinflation had reached over 33,000 per cent (1987), 55 per cent of the electorate voted out the *Sandinistas* in 1990, embracing Pedro Joaquín Chamorro's daughter, Violeta Chamorro, as the new president at the head of the conservative UNO party. With Violeta Chamorro (1990–95) and subsequent conservative presidents (1996–2006) abiding by the tenets of neoliberalism, illiteracy rose again to 34 per cent, and 70 per cent of Nicaraguans became unemployed. With 40 per cent of the population earning less than $1 a day, Nicaragua became, after Haiti, the poorest country in Latin America. Worthy of note is that sixteen years after Violeta Chamorro won the 1990 elections, the Sandinistas were voted back into power, with Daniel Ortega returning to the presidency, albeit advocating a more moderate agenda than that of 1979.

## Processes of democratisation

The 1979 *Sandinista* Revolution marked the beginning of a generalised trend towards democratisation in Latin America. Nevertheless, it was exceptional in the sense that most Latin American dictatorships established the foundations of democracy themselves, without being overthrown. Excluding Nicaragua, Argentina, Panama and Haiti, the processes of democratisation that became hegemonic in the region *c.*1985–*c.*2000 were actually initiated by the very authoritarian regimes that had come to power either in the 1960s–1970s or earlier. In Argentina, the defeat suffered by the Argentinean troops during the 1982 *Malvinas*/Falklands War against Britain resulted in the collapse of the military junta. In Panama and Haiti, US military intervention led to the fall of their dictators. Elsewhere, however, it was the governing elites who gave in to internal and international pressures, and paved the way towards democratisation through parallel stages of *apertura/abertura* ('opening').

In Chile, it was the overconfidence of the Pinochet regime that laid the groundwork for the transition to democracy. Following the consolidation of Pinochet's authority (1973–78), he set about giving his rule constitutional legitimacy. He prevented the constitutional commission, made up of conservative leaders, from calling elections in 1985. Instead he ensured that the Constitution (coercively approved in 1980) prioritised issues of national security over issues of popular sovereignty, transformed the army into the 'guarantor' of the nation's institutions, and banned the existence of certain political parties and ideologies. However, Pinochet gave in to the idea of holding a plebiscite in 1988 or 1989, whereby a candidate, potentially Pinochet, would be ratified for a further eight-year term in office. The idea of the plebiscite gave the 1980 Constitution a certain, albeit highly questionable, aura of democratic values. Pinochet was not openly stating that he would remain Supreme Chief of the Nation for life, and it was in tune with the Constitution's aim to forge a so-called 'modern and protected democracy'. Evidently, neither Pinochet nor his cronies believed that he would actually lose the plebiscite when it occurred. Nevertheless, when the plebiscite was called, in 1988, all the moderate politicians joined forces and registered their coalition of parties under the title of Party for Democracy, to push for a 'No' vote. The illegal Communist Party and other radical left-wing parties refused to participate, given that they believed participation amounted to legitimising the Pinochet regime. Notwithstanding the communists' boycott, the Party for Democracy, benefiting from international pressure to conduct the plebiscite fairly, carried out a major door-to-door campaign. Much to the dismay of the regime, in spite of the fact that it had the media at its service, 92 per cent of the eligible population went to the polls, and the opposition's 'No' vote won in all but two of Chile's twelve regions. To prevent the regime from having any possible excuse to ignore this result, alleging the country's security was threatened, the Communist Party played a key role in ordering its militants to refrain from celebrating the outcome with demonstrations. Pinochet had no choice but to stand down and allow the transition to get under way, with the election of Patricio Aylwin to the presidency, at the head of the Christian Democratic Party, on 14 December 1989.

To claim, however, that democracy was fully restored in Chile in 1989 remains a controversial matter. Although Pinochet ceased to be dictator in March 1990, he remained Head of the Armed Forces (1989–97) and became senator for life. Although the 1980 Constitution was reformed, many of its institutions remained in place, notably a military-dominated National Security Council, which could overrule any legislation if this were deemed to threaten the country's 'security'. Although a Commission on Truth and Reconciliation was set up, with the exception of General Manuel Contreras, no high-ranking officers were sentenced for their involvement in the dictatorship's crimes. It would only be in the wake of Pinochet's arrest in London, in October 1998, with his subsequent arrest in Chile, that the process of democratisation would appear to gather momentum. Following socialist Ricardo Lagos' term in office (2000–06), and Michele Bachelet's subsequent electoral victory, it can be said that democracy has become fully established in Chile. Having said this, Pinochet, who died in December 2006 at the age of 91, escaped judgement due to much judicial prevarication. Although more than 3,000 people died, and a further 28,000 were tortured during his rule, one in three Chileans maintains to this day that 'he saved Chile from Marxism, from becoming a satellite colony of Soviet–Cuban imperialism'.

Most other Latin American countries that have joined this third wave of democracy share several of Chile's contradictions. This is inevitable given that it was the authoritarian regimes of the 1960s–1980s that allowed the transitions to democracy to take place, seeking, in doing so, to retain certain privileges and institutions, and to protect the military and politicians from facing trials for corruption or abuse of human rights. It is still too early to know whether the processes of democratisation that characterised the last two decades of the twentieth century will prove long lasting. The ideal of democracy remains, as yet, unfulfilled, if we interpret democracy as a system in which the following factors are essential prerequisites:

1   The absence of reserved domains of power for the military and/or other actors who are not accountable to the electorate.
2   The existence of horizontal accountability of office holders, constraining executive power, protecting constitutionalism, legality and a deliberative process.

3   The guarantee of political and civic pluralism, with ongoing processes of representation and articulation, periodic elections and the safeguarded right of every individual and/or group to freedom of belief and speech.
4   The consolidation of a 'rule of law' which ensures that all citizens have legal and political equality and that everybody, without exception, is subject to the law.

While many Latin American countries have made great strides towards achieving these goals, democracy remains fragile in Latin America. It is true to state, however, that the processes of democratisation became hegemonic in the region by 2000, with Cuba remaining the one notable exception. The defeat of the PRI in the 2000 Mexican elections, and the resignation and exile of the Peruvian president Alberto Fujimori (1990–2000), whose 1992 self-inflicted coup (*autogolpe*) represented one of the last attempts in twentieth-century Latin America to impose a return to authoritarian rule, followed by Alejandro Toledo's electoral victory in June 2001, confirmed that authoritarianism was finally losing ground in the region.

For many, this hopefully permanent democratic wave was in part a by-product of the end of the Cold War, following the collapse of the Berlin Wall and the demise of the Soviet Union (1989–91). With the need for US interventionism becoming less acute as a result of the end of a much-mythicised Soviet-backed communist threat in Latin America, democracy was able to surface. The United States' shift from supporting dictatorships to democracies was conducive to the collapse of authoritarianism in the region. Another important contributing factor to the collapse of authoritarian rule in the mid to late 1980s was, paradoxically, the adoption of neoliberal economic measures throughout the region after the mid 1970s. As was the case with General Francisco Franco's dictatorship in Spain (1939–75), the abandonment of autarkic, ISI-inspired measures and the endorsement of free market economics created a contradiction for those authoritarian regimes who pursued neoliberal policies. How could the economy be free when the people were not? How could the State of a country dismantle its control of the nation's economic mechanisms, privatising its industries, opening its doors to world market forces in what amounted to a global competitive free-for-all, while strengthening its control, through repressive and dictatorial measures, of its population's rights and liberties? Sooner or later, something would have to give. In the end, it was the authoritarian regimes.

The paradox was that few of the neoliberal austerity measures that were implemented post-1980 could have been put in place had the different countries been governed democratically. The success of the South East Asian newly industrialising countries (NICs) (South Korea, Taiwan and Singapore) represented an authoritarian, State-led, rather than free market-driven, neoliberal model that many Latin American elites thought worth emulating. After all, the wave of popular resistance these measures would have met in countries where social inequality is so great and poverty so widespread would have prevented elected governments from carrying them through. Democracy, in the context of the 1970s, was not compatible with economic development, especially since 'development' entailed drastic measures that would inevitably generate acute social tension. A system that permitted democratic contestation and legal challenges to any proposed draconian economic measures was seen as too major an obstacle for the governing elite.

Taking Peru as an example, in the 1990 presidential elections the majority rallied behind the then unknown Alberto Fujimori, rather than support Mario Vargas Llosa, precisely because, unlike the novelist, Fujimori did not advocate implementing a tough neoliberal 'shock' programme once he came to power. Ironically, once elected, the so-called 'Fujishock' that followed, with major cuts in State expenditure, further cuts in tariffs, the relaxation of foreign investment laws and the initiation of a dramatic privatisation programme, was far more brutal than that which Vargas Llosa had recommended. When, in 1992, Fujimori's unpopular economic measures were blocked by Congress, his response was to dissolve it with his military-backed *autogolpe*. In Latin America, it was easier to implement neoliberal policies under authoritarian rule than to do so within a democratic framework. The paradox was that once the economy was liberalised, it became increasingly difficult for the authoritarian governments to survive for a lengthy period of time. The very tenets of neoliberalism contradicted the key principles of authoritarian rule. Economic modernisation could lead to political modernisation: that is, democracy.

## Globalisation, the impact of neoliberalism and the rise of the New Left

There is no doubt that the most important issue affecting Latin America during the last two decades of the twentieth century was the generalised implementation of neoliberal policies in the region. There are several reasons that account for the emergence of neoliberalism as a dominant force. One cannot avoid stressing the importance of globalisation as a phenomenon which affected the world at large (as suggested by the term itself), in the wake of the collapse of the Soviet Union. This collapse, and the subsequent end of the bipolar (US–Soviet) world that emerged after the Second World War, gave way to a tripolar one (US–Japan and the NICs of east Asia–European Union), in which capitalism became hegemonic in global terms. This new world order resulted in an international capitalist system which, based on free market economics, broke with traditional boundaries. Geographical–national differences ceased to matter, as a more homogenised world of global corporations came into being. Integration into the world market became both a necessity and a remarkably fast process (accelerated by the advances made in information technology). The World Bank, the International Monetary Fund (IMF), the World Trade Organization (WTO) and the increasingly powerful multinational companies undoubtedly became the decision-making institutions of the world, leaving little space for manoeuvre at a local or national level. The supremacy of these institutions made the implementation of any feasible alternative political or economic strategy a near impossibility. In order to prosper, it became essential for all governments to conform to these bodies' economic rules. As a result, as the century drew to a close, the differences between the main political parties in the world became difficult to discern, as it became evident that, regardless of one's original inclinations, neoliberal policies had to be adopted in order to survive.

From a more specifically Latin American outlook, the triumph of neoliberalism emerged as a result of several historical patterns. First, the inward orientation of the ISI policies that were implemented (c.1940–c.1970) proved to be unsuccessful in terms of Latin American trade. Latin America's participation in world trade declined to the extent that its exports, as a percentage of total world exports, went from 13.5 per cent in 1946 to 4.4 per cent in 1975. Latin American trade stagnated and its currencies became prone to hyperinflation. The subsequent need to borrow vast sums of money from the international banking community led to the devastating debt crisis that exploded in August 1982, when Mexico became the first Latin American country to declare a moratorium on its debt repayments. The rising national debts, coupled with the inability of most Latin American countries to service them, resulted in a breakdown of confidence on the part of the international banking community. The loans were cut abruptly as long as the past debts were not repaid. Given that the United States refused to support a 1980s version of the Marshall Aid Plan for Latin America, most Latin American governments were faced with the near-impossible task of regenerating the kind of economic stability that was required to attract further international loans and investment.

The collapse of the Soviet Union, and what this represented in terms of proof that the inward-looking, socialist, State-led economy had failed, gave the neoliberal proposal further weight as the only acceptable model in a global context in which capitalism had finally triumphed. For Latin America, there appeared to be no way out other than to attempt to conform with the demands of the global market, as represented by the World Bank, the IMF, the WTO and the multinational companies. In order to bring an end to the endemic problems associated with the debt crisis, it became evident that most governments would have to significantly reduce all State expenditure (affecting social services such as health and education). Likewise, they would have to open up their economies in a bid to encourage foreign investment (accepting that uncompetitive sectors, such as Latin American industry, would have to be sacrificed). This, in turn, meant that most Latin American exports would again be centred on primary products, importing manufactured goods from the United States, Europe and east Asia. Nevertheless, at least in countries such as Mexico, Argentina, Chile, Venezuela and Brazil, monoculture was avoided to a certain extent. In other words, a number of Latin American countries were able to base a number of exports (e.g. cars and textiles) on the diversified economy that was forged during the ISI years. Having said this, coffee remained the main (legal) product of Colombia, as did bananas in most of Central America and sugar in the Caribbean.

For those Latin American intellectuals who endorsed neoliberalism, the majority educated in US universities (in Chile they became known as the 'Chicago boys'), there were reasons to support the neoliberal model other than that of surviving in an increasingly globalised economic context. The large bureaucratic states that had been formed (c.1930–c.1970) stifled economic activity and were riddled with corruption. Protected subsidised nationalised industries, not having to compete with private or foreign enterprise, lacked any incentive to develop or modernise. The medicine of neoliberalism, albeit hard to swallow initially because of the short-term upheaval it entailed, was, they argued, 'a good thing' in the long run. Reducing state interventionism amounted, in theory, to tackling corruption and creating a more technical, transparent and efficient

*didn't help*

management of the economy. Slashing public expenditure strengthened the economy and attracted foreign investment. Privatisation programmes ended inefficient and stagnant state businesses, allowing industry, in private hands, to be more efficient and dynamic. Despite the initial shock (which inevitably entailed a dramatic increase in unemployment and poverty), most neoliberals argued that, in the long run, gradual improvement of the economy would increase employment and improve the conditions of the majority. Once stability was achieved and the economy was thriving, the wealth of the few would gradually trickle down and benefit the majority. This hope or promise has yet to be fulfilled.

Since the advent of neoliberalism, unemployment has increased dramatically (at present between 30 and 50 per cent of the working population are unemployed). Real wages have also declined in order to make Latin American businesses more profitable. Likewise the power of trade unions has been significantly curtailed. Inequalities between the reduced percentage of the population that has benefited from the reforms and the majority have widened dramatically. In Mexico, for example, in 1994 there were as many dollar-billionaires as in Britain (i.e. seven), while 16 per cent of the population (13.5 million), according to government figures, were classified as living in 'extreme poverty', and a further 23.6 million were defined simply as 'poor'. Latin American economies have become, once more, highly dependent on external finance and vulnerable to global economic shifts.

The moves to protect them within the frameworks of common markets such as MERCOSUR (Argentina, Brazil, Paraguay and Uruguay) or NAFTA (Canada, Mexico and the United States) have not yet proven entirely successful. The asymmetries in the world economy between Latin American countries and the centre countries of the world economy have increased. In 1978, the per capita income enjoyed by an average Western European was twelve times higher than that of an average Latin American. By 1995, it was thirty times higher. It remains deeply disturbing that most of the views that were sustained by the Uruguayan intellectual, Eduardo Galeano, in his combative *Las venas abiertas de América Latina* (first published in 1971), remain as relevant at the turn of the century as they were more than three decades ago. As Galeano noted, in what amounts to a condemnatory history of the European and US capitalist exploitation of Latin America, 'We lost; others won. Although it remains the case that those who won did so because we lost. The history of the underdevelopment of Latin America...[is] the history of the development of world capitalism'.

Latin America found itself, in the last decades of the twentieth century, in a no-win situation. If the governments attempted to conform with the demands of the IMF and the World Bank, servicing the debt, liberalising the economy and pursuing austerity policies that reduced public spending, trimming down the State and privatising all national industries, they met the fierce opposition of an impoverished majority whose already precarious conditions were made markedly worse. Political instability, paired with a rise in crime and armed rebellions, such as the *Zapatista* revolt in Mexico (1994–), appeared to be the inevitable outcome of neoliberalism. It is worth noting here that one of the slogans of the **Subcomandante Marcos** and the *Zapatistas* was: 'We are the globalised fighting against the globalisers.' On the other hand, if the governments attempted to resist the international pressures of the main world banking institutions and the leading multinationals, by refusing to pay the debt, nationalising all commercial business, expropriating all companies, regardless of whether they were foreign-owned or not, and increasing public expenditure, they met the fierce opposition of the international capitalist community. Funds ceased to be invested in the country, foreign trade collapsed, the wealthier members of society swiftly transferred their funds to banks abroad, and in some cases trade embargoes and diplomatic ruptures further isolated the socialist-inclined governments, to the extent that global economic marginalisation prevented the countries in question from recovering from their fragile situation. In other words, despite the great strides taken towards democratisation towards the end of the twentieth century, it remained nonetheless difficult to discern whether the levels of poverty in Latin America would actually be reduced.

Notwithstanding these bleak considerations, the electoral gains made by socialist governments in the first decade of the twenty-first century, the so-called Pink Tide, signalled a disposition on the part of a majority of Latin Americans to seek a democratic response to globalisation and neoliberal practices that seriously attempted to tackle the asymmetries of wealth and acute social injustice afflicting their populations. In Chile, Brazil, Argentina, Uruguay, Peru, Ecuador and Nicaragua, the governments that came into being sought to improve the conditions of the majority, while not breaking with the IMF or the World Bank, pursuing social democratic policies that attempted to inject investment into community and welfare programmes, while encouraging their export economies to thrive at the same time. This so-called Third Way, seeking a halfway mark between the confrontational anti-US, anticapitalist agenda of Hugo Chávez's Venezuela and a sheepish acceptance of IMF orthodoxy, would find a clear exponent in the case of the government of Luiz Inácio Lula da Silva (2002, re-elected 2006) in Brazil.

Lula, a working-class leader who started his working career as a shoeshine boy, made history by becoming the first president of Brazil to have risen to power from a poor background. Although in business circles there was a fear that he would challenge

> ### *Subcomandante Marcos (1957–)*
>
> Born Rafael Sebastián Guillén, in Tampico, the *Subcomandante* studied philosophy in the UNAM (Mexico City), and taught at the UAM (Mexico City), before becoming affiliated with left-wing guerrilla organisations. After a period of training in Nicaragua (1981) and Cuba (1982), he moved to the southern state of Chiapas in 1984. For the next ten years, he prepared for the revolt that broke out on 1 January 1994, on the same day Mexico became formally integrated into NAFTA (North American Free Trade Agreement). At the head of the *Zapatista* National Liberation Army (EZLN), named after the 1910s revolutionary, Emiliano Zapata, the *Subcomandante* Marcos became notorious for his poetic email declarations (he was the first 'Internet revolutionary') and his enigmatic appearance, always wearing a balaclava. Although cornered by the Mexican army in the Lacandón jungle, his writings have become extremely influential, defending the rights of the indigenous people of Mexico (and the oppressed in general) and condemning neoliberalism.

the IMF and the USA, and usher in a new era of Marxist-style populism in the region, he succeeded in pursuing a progressive form of neoliberalism that has used the boom in Brazilian exports (sugar, coffee, beef, orange juice, soya beans, aircraft, vehicles, iron ore, steel, textiles and footwear) to fund an extensive range of social welfare programmes. The *pai dos pobres* (father of the poor) has thus been responsible for paying Brazil's foreign debts and attracting investment, while raising some six million Brazilians out of poverty (the percentage of people living in poverty fell from 27.3 in 2003 to 25 in 2004) and increasing the per capita income of the most deprived half of the population by 14 per cent. There is little doubt that his re-election in 2006, having succeeded in over-coming a major corruption scandal that rocked his Workers Party (PT), can be attributed to the wide range of policies he has implemented to alleviate poverty. There are, nonetheless, those who criticise him for not having gone far enough in his reforms, given that despite Lula's years in power, Brazil remains one of the most economically unequal countries in the world. A film such as Fernando Meirelles' *Cidade de Deus* (2002) serves to remind us of the conditions in which 33.2 per cent of a population of 188 million continues to live. It is in this sense that it is not surprising that there are those who view Hugo Chávez's Bolivarian revolution as the real answer to globalisation.

Unlike Lula and the other Third Way presidents in Latin America, Hugo Chávez was confrontational from the moment he won the elections in Venezuela in 1998. However, albeit more radical, his so-called Bolivarian revolution (in honour of the 'Liberator', Simón Bolívar) has been founded on democratically conducted elections and referendums. A former army major, Chávez swore that his actions would be subject to the will of the people, and accordingly each of his sweeping reforms was initially put to the vote. In 1999 alone, Chávez held referendums on whether the people wanted a new constituent assembly and on whether they approved of the new constitution that was drafted (71 per cent did), holding elections, as well, for the assembly. Ever since, his government has striven to improve the conditions of the majority of the population, using the wealth generated by Venezuela's oil to fund a far-reaching educational programme (the *Misiones Robinson*), a major subsidy programme for popular markets (the Mercal system), and a marked increase in access to health care. When in April 2002 a coup was orchestrated against him by the disgruntled Venezuelan elites, with the endorsement of the USA, the people of Caracas came down from the popular barrios, converged in the centre of the capital, and succeeded in having their president freed. Bearing in mind the millions of dollars Chávez has invested in social programmes, it is not surprising that he has been re-elected twice, gaining 61 per cent of the vote in 2006. Under Chávez, inflation went from 38 per cent in 1998 to 16 per cent in 2006, and the proportion of people living in poverty went from 44 per cent to 34 per cent. In 2007, moreover, to demonstrate his commitment to developing an alternative economic vision for Latin America, he withdrew Venezuela from the World Bank and the IMF. He has also sought to spread his Bolivarian revolution abroad, to counterbalance the influence the USA has in the region, and has funded welfare and educational initiatives in other Latin American countries, including Cuba and Bolivia. In a similar vein, and to counter the influence of the IMF and the World Bank, he has offered Latin American countries alternative forms of credit and financial support, developing his so-called

'Bank of the South'. As a result, the USA has consistently demonised him, and Chávez, in turn, using a marked sense of humour, has countered the accusations of evildoing with parallel religious terminology (see Exhibit 6.2).

Evo Morales, the first indigenous president of Bolivia, was elected in 2006 with the open backing of Chávez. Like Chávez, Morales has striven to nationalise operational control of the country's resources. While Chávez has led a nationalisation programme of oilfield projects managed by foreign companies, Morales announced on 1 May 2006 that Bolivia would renegotiate the terms of the ownership of the Andean country's natural gas fields, pipelines and refineries. A former coca farmer, Morales' appeal (he won the elections with 54 per cent of the vote) has been based on his defence of indigenous rights (see Exhibit 6.1) and his determination to tackle the country's poverty and social injustice, while championing the cause of the coca growers.

Whether the reforms that are being implemented by Chávez, Morales and the governments of other socialist Latin American countries (Chávez's 'Axis of Good') constitute a meaningful empowerment of the majority of their countries' populations, or whether these are purely populist gimmicks employed by demagogues who intend to 'buy' the votes of the poor to stay in power, remains to be seen. The USA, the IMF, the World Bank, the international media and a high percentage of the middle classes in these countries, view Chávez and his allies as incipient dictators. Chávez's announcement that he would inaugurate a new era of 'maximum revolution' by presidential decree, followed by his closure of the anti-Chávez TV channel RCTV in 2007, appeared to confirm his critics' accusation that he was becoming increasingly authoritarian. Notwithstanding the arguable dictatorial tendencies of these twenty-first-century socialists, the case remains that they have a vast following, which begs the question whether their alleged 'populism' is not, in reality, a consequence of democracy having finally become firmly established in countries where the deprived majority are understandably backing leaders committed to improving their situation.

## Migration

One key result of the deteriorating economic condition of the peasant and working classes in Latin America was the emergence of international migration as one of the most important issues to concern the Americas and the world at large. While political repression was, at least initially, one of the prime causes behind the migration of numerous Latin American refugees from the 1950s to the 1980s, by the 1980s economic reasons had gained ascendancy. Legal and illegal immigration has been on the increase since the 1960s. Within Latin America, Venezuela, Argentina and Mexico have been the main destinations for unemployed peasants and workers desperate to make a living. However, none of their figures compare with the increasing flow of Latin American migrants that the United States has had to deal with over the last decades of the twentieth century. In terms of legal and documented migration figures (in other words, the very tip of the iceberg), the number of Latin American migrants crossing into the United States per year rose from 330,000 in the 1960s, to 450,000 in the 1970s and 600,000 in the 1980s. According to one estimate, in 1986 there were about 5 million

Latin American 'illegal aliens' living in the United States, of which 60 per cent were Mexican in origin. By 1990, the US census established that there were 22.4 million people of Latin American descent living legally in the United States (i.e. 8 million more than had been enumerated in the 1980 census). By the year 2000, Los Angeles had become the second-largest Spanish-speaking city in the world, after Mexico City, and there were an estimated 30 million Latin American immigrants living in the USA, of which 28 per cent were undocumented aliens.

One of the effects of globalisation has clearly been to heighten the disparity between the wealth of the United States, Canada, the European Union and Japan and that of the rest of the world. Given that neoliberal policies have resulted in an increase in poverty in the so-called Second and Third Worlds, migration has become an inevitable consequence. Africans, Eastern Europeans and Asians have been attempting to migrate to Western Europe since the 1970s, in a desperate quest to find employment and make a living. In the Americas, it has been a fast-increasing population of Latin American migrants who have been struggling to reach the United States. The stories of the individual migrants are not always positive. As depicted in Gregory Nava's harrowing film *El norte* (1983), which traces the journey of two Guatemalans to the United States, the hardships endured by Latin American migrants in order to reach the 'land of opportunity' and then survive are appalling. Oppressed and persecuted at home, exploited and marginalised abroad, migration, in itself, does not necessarily appear to be the solution to the plight of so many impoverished Latin Americans.

Furthermore, the rising numbers of destitute *Latinos*, as they have become known, often forced by their circumstances into crime to survive in the ghettoised, run-down parts of the major cities of the southern states of the USA, has further tarnished the manner in which many Americans view Latin America. As is eloquently depicted in T. Coraghessan Boyle's ironic novel, *The Tortilla Curtain* (1995), even for the more liberal-minded, chattering classes of California, having to contend with the increasing proximity of *Latinos* is equated with the problems posed by the coyotes that rummage through their dustbins at night. Regardless of the fact that it is precisely this 'plague' of 'illegal aliens' that is doing all that work no one else wants to do, for hardly any money at all, the mainstream US perception of 'them', and by default of Latin America, remains one of prejudiced distrust and contempt. Following the terrorist attacks of 11 September 2001, moreover, the US government militarised its response to immigration, viewing it as a problem that was part of its combined wars on terror and drugs. At the time of writing, a 2,100-mile wall is being built along the US–Mexican border, in a flawed attempt to keep the immigrants out.

Between *c.*1950 and *c.*1990, US fear of communism spreading throughout Latin America determined its policies towards the region. Since the 1970s, two new issues have gained prominence, becoming all-important by the end of the century. Albeit very different, these two issues would eventually be perceived as interrelated. The first was the problem of migration, and the second was the problem of drugs. If one decodes the somewhat obvious message of a popular 1980s US TV police series such as *Miami Vice*, it becomes clear that the mainstream view of Latin Americans in the USA, in the 1980s and 1990s, was that all criminals in Miami, and by default in the USA, were Latin

American migrants, and that all Latin Americans were drug dealers. From every Latin American being a potential Fidel Castro, the US media and, perhaps more worryingly, government had gone on to view every Latin American as a potential Pablo Escobar (the notorious drug baron of Medellín).

## Drug trafficking

For thousands of years, coca has been grown and used, on a small scale, by peasant farmers in numerous Latin American countries, particularly in the Andean region. Its qualities have served a number of medicinal purposes. Up in the heights of the Andes, where most people are prone to suffering from *soroche* (altitude sickness), chewing coca leaves or drinking *mate de coca* is a recommended remedy. During times of need, coca also has the 'virtue' of dulling people's sense of hunger. Ever since the silver, tin and copper mines of the Andes were worked by countless impoverished labourers, coca eased the pain of hard labour and kept the pangs of hunger at bay. For many Indian communities in the Andes, coca has also played an integral part in their religious ceremonies. However, what had always been a minor economic operation was transformed into a major industry as the US and European demand for drugs began to expand at the end of the 1960s. Rock and roll, 'swinging', nihilism, punk, raves and modernity were all western cultural phenomena that erupted in a context where drugs became, albeit illegal, very much an essential ingredient.

As a result, by the 1980s the most lucrative Latin American export was cocaine, a derivative of coca. In tandem with coca, marijuana and poppy cultivation and processing (for heroin) also increased. According to the United Nations, by the mid 1990s it was estimated that the annual revenue generated by the illegal drug industry amounted to $460 billion (i.e. 8 per cent of total international trade). At a time of economic disarray, with the impact of the debt crisis and the implementation of drastic neoliberal programmes weighing heavily on the lives of many Latin American peasants, coca and poppies became the most viable cash crops for the majority of small farmers. The wealth the drug trade generated for those individuals who controlled the illegal plantations and processing plants is astronomical. By the time he was tracked down and killed in 1993, the notorious drug baron of the Medellín cartel in Colombia, Pablo Escobar, had acquired one of the most substantial fortunes in the world ($3,000 million).

The drug trade has had a number of major repercussions in Latin America. Beyond creating employment, it has become an increasingly destabilising force in politics. The drug cartels in Colombia, Mexico and Bolivia have, with time, become a force to be reckoned with. Due to the illegality of the drug trade, the drug cartels have had to use a wide range of strategies to avoid persecution from the authorities. These have entailed bribing politicians, policemen and army officers, killing and kidnapping outspoken politicians and journalists, and, in some cases, such as in Colombia, financing either guerrilla movements such as the FARC or their opposed right-wing paramilitary armies and death squads, depending on circumstances. The spiral of violence that has characterised the modern history of Colombia has no doubt become even more acute since the advent of the drug trade boom. Gabriel García Márquez, in his novelistic account of the kidnapping of a group of journalists in the early 1990s, *Noticia de un secuestro* (1996), referred to the drug barons' use of violence as a holocaust of biblical proportions.

The US policy that was subsequently enforced to tackle the drug trade has, unfortunately, done little to improve the situation. Some would argue that it has made it worse. Based on the premise that the main priority should be to destroy the supply of drugs in Latin America rather than cut the demand at home, it has increasingly involved armed intervention in Latin America, raising issues of sovereignty, democracy and human rights. By the time George Bush implemented the 1990 Andean Initiative, $2.2 billion had been invested in the antidrug campaign. Under President Bill Clinton, the militarisation of the 'war on drugs' continued, with the cost rising to $10.5 billion in 1995. The United States has actively assisted the Colombian, Bolivian and Peruvian governments with military, legal and economic aid, with the Drug Enforcement Agency (DEA) and the CIA training their respective armies in counterinsurgency tactics. They have formed and hired private armies of paramilitaries along parallel lines to those used in Nicaragua. And they have sought to destroy those plantations that have been found, either in the jungle or in the highlands, using highly toxic chemicals. By ignoring the importance of the demand issue at home (an estimated 20 million US drug consumers), the US 'war on drugs' is viewed by many Latin Americans as another example of US imperialism. The popularity of the *narcocorridos* (popular Mexican songs that celebrate the feats of drug dealers and smugglers) is a curious cultural expression of defiance vis-à-vis the DEA's heavy-handed behaviour. The fact that much of the military and economic aid has been used to fight the guerrillas rather than the drug cartels has been equally criticised. The destruction the war has entailed has also seriously jeopardised the prospects of employment for numerous peasant communities, damaging economic growth.

## The challenges of the twenty-first century

At the beginning of the twenty-first century, the drug trade remains one of the most disturbing issues to affect Latin America. Its impact is far-reaching and affects the everyday lives of thousands of people, as captured in both Steven Soderbergh's *Traffic* (2001) and Joshua Marston's *María llena eres de gracia* (2004). The short-sightedness that has characterised US policies on the one hand, and the arguably extreme apprehension of many Latin Americans towards what they perceive to be another example of US imperialism on the other, does not bode well for the near future. As long as the demand for drugs remains high in the western world, it is difficult to see how the war on the suppliers will succeed. Although political democracy appears to be on the path to consolidation throughout the region, the levels of poverty and inequality that characterise most Latin American countries remain one of the greatest challenges to be overcome. The hegemonic standing of neoliberalism does not, at least at present, appear to provide the solution to poverty. While the Mexican government forecast in 2000 that poverty would be eradicated in the Republic by the year 2030, many analysts are less optimistic. Most Latin American countries remain profoundly in debt (with it having tripled since 1982). Most Latin American economies have become, once more, highly dependent on their exports, and thus vulnerable to the fluctuations of the world market. The so-called New World Order that emerged with the end of the Cold War does not appear to show concern for countries that are on the periphery of the major economies. As an example, the need for oil inspired the rapid military intervention of the United States and Britain when Iraq invaded Kuwait in 1989. In contrast, little was done to avert or prevent the eruption of a parallel conflict, in a region where global economic interests were not so obviously jeopardised: the Ecuador–Peru War (1995).

Nevertheless, the contestation of social injustice and increasing global inequality remains active and dynamic in the region. While the struggle for true independence is ongoing, there is no doubt that great strides have been taken towards consolidating freer and fairer societies since independence was achieved almost 200 years ago. As Rodó's Próspero reminded his students, 'You cannot aspire to achieve a definitive victory immediately.' There was, in 1900, just as in 2000, a long way to go. He warned his pupils that they could not even hope to be the founders of a new Latin America, but that they might be the precursors of those who were. It was thus essential that the young ensured that they had 'facilitated better conditions for the struggle', so that future generations of young Latin Americans, building on their predecessors' exertions, might one day see the dream of a free Latin America come true. Although at times it may be difficult to find, hope for a better future still lives on.

## Exhibit 6.1: Excerpt from Evo Morales, *Discurso de posesión del Presidente Constitucional de la República* (22 January 2006)

Los pueblos indígenas que son mayoría de la población boliviana, para la prensa internacional, para que los invitados sepan: de acuerdo al último censo del 2001, el 62.2% de aymaras, de quechuas, de mojeños, de chipayas, de mulatos, de guaraníes. Estos pueblos, históricamente hemos sido marginados, humillados, odiados, despreciados, condenados a la extinción. Esa es nuestra historia; a estos pueblos jamás los reconocieron como seres humanos, siendo que estos pueblos son dueños absolutos de esta noble tierra, de sus recursos naturales. Esta mañana, esta madrugada, con mucha alegría he visto a algunos hermanos y hermanas cantando en la plaza histórica de Murillo, la Plaza Murillo como también la Plaza San Francisco, cuando hace 40, 50 años no teníamos derecho a entrar a la Plaza San Francisco, a la Plaza Murillo… Esa es nuestra historia, esa nuestra vivencia. Bolivia parece Sudáfrica. Amenazados, condenados al exterminio estamos acá, estamos presentes. Quiero decirles que todavía hay resabios de esa gente que es enemiga de los pueblos indígenas, queremos vivir en igualdad de condiciones con ellos, y por eso estamos acá para cambiar nuestra historia, este movimiento indígena originario no es concesión de nadie; nadie nos ha regalado, es la conciencia de mi pueblo, de nuestro pueblo… Estamos acá en democracia, y quiero que sepan…: queremos cambiar Bolivia no con bala sino con voto, y esa es la revolución democrática. ¿Y por qué hablamos de cambiar ese estado colonial?, tenemos que acabar con el estado colonial. Imagínense: después de 180 años de la vida democrática republicana recién podemos llegar acá, podemos estar en el Parlamento, podemos estar en la presidencia, en las alcaldías. Antes no teníamos derecho. Imagínense… Para cambiar ese estado colonial habrá espacios, debates, diálogos. Estamos en la obligación, como bolivianos, de entendernos para cambiar esta forma de discriminar a los pueblos.

*Source*: www.democraciasur.com/documentos/BoliviaEvoMoralesAsuncionPres.htm

## Exhibit 6.2: Excerpt from Hugo Chávez, *Discurso ante la ONU* (address to the United Nations, 20 September 2006)

Ayer vino el Diablo aquí, ayer estuvo el Diablo aquí, en este mismo lugar. Huele a azufre todavía esta mesa donde me ha tocado hablar. Ayer señoras, señores, desde esta misma tribuna el Señor Presidente de los Estados Unidos, a quien yo llamo 'El Diablo', vino aquí hablando como dueño del mundo… Como vocero del Imperialismo vino a dar sus recetas para tratar de mantener el actual esquema de dominación, de explotación y de saqueo a los pueblos del mundo… El Imperialismo norteamericano…está haciendo desesperados esfuerzos por consolidar su sistema hegemónico de dominación. Nosotros no podemos permitir que eso ocurra, no podemos permitir que se instale la dictadura mundial… El discurso del Presidente 'tirano' mundial, lleno de cinismos, lleno de hipocresía, es la hipocresía imperial, el intento de controlar todo, ellos quieren imponernos el modelo democrático como lo conciben, la falsa democracia de las elites, y además un modelo democrático muy original, impuesto a bombazos, a bombardeos y a punta de invasiones y de cañonazos. ¡Vaya qué democracia!… Dice el presidente de los Estados Unidos ayer…cito: 'Hacia dónde quiera que usted mira, oye a extremistas que le dicen que puede escapar de la miseria y recuperar su dignidad a través de la violencia, el terror y el martirio'. Adondequiera que él mira ve extremistas… No, no es que somos extremistas, lo que pasa es que el mundo está despertando y por todos lados insurgimos los pueblos… Por donde quiera que vea vamos a surgir nosotros, los que insurgimos contra el imperialismo norteamericano. Los que clamamos por la libertad plena del mundo, por la igualdad de los pueblos, por el respeto a la soberanía de las naciones, sí, nos llaman extremistas, insurgimos contra el Imperio, insurgimos contra el modelo de dominación.

*Source*: www.alterinfos.org/spip.php?article536

# Topics for discussion in class

- Does Exhibit 6.1 strike you as being extremist, populist or simplistic?

- What rhetorical strategies does Evo Morales use in Exhibit 6.1 to give his words a definite emotional charge?

- Who do you think Evo Morales is addressing in Exhibit 6.1? The indigenous peoples of Bolivia? The white elites? The international community?

- Does Exhibit 6.2 strike you as being extremist, populist or simplistic?

- How does Hugo Chávez use humour in Exhibit 6.2?

- Who do you think Chávez is addressing in Exhibit 6.2? The United States government? The international community? His supporters in Venezuela?

- Are there any similarities between Exhibits 6.1 and 6.2?

# Topics for essays and presentations

Making use of the recommended texts (see Further reading, p. 161) and/or others that may be available to you in your local library, write an essay/give a seminar presentation on **one** of the following topics.

1 Analyse the process of democratisation undergone in *one* of the following countries: Mexico, Argentina, Uruguay, Paraguay or Chile.

2 'Mr [Carlos] Salinas's economic policies...widened already-huge disparities of wealth' (*The Economist*, 22 January 1994). Assess the extent to which the adoption of neoliberal economic policies has led to a dramatic increase in the disparity between the few and the many in *one* of the following countries: Mexico, Chile or Argentina.

3 Discuss the origins of the *Zapatista* revolt in Chiapas (Mexico) of 1 January 1994.

4 'The new populists [Hugo Chávez, Evo Morales] are coming to power in large measure because of successful mobilisation of indigenous peoples against the Hispanic or Ladino elites who have dominated Latin American politics since the era of conquest and colonisation' (Niall Ferguson). Discuss.

# Further reading

## 1 The late colonial period and the wars of independence (1780–1825)

Timothy E. Anna, *The Fall of the Royal Government in Peru.* Lincoln: University of Nebraska Press, 1979.

Christon I. Archer (ed.), *The Wars of Independence in Spanish America.* Wilmington, DE: Scholarly Resources, 2000.

David A. Brading, *The First America: The Spanish Monarchy, Creole Patriots, and the Liberal State 1492–1867.* Cambridge: Cambridge University Press, 1991.

Simon Collier, *Ideas and Politics of Chilean Independence 1808–1833.* Cambridge: Cambridge University Press, 1967.

Rebecca A. Earle, *Spain and the Independence of Colombia 1810–1825.* Exeter: University of Exeter Press, 2000.

Tulio Halperín Donghi, *Politics, Economics, and Society in Argentina in the Revolutionary Period.* Cambridge: Cambridge University Press, 1975.

Brian R. Hamnett, *Roots of Insurgency: Mexican Regions, 1750–1824.* Cambridge: Cambridge University Press, 1986.

John Lynch, *The Spanish American Revolutions 1808–1826.* London: Weidenfeld & Nicolson, 1973.

John Lynch (ed.), *Latin American Revolutions 1808–1826: Old and New World Origins.* Norman: University of Oklahoma Press, 1994.

John Lynch, *Simón Bolívar: A life.* Yale, CT: Yale University Press, 2006.

Kenneth R. Maxwell, *Conflicts and Conspiracies: Brazil and Portugal 1750–1808.* Cambridge: Cambridge University Press, 1973.

Jaime E. Rodríguez O., *The Independence of Spanish America.* New York: Cambridge University Press, 1998.

## 2 Early national period (1825–1850)

Leslie Bethell (ed.), *The Cambridge History of Latin America. Vol. III.* Cambridge: Cambridge University Press, 1985.

David Bushnell, *Reform and Reaction in the Platine Provinces, 1810–1852.* Gainesville: University Press of Florida, 1983.

David Bushnell and Neill Macaulay, *The Emergence of Latin America in the Nineteenth Century.* New York: Oxford University Press, 1988.

Emilia Viotti da Costa, *The Brazilian Empire.* Chicago, IL: Dorsey Press, 1985.

Will Fowler, *Mexico in the Age of Proposals, 1821–1853.* Westport, CT: Greenwood, 1998.

Will Fowler, *Tornel and Santa Anna: The Writer and the Caudillo, Mexico 1795–1853*. Westport, CT: Greenwood, 2000.

Will Fowler, *Santa Anna of Mexico*. Lincoln and London: University of Nebraska Press, 2007.

John Lynch, *Argentine Dictator: Juan Manuel de Rosas 1829–1852*. Oxford: Clarendon Press, 1981.

John Lynch, *Caudillos in Spanish America 1800–1850*. Oxford: Clarendon Press, 1992.

Ralph Lee Woodward, Jr., *Rafael Carrera and the Emergence of the Republic of Guatemala, 1821–1871*. Athens: University of Georgia Press, 1993.

## 3 The rise of the neocolonial order (1850–1880)

Jan Bazant, *Alienation of Church Wealth in Mexico: Social and Economic Aspects of the Liberal Revolution, 1856–1875*. Cambridge: Cambridge University Press, 1971.

Robert E. Conrad, *The Destruction of Brazilian Slavery 1850–1888*. Melbourne: Krieger, 1993.

James Dunkerley, *Americana: The Americas in the World, Around 1850*. London and New York: Verso, 2000.

Rebecca Earle (ed.), *Rumours of Wars: Civil Conflict in Nineteenth-Century Latin America*. London: ILAS, 2000.

Lowell Gudmundson and Hector Lindo Fuentes, *Central America, 1821–1871*. Tuscaloosa: University of Alabama Press, 1995.

Charles A. Hale, *The Transformation of Liberalism in Late Nineteenth-Century Mexico*. Princeton, NJ: Princeton University Press, 1991.

Brian Hamnett, *Juárez*. London: Longman, 1994.

John Mayo, *British Merchants and Chilean Development, 1851–1886*. Boulder, CO and London: Westview Press, 1987.

Frank Safford, *The Ideal of the Practical: Colombia's Struggle to Form a Technical Elite*. Austin: University of Texas Press, 1976.

## 4 The development and fall of the neocolonial order (1880–1930)

Bill Albert, *South America and the First World War: The Impact of the War on Brazil, Argentina, Peru, and Chile*. Cambridge: Cambridge University Press, 1988.

Charles Bergquist, *Labor in Latin America*. Stanford, CA: Stanford University Press, 1986.

Leslie Bethell (ed.), *The Cambridge History of Latin America. Vol. V*. Cambridge: Cambridge University Press, 1986.

Harold Blakemore, *British Nitrates and Chilean Politics, 1886–1896*. London: University of London, 1974.

Peter Blanchard, *The Origins of the Peruvian Labor Movement, 1883–1919*. Pittsburgh, PA: University of Pittsburgh Press, 1982.

Paul Garner, *Porfirio Díaz*. London: Pearson, 2001.

Alan Knight, *The Mexican Revolution*, 2 vols. Cambridge: Cambridge University Press, 1986.

Frederick B. Pike, *The United States and Latin America: Myths and Stereotypes of Civilization and Nature*. Austin: University of Texas Press, 1992.

Richard V. Salisbury, *Anti-Imperialism and International Competition in Central America, 1920–1929*. Wilmington, DE: SR Books, 1989.

Hans Schmidt, *The United States Occupation of Haiti, 1915–1934*. New Brunswick, NJ: Rutgers University Press, 1995.

## 5 Reaction and revolution (1930–1970)

Carol Andreas, *When Women Rebel: The Rise of Popular Feminism in Peru*. Westport, CT: Greenwood, 1985.

Marjorie Becker, *Setting the Virgin on Fire: Lázaro Cárdenas, Michoacán Peasants, and the Redemption of the Mexican Revolution*. Berkeley: University of California Press, 1996.

Leslie Bethell (ed.), *The Cambridge History of Latin America. Vol. VI. Part I*. Cambridge: Cambridge University Press, 1994.

Leslie Bethell (ed.), *The Cambridge History of Latin America. Vol. VI. Part II*. Cambridge: Cambridge University Press, 1994.

Jorge Castañeda, *Compañero. The Life and Death of Che Guevara*. London: Bloomsbury, 1997.

Michael L. Conniff, *Urban Politics in Brazil: The Rise of Populism, 1925–1945*. Pittsburgh, PA: University of Pittsburgh Press, 1982.

Michael L. Conniff (ed.), *Populism in Latin America*. Tuscaloosa: University of Alabama Press, 1999.

Nikki Craske, *Women and Politics in Latin America*. Cambridge: Polity, 1999.

James Dunkerley, *Power in the Isthmus: A Political History of Modern Central America*. London: ILAS, 1988.

Joel Horowitz, *Argentine Unions, the State, and the Rise of Perón, 1930–1945*. Berkeley, CA: Institute of International Studies, 1990.

Brian Loveman and Thomas M. Davies (eds), *The Politics of Antipolitics: The Military in Latin America*. Lincoln: University of Nebraska Press, 1978.

Hugh Thomas, *The Cuban Revolution*. London: Weidenfeld and Nicolson, 1986.

Knut Walter, *The Regime of Anastasio Somoza, 1936–1956*. Chapel Hill: University of North Carolina Press, 1993.

## 6 Dictatorship and democracy since 1970

Charles W. Bergquist, Ricardo Peñaranda *et al.* (eds), *Violence in Colombia*. Wilmington, DE: SR Books, 1992.

Sylvia Chant (ed.), *Gender and Migration in Developing Countries*. London: Belhaven Press, 1992.

Jack Child, *The Central American Peace Process, 1983–1991.* Boulder, CO: Lynne Rienner, 1992.

Pamela Constable and Arturo Valenzuela, *A Nation of Enemies: Chile under Pinochet.* New York: W.W. Norton & Company, 1991.

Larry Diamond, Jonathan Hartlyn, Juan L. Linz and Seymour Martin Lipset (eds), *Democracy in Developing Countries: Latin America.* Second edition. Boulder, CO and London: Lynne Rienner, 1999.

Charles Guy Gillespie, *Negotiating Democracy: Politicians and Generals in Uruguay.* Cambridge: Cambridge University Press, 1991.

Richard Gott, *Hugo Chávez and the Bolivarian Revolution.* London and New York: Verso, 2005.

Robert N. Gwynne and Cristobal Kay (eds), *Latin America Transformed: Globalization and Modernity.* London: Arnold, 1999.

Richard L. Millet and Michael Gold-Biss (eds), *Beyond Praetorianism: The Latin American Military in Transition.* Miami, FL: North–South Center Press, 1996.

Frederick M. Nunn, *The Time of the Generals: Latin American Professional Militarism in World Perspective.* Lincoln: University of Nebraska Press, 1992.

Harry E. Vanden and Gary Prevost, *Democracy and Socialism in Sandinista Nicaragua.* Boulder, CO: Lynne Rienner, 1992.

Timothy P. Wickham-Crowley, *Guerrillas and Revolution in Latin America.* Princeton, NJ: Princeton University Press, 1992.

## General

Peter Bakewell, *A History of Latin America.* Malden, MA: Blackwell Publishers, 1997.

Victor Bulmer-Thomas, *The Economic History of Latin America Since Independence.* Cambridge: Cambridge University Press, 1994.

John Charles Chasteen, *Born in Blood and Fire: A Concise History of Latin America.* New York: W.W. Norton & Company, 2001.

Lawrence A. Clayton and Michael L. Conniff, *A History of Modern Latin America.* Fort Worth, TX: Harcourt Brace & Company, 1999.

Simon Collier, Thomas E. Skidmore and Harold Blakemore, *The Cambridge Encyclopedia of Latin America and the Caribbean.* Cambridge: Cambridge University Press, 1992.

Will Fowler (ed.), *Authoritarianism in Latin America Since Independence.* Westport, CT: Greenwood, 1996.

Will Fowler (ed.), *Ideologues and Ideologies in Latin America.* Westport, CT: Greenwood, 1997.

Tulio Halperín Donghi, *The Contemporary History of Latin America.* Basingstoke: Macmillan Press, 1993.

Hugh M. Hamill (ed.), *Caudillos: Dictators in Spanish America.* Norman and London: University of Oklahoma Press, 1992.

Brian Hamnett, *A Concise History of Mexico.* Cambridge: Cambridge University Press, 1999.

Benjamin Keen and Keith Haynes, *A History of Latin America*. Boston and New York: Houghton Mifflin Company, 2000.

Rory Miller, *Britain and Latin America in the Nineteenth and Twentieth Centuries*. London and New York: Longman, 1993.

David Nicholls, *From Dessalines to Duvalier: Race, Colour and National Independence in Haiti*. Cambridge: Cambridge University Press, 1979.

Gavin O'Toole, *Politics Latin America*. London: Pearson Longman, 2007.

Frederick B. Pike, *The United States and Latin America*. Austin: University of Texas Press, 1992.

Edwin Williamson, *The Penguin History of Latin America*. Harmondsworth: Penguin, 1992.

Ralph Lee Woodward, Jr., *Central America*. Oxford: Oxford University Press, 1985.

# Index